DATE			

INTERVIEWS WITH
SIXTY-FIVE AUTHORS
OF BOOKS
FOR CHILDREN

More Books by More People

Lee Bennett Hopkins
Curriculum and Editorial Specialist
Scholastic Magazines, Inc.

Citation Press ✳ *New York* ✳ **1974**

For reprint permission, grateful acknowledgment is made to:

Harcourt Brace Jovanovich, Inc. for "I Learned About Clocks" by Harry Behn from ALL KINDS OF TIME, copyright, 1950, by Harry Behn.

The Macmillan Company for "Such Things I Praise" by Elizabeth Coatsworth from POEMS, copyright 1931, 1933, 1936, 1938, 1942 by Elizabeth Coatsworth Beston, renewed 1970 by Elizabeth Coatsworth Beston.

The Westminster Press for "Spring Is . . ." by Sister Noemi Weygant, O.S.B. from IT'S SPRING, copyright © MCMLXIX Sister Noemi Weygant, O.S.B.

Cover and design by
SPRING

For **Jennifer Lee Venturi**

(born July 1, 1972),

And her sister, **Kim**—
who will never outgrow
the joy of being read to.

*
* Acknowledgments
*

To do a book about people one needs the assistance of many individuals. I would like to thank the following people in publishing for the generous help they have given me in the preparation of this volume:

Evelyn Diggs, Little, Brown; Jean Karl, Atheneum; Marjorie Naughton, Seabury Press; Christine B. Stawicki, The Children's Book Council; Lee Randhava, Doubleday; Deborah Piggins, E. P. Dutton; Laura Kubarmann and Michael di Capua, Farrar, Straus & Giroux; Sandra Griefenstein, Follett; Hilda B. Lindley, Harcourt Brace Jovanovich; Bill Morris and Joan Robins, Harper & Row; Barbara M. Geraghty and Diane Lewis Majer, Holt, Rinehart & Winston; Ann Greenaway, formerly Houghton Mifflin; Caroline Y. Soule, formerly Little, Brown; Jimmy Sarno, McFadden, Strauss and Irwin; Janet Schulman, Macmillan; Sally M. Brooke, William Morrow; Fabio Coen, Pantheon; Pat Ross and Georgia Van Dusen, Random House; Trudy Schaeffer and Harry Simmons, Viking Press; Barbara S. Bates, Westminster Press; and Susan T. Halbreich, Scholastic Book Services.

Special thanks also to my excellent editor, Mary L. Allison, for her constant encouragement, Charles J. Egita, for his help, Nancy Larrick who suggested the title, and to Misha Arenstein, teacher and friend, without whom this work would never have come to be.

Contents

*
* * Preface

In this continuation of his *Books Are By People: Interviews with 104 Authors and Illustrators of Books for Young Children* Lee Bennett Hopkins introduces us to 65 more authors and illustrators of books for older children. We join him as he visits their homes, asks questions, chats about favorite stories and characters, and departs with a notebook full of comments.

As the world has grown more sophisticated and the pace of life has speeded up, it has become increasingly difficult to continue some of the pleasant customs of the past that once added another dimension to life. The informal drop-in calls on neighbors that kept people-to-people communications flowing have become anachronistic, yet here is a good substitute for that pleasant custom. With Lee we again go visiting. Into each account of his personal conversation he has woven the facts that children feel they need for a report on an author and that adults need to jog their memories about places, publishers, and story lines.

Although no attempt has been made to write full biographies, there are enough salient facts given about each author to satisfy the casual reader and spur the student on to further research. It's fun to discover how such widely divergent minds answer the same basic questions and to note differences in working habits and life styles. After reading emphatic pro and con answers to the query, "Do you try your books out on children," one realizes Madeleine L'Engle's statement is the arbiter of the dispute: "I write for the children in everybody, that part of us that is aware and open and courageous. It's also that part of us that isn't afraid to explore the mythical depths, that vast part of ourselves we know little about, and which we often fear because we can't manipulate or control it. That's where art is born."

When the visits are over and the book finished, we close it with the satisfaction of having made new friends and shared for a time true experiences in their lives and the qualities that make the writing great—the romance of Mary Stolz meeting her doctor husband and discovering her great talent during a three-month hospital stay; the miracle that stored away the memory of Wales in Lloyd Alexander's mind until the right moment to develop the chronicles of Prydain; the give and take of two writers in one household, Arnold Adoff and Virginia Hamilton, both writing while their children are in school and trying out ideas on each other; the imagination of Robert Burch thinking of his books as his children and finding some of his less successful ones more comfortable to be around than their more highly praised siblings. Mr. Hopkins' descriptions of these people who have written books for children and the stories of how their books came to be are reassuring and heartwarming for they prove that at this very minute more books are being created by more people.

Anne Izard
Children's Services Consultant
Westchester Library System, White Plains, New York
President, Children's Services Division, ALA, 1972–73

✳ Looking Back

Here are some people like you, some like me, and some like neither of us. They have only one thing in common—they write and illustrate books for children. These people have created more memorable characters and situations than any other media.

Where else could you find such fantastic creatures as an English nanny who can fly with an umbrella, an Assistant Pig-Keeper who fights against evil, or a farmer's young daughter who names a pet pig Wilbur and raises him in a doll buggy?

Although most characters in books for children are fictitious, people such as "the ferociously intelligent" orphan, Gilly Ground, the beautiful Miyax who survives the perils of the Alaskan tundra, or Mario, whose parents run a newsstand in the subway station of New York's Times Square, really do seem to live and breathe!

Pick up any travel brochure. Look through it carefully. Certainly none of the places on any of the world's continents sound or are as exciting as the places one can travel to in the world of children's literature. Such places as Prydain, where Cauldron-Born creatures live on even after death, or the village of Instep, whose inhabitants are cast in a spell by the Megrimum that lurks on the mist-wreathed peak of Kneeknock Rise, whets one's appetite for adventure far more than a trip to Paris or London would.

In books animals are more extraordinary than any real animal could ever hope to be. There are the unforgettable horses, Man O' War and Black Stallion, the powerful and swift red fox, Vulpes, the Damon Runyan-type animals — Chester Cricket, Tucker, the Mouse, and Harry, the Cat — a spider named Charlotte, a fox named Francois, and even a cat who went to heaven.

Tiny chuckles and hearty laughs are to be found in children's books. The adventures of Ramona and Henry Huggins and of Betsy and Irma Baumlein are riotously funny. And there are quiet moments to sigh and silent tears to shed, too, when Sounder crawls under the cabin to die, when a young girl is sent to endure harsh years in a Siberian work camp, or when the proud Amos Fortune is stripped of his dignity and made a slave.

People — book people — have given us a wide world to enjoy — a world reflecting the complexities of the real world in which we live.

A question I have been most asked since I wrote *Books Are By People* (New York: Citation Press, 1969) is, "How do you select the individuals you are going to include from such a myriad of personalities?" Well, how does one? You listen to comments by children, parents, children, teachers, children, librarians, children, educators on every level — and children! You strive for a balance to present a small, yet broad picture of children's literature, so you include poets, anthologists, writers of nonfiction, writers of popular novels, newcomers, and writers of books many of us grew up on. You try to include award-winning authors. Some writers you want to interview manage to spare precious hours talking with you; others you just never hear from or some cannot afford time for you.

Several popular authors of middle-grade books are not in this volume because they were interviewed earlier in *Books Are By People*—for example, James Daugherty, winner of the 1940 Newbery Award for *Daniel Boone* (Viking, 1939), Lois Lenski, winner of the 1946 Newbery Award for *Strawberry Girl* (Lippincott, 1945), and poets such as Eve Merriam and Myra Cohn Livingston. Many of these people's writings are so diverse that their words speak to children young and old.

A lot of reading, talking, meeting, re-meeting, and much back-and-forth correspondence is necessary to include the people you want. But the end result is worth all the effort. For through a book such as this authors share themselves with children and adults. They reveal inner feelings, they tell how and why they write books, they become living human beings— more than just a name on a book spine or a title page.

Through my work with children and adults, I know how much more exciting books become when readers know a little something about the authors. Who might imagine that William H. Armstrong raises sheep, that Madeleine L'Engle was once an actress, that Virginia Hamilton almost gave up a writing career to become an athletic instructor or a singer or an anything other than a writer of children's books?

Few children imagine that people who write books are real people—that they grow up all over the world, that they have children, grandchildren, great-grandchildren, that they are involved with life problems ranging from building a new home to involvement with social issues from women's liberation to preserving what is left of our environment—that authors really and truly live!

It is my hope that when children find out that books are indeed by people, they will come to have a greater understanding of the works they read and that they will reap much more enjoyment from the world of children's literature. It is my hope that you will, too.

Lee Bennett Hopkins
New York City
1973

*MORE BOOKS *
by MORE PEOPLE

$\underset{*}{\overset{*}{*}}$ Arnold Adoff

Arnold Adoff (Ā-doff) burst on-
to the literary scene like a man
shot out of a circus cannon,
producing outstanding volumes
of prose, poetry, biography,
and picture books in less than
five years. His first book, *I Am
the Darker Brother: An Anthology of Modern Poems by
Negro Americans* (Macmillan) was published in 1968.
It grew out of years of collecting Black American poetry
for use in his own classrooms.

"I began collecting literature for my classes while
teaching in the late 1950s and early 1960s in Harlem
and the Upper West Side of New York," he explained.
"I have been a poet, deep inside, since I began writing
as a teen-ager. By thirty I was enough of a man to
start to put things together and realize where the thrust
should be directed. I wanted to influence the kids coming up—not a small group of academic anemics who
try to control aspects of the literature of this country.
I felt that if I could anthologize adult literature of the
highest literary level and get it into classrooms and
libraries for children and young adults, I could make
my share of the revolution. I guess when I realized I
was too old to learn how to make bombs, I threw myself full-force into creating books for children.

"After I discovered the totally racist nature of text-books and almost all poetry anthologies, I thought *I Am the Darker Brother* would be an ending—but it was only the beginning of a continuing series of anthologies, each of which grabs ahold of me and won't let go until it is done and in print.

"I found books in the schools were called American literature or poetry, but the work was almost always White. I had little knowledge of some of the writing by Black writers myself, because my education at City College and Columbia University was as lily-White as most college curricula were during the 1940s and 1950s. I started to dig and find and collect poetry by Black writers for my Black, White, and Puerto Rican students on 129th Street and Amsterdam Avenue. It wasn't until years later that I knew this collection should become a book. The idea is to believe in the truth—and the truth is the whole thing, the whole culture, the whole literature.

"One book followed another, and though not all of them have been collections of Black literature, the principle is the same. Find the best writing and present it to young people; they will dig it. This has happened with all my books."

In *I Am the Darker Brother,* Mr. Adoff brought together poems by Black writers from earlier poets—Paul Laurence Dunbar and Countee Cullen—to today's contemporary writers—Gwendolyn Brooks, Langston Hughes, and LeRoi Jones *(Imamu Ameer Baraka).* This range gives the mature reader great insight into the varied experiences and attitudes of Black Americans as *Black* Americans.

Following the success of his first volume, Mr. Adoff compiled *City in All Directions: An Anthology of Modern Poems* (Macmillan, 1969), which contains eighty-one poems written over the past fifty years by poets in many different countries and representing most of the poetic forms developed in this century.

Other anthologies include *Black Out Loud: An Anthology of Modern Poems by Black Americans* (Macmillan, 1970) and *It Is the Poem Singing into Your Eyes: Anthology of New Young Poets* (Harper, 1971).

Black Out Loud was the first anthology of Black poetry to be published for young readers since 1941, when Arna Bontemps compiled *Golden Slippers.** *Black Out Loud* contains works by acclaimed Black poets as well as by promising young poets.

"This volume was especially pleasing to do," the anthologist commented. "With this book I wanted to reach the kids who don't get to discover the world of their heritage until they are teen-agers."

To compile *It Is the Poem Singing into Your Eyes,* Mr. Adoff drew from more than six thousand manuscripts submitted by children from forty states, Canada, Denmark, Japan, and Mexico. In this volume one reads, hears, and feels the voices of youth calling out through poetry. They speak of their concerns,

---

*An interview with Mr. Bontemps appears on pp. 48-53.

and the issues of today and write freely on topics ranging from the Defense Department in "The War Dead," a poem by a fifteen-year-old girl, to pollution in an interestingly executed concrete poem by a thirteen-year-old girl in which the letters in the word pollution form a map of the United States; the poem is satirically titled "America the Beautiful."

At the time of this interview, Mr. Adoff had just completed a large, comprehensive collection of over six hundred poems by one hundred fifty-two Black American poets titled *The Poetry of Black America: Anthology of the Twentieth Century* (Harper, 1973).

Discussing his anthologies further, Mr. Adoff stated: "I want my anthologies of Black American writing to make Black kids strong in their knowledge of themselves and their great literary heritage—give them facts and people and power. I also want these Black books of mine to give knowledge to White kids around the country, so that mutual respect and understanding will come from mutual learning. We *can* go beyond the murders and muddles of the present.

"Children have to understand that the oversimplifications they get in classrooms, along with the token non-White artists represented, are not the true American literature—not the true America. Melvin Tolson stands with Robert Frost as does Robert Hayden with Robert Lowell. The great force and numbers of the current, most exciting generation of Black writers in the history of this country is overwhelming to the White educator, textbook writer, and guardian-of-the-culture who wish to preserve the mainstream culture in its basic White dress. But for those who want the truth, for themselves and for their students, using an anthology is the first step to discovery. The anthology then leads to individual works of the writers.

"All young people—Black and White—are entitled to the power fist. It shows a pride and sense of self. But the fist inside keeps the back straight and the head sharp; that fist must be fueled with truth and love and the music of fine writing. All this requires the open classroom where the books can be available and the open minds of parents, teachers, and librarians who can make a difference."

Mr. Adoff's life is now totally immersed in writing. He is married to Virginia Hamilton, author of such books as *Zeely* (1966), *The House of Dies Drear* (1967), and the 1971 Newbery Honor Book, *The Planet of Junior Brown* (1970; all published by Macmillan).*

The Adoffs and their two young children, Leigh and Jaime, recently moved from New York City to settle in Yellow Springs, Ohio. They live in a new redwood house that they built on a part of the old back field where Zeely once roamed feeding her hogs. It is situated behind Ms. Hamilton's mother's house.

"The kids can run down the field to granny for cookies, look at the old photographs in her album, and just bask in the warmth of the old house," Mr. Adoff

---

*An interview with Ms. Hamilton appears on pp. 199-207.

remarked. "We are about a mile from town, and we walk in very often. Sometimes I pull Jaime-boy in his red wagon up to nearby Antioch College to use its facilities; sometimes we bike in."

There is much company in the Adoff house, good talk, and a relaxed atmosphere that accepts people for what they are.

"But the greatest thing about living here, after New York is the good clean air. You can take great gulps of it and almost taste it," Mr. Adoff declared.

Life with two writers and two young children in one house can sometimes be hectic.

"We are a two-typewriter family," Mr. Adoff chuckled. "There is always a writing project going on upstairs and down. It is exciting, nerve-frazzling, hard on the kids at times, and always hard on us. There is never enough time to just quietly talk by a roaring fire or sit out on the deck and watch the redbirds. But our life is full of ideas and alive with the lives of others— DuBois, Robeson, Malcolm X, a new young poet, the latest crisis of a college student who writes or comes over for advice, and the characters in Virginia's novels who live with us, like little Jahdu running along beside us on especially lucky days." (Jahdu is the character in Ms. Hamilton's book *The Time-Ago Tales of Jahdu,* Macmillan, 1969.)

"But," he continued, "Leigh and Jaime understand; they have learned to live within it all and are making themselves individuals despite so much of our grown-up selves. Sometimes I yell pretty loud, sometimes I am short-tempered, irritable, and unhappy. I work at home, so when things go wrong, it dribbles over onto the lives of all of us. This is never good, but it can't be helped.

"I work each morning while the kids are in school and in the evenings when they go to bed. We get very little sleep when the heat is on and deadlines have to be met. I take a long time with my books, maybe even two years on an anthology, and so I work on more than one book project at a time. You must mix things up, and keep your head interested by changing the pace. I will work on a new poem or a new book and when I'm up against the wall, I read some Black plays or short stories or write letters to new, young poets asking for contributions to another anthology.

"When my neck gets really tired and bleary eyes signal fatigue, then it is time to put everything down and relax with a cup of coffee and good conversation. If I really hit the time right, Virginia will be coming downstairs with the latest chapter of a new novel, and I can sit and listen while she reads it to me. Fortunately Virginia loves to read her new work aloud for a give-and-take of ideas and feeling—a testing out that is important to her. For me it is a great treat, great fun. Then I go back to my own work.

"I work and rework my material many, many times, whether it is original writing of my own or work for an anthology. The key is sitting with it, letting it grow inside, become a part of your body for weeks and months and learning to work it over and over like my daughter will do with a piece of clay.

"I go out to many schools and colleges during the

year and have a chance to talk with people from six to sixty. I also talk and listen to the many kids who come to our house. I couldn't continue to grow if I couldn't go out and see kids. Aside from their feelings about my work, just talking and listening to young people helps to balance my natural inclination towards a pessimistic view of the future of humanity."

I asked Mr. Adoff if he would give me his definition of poetry. He did.

"There are as many definitions of poetry as there are different kinds of poems, because a fine poem combines the elements of meaning, music, and a form like a living frame that holds it all together. There are things I look for in any poem. My own personal preference is the music first that must sing out to me from the words. How does it sing, sound—then how does it look?

"I look for craft and control in making a form that is unique to the individual poem, that shapes it, holds it tight, creates an inner tension that makes a whole shape out of the words. I really want a poem to sprout roses and spit bullets; this is the ideal combination, and it is a tough tightrope that takes the kind of control that comes only with years of work."

The poet-anthologist-author was born in the East Bronx section of New York City. "I was a Cancer crab who was born on a hot July Sunday in 1935. I grew up in and around the Bronx and all over the city and loved New York and its potential for power, excitement, and discovery. There was too much to see, always too much to read, always another place to go. The neighborhood had a character—a solid, respectable Jewish middle-class, the butcher, the grocer, my father's pharmacy on the corner, the old ladies sitting in front of the stoops, mothers waiting with jars of milk for their kids' afternoon snacks after school before running to Crotona Park to play ball.

"There were values, a sense of self-importance because we felt we Jewish kids were better than the Christian kids who could get dirtier, a love of music, art, literature—as long as they didn't threaten the family and greater ethnic family that spelled survival in a land of hostile strangers. There was a great humanity in these values, and the trick has been to apply that sense of justice-with-love to life in the complex world of a big country suffering its way to the future. For the rest, see Malamud, Bellow, Roth, and other contemporary novelists. It is all true—even in its contradictions."

Also by Mr. Adoff

For young readers

Malcolm X (T. Y. Crowell, 1970).

MA nDA LA (Harper, 1971).

For older readers

Black on Black: Commentaries by Negro Americans (Macmillan, 1968).

Brothers and Sisters: Modern Stories by Black Americans (Macmillan, 1970).

✱ Lloyd Alexander

While working one day with a small group of sixth-grade youngsters in a New York City public school, I asked, "Where would you like to go for a vacation if you could choose anywhere in the world?" Without a moment's hesitation, Jeffrey, a very bright lad of eleven, answered, "Prydain!"

"Why would you go there," I asked, "and how would you get there?"

"I'd go there to find adventure," he replied. "And I'll go there by closing my eyes. I know there's no such real place as Prydain, but man, I wish there was!"

All of us, no matter what our age, can go to Prydain. It's a long trip but an inexpensive one. You can go hardcover deluxe for about $20,* or you can go paperback economy for under $5.** No matter what your wallet or purse can afford, you will have an unforgettable experience. You'll discover a new land with places to visit such as the Marshes of Morva, the Hall of Warriors, Fair Folk Mine; you can travel rivers such

---

*Unless otherwise noted, all books mentioned were published by Holt, Rinehart & Winston.
**Mr. Alexander's five chronicles of Prydain are published in paperback by Dell.

as the Ystrad, Tevvyn, and Kynvael, climb the Eagle or the Llawgadarn Mountains, and meet a multitude of interesting people—Taran the Assistant Pig-Keeper, Fflewddur Fflam, Eilonwy, Glew, Gwystl, and an assortment of kings with odd-sounding names. You can also meet a variety of new animals—Hen Wen, Llvagor, Islimach, Llyan, Kaws, and Gwythaints.

They haven't opened a souvenir shop in Prydain as yet, but if they do you might bring home replicas of magic wallets, swords, harps, silver horns, or rings. In short, it would be some trip!

This fascinating land can be reached by reading Lloyd Alexander's fantasy chronicles of Prydain: *The Book of Three* (1964), *The Black Cauldron* (1965), *The Castle of Llyr* (1966), *Taran Wanderer* (1967), and *The High King,* (1968). There hasn't been a series so acclaimed in the field of children's literature for some time. The first three titles were selected as American Library Association Notable Books; the second was designated as a Newbery Honor Book, and the fifth won the 1969 Newbery Medal.

The man who founded Prydain is a thin, wispy sort of fellow who has been described as resembling Hans Christian Andersen or a character from one or several of his books. But Lloyd Alexander is Lloyd Alexander, a most interesting individual who brims over with life and love.

The author was born on January 30, 1924, in Philadelphia, Pennsylvania, and grew up there and in a nearby suburb, Drexel Hill, where his wife, Janine, and he still live.

"Family life as a child was unextraordinary. My childhood was certainly no more miserable than anyone else's, although at the time, I thought it was. I learned to read quite young and have been an avid reader ever since, even though my parents and relatives were not great readers. I was more or less left to my own devices and interests, which, after all, may not be such a bad idea. My relatives were as Dickensian an assortment of people as anyone could imagine, and that might have been an advantage, too," he told me.

At fifteen, in his last year of high school, he decided to become a poet. "Poetry, my father warned, was no practical career; I would do well to forget it. My mother came to my rescue. At her urging, my father agreed I might have a try, on condition that I also find some sort of useful work. For my part, I had no idea how to find any sort of work—or, in fact, how to go about being a poet. For more than a year I had been writing long into the night and studying verse forms to the scandalous neglect of my homework. My parents could not afford to send me to college and my grades were too wretched for a scholarship."

Besides writing, he read a great deal. His favorite shop along 52nd Street in Philadelphia was a stationery store with a few shelves of children's books. One night he found *King Arthur and His Knights* and began reading and enjoying hero tales.

After graduating from high school, he worked as a bank messenger in Philadelphia where he felt "like Robin Hood chained in the Sheriff of Nottingham's dungeon." This wasn't for him! He attended Lafayette College but quit at the end of one term. He wanted adventure, so he joined the United States Army during World War II. He didn't find much adventure, however. He was shipped to Texas and later to Maryland. One autumn his company was ordered to Wales to be outfitted for combat. The country fascinated him.

"Wales was an enchanted world," he recalled. "Here, it seemed, I recognized faces from all the hero tales of my childhood. My sense of Wales was of a land far more ancient than England, wilder and rougher hewn. The companions of Arthur might have galloped from the mountains, and I would not have been surprised. Wales, to my eyes, appeared still a realm of bards and heroes; even the coal tips towered like dark fortresses. Not until years afterward did I realize I had been given, without my knowing it, a glimpse of another enchanted kingdom."

From Wales he was sent to France to join the Seventh Army in Alsace-Lorraine. When the war ended, he was attached to a counter-intelligence unit in Paris. There he met and married Janine. After his discharge from the Army, he attended the University of Paris, but homesickness attacked him so badly that he and his wife went back to Pennsylvania. There he dabbled at a variety of jobs by day, and wrote by night. His first three novels were rejected; his fourth, *And Let the Credit Go,* was accepted for publication. "As was to be expected, this book was based on my own adolescence—my first job, falling in love, a young man's typical rites of passage. The book has long been out of print. I had also translated novels by Jean-Paul Sartre and the poetry of Paul Eluard. I had written some biographies for young adults, but my first attempt at fantasy was *Time Cat* (1963). For over ten years I had been writing for adults and had never imagined I'd ever write for children. It wasn't until I was about forty that somehow I began to sense that there were things I wanted to say that could best be said through books for young people. While doing historical research for *Time Cat,* I had stumbled across a collection of Welsh legends, *The Mabinogion,* which were medieval stories found in two manuscripts. It was as if all the hero tales, the games, the dreams, and imaginings of my childhood had suddenly come back to me; and Prydain itself was the Wales I had sensed twenty years before.

"Ann Durrell, my editor, gave me a priceless gift —the freedom to write the tales of Prydain as I chose, without questioning why, when, or how. The result was a fantasy adventure for children, but for myself, it was a true adventure and a most joyous one."

I asked Mr. Alexander how he felt now that the last trip to Prydain has been taken in *The High King.* "Coming to the last page of *The High King* was by no means a happy moment," he answered. "For close to seven years I had been so caught up in my work and it had come to mean so much to me in very deep, personal ways, that instead of feeling jubilant, I felt very sad indeed, a sense that something I had greatly loved had come to a sort of conclusion.

"There is surely in the chronicles of Prydain as much of my own life as there is of ancient legends, half-forgotten, half-remembered, as our dreams change and color happenings in our waking lives. My harp, still broken-stringed, is on my mantelpiece. Does it really belong to me or to the would-be bard Fflewddur Fflam, with his incorrigible habit of stretching the truth? Are the dreams of an awkward Assistant Pig-Keeper so different from mine as a child or those of all children? Or Gurgi's fearfulness, or Doli's striving for the impossible?

"Prydain still fascinates me. There are still unexplored areas and ideas. Even though the chronicles of Taran are finished, I can't rule out the possibility of further discoveries. I just don't feel I've said all I could hope to say. Time will tell!"

Younger children and/or slower readers in grades three and up can get a taste of Prydain via two picture-book tales: *Coll and His White Pig* (1965), based on an incident from *The Book of Three,* and *The Truthful Harp* (1967), a tale of King Fflewddur Fflam. Both texts are illustrated by the Caldecott Award-winning artist, Evaline Ness, and both are available in paper-back editions from Holt.

In 1971, Mr. Alexander received the National Book Award for *The Marvelous Misadventures of Sebastian*

(Dutton, 1970), the story of an optimistic fiddler set in the imaginary eighteenth century country of Hamelin-Lorring. I asked the author about this book's evolution.

"*The Marvelous Misadventures of Sebastian* is closely and directly connected with my own feelings at completing the Prydain chronicles. Writing the books of Prydain had been such a profound, amazing experience for me, as if, after all these years, I had caught a brief glimpse of creativity—of having experienced something that had considerably changed my own life. And I suppose I was trying to think of some way to express that idea. Though I'm a miserably bad fiddler, trying to learn to play the violin as an adult gave me insights into music; by the same token, writing for young people gave me an insight into my own personality and perhaps into the nature of art as well. So *Sebastian* was the result. Below the surface adventure, it's a very personal, very meaningful story for me. *Sebastian* is a metaphor, I suppose, for the creative process—the demands that creativity makes on us and our own commitment to it."

I asked how it felt to receive two such prestigious awards just two years apart. He replied: "These surely must be the most exciting, moving, and miraculous things that any writer could hope for. Most important, the awards have made me very much aware of a responsibility to create, to accept the idea of a basic commitment to literature, and to continue trying to improve and grow as an artist. The effect is not one of resting on one's laurels but of an obligation to explore still further."

Mr. Alexander's writing day consistently starts at 4:00 a.m. "That is," he explained, "barring the occasional household disasters, naturally. It lasts until I have the impression that's about all that's going to happen for the day. I rework constantly and continually, until I'm more or less resigned to the fact that that's the best I can do at this particular moment. I don't try out my ideas on children. Story ideas seem to evolve from my own personal attitudes and ongoing explorations of life, from trying to understand where my head is.

"I had no formal writing training, but I did have the greatest teachers in the world, for example, the great works of literature. In fact, I really had very little formal education—bits and pieces of schooling here and there. Mainly, I read and studied on my own."

When not writing, he enjoys the music of Mozart, animals, especially cats, drawing, and printmaking. "I'm now learning etching and lithography," he told me. "I practice the fiddle, which doesn't seem to get any better. I play the violin with an amateur string quartet regularly—and very, very badly."

Currently he is author-in-residence at Temple University in Philadelphia.

As a last question I asked Mr. Alexander if there was anything in particular he felt a child would like to know about him. His answer confirmed my own beliefs and is the reason I have written two volumes of author interviews. He stated: "From what I've seen during my visits to schools, what children really want to know— and I think it's most important for them to know—is that writers are genuine human beings, that they're real people, with real lives, problems, ups and downs; that we aren't abstractions or textbook figures. Even though we're adults, we really are alive."

Also by Mr. Alexander

For younger readers

The King's Fountain (Dutton, 1971).

The Four Donkeys (Holt, 1972).

The Foundling (Holt, 1973).

*William H. Armstrong

Soon after William H. Armstrong joined the faculty of Kent School in Kent, Connecticut, where he teaches history, he bought twenty acres of land about two miles from the school. The area lies at the base of Skiff Mountain along the west shore of the Housatonic River.

He proceeded to build a house a couple of hundred yards up from the river and designed it to fit into the rocky terrain of Skiff Mountain. The house is large, featuring much use of knotty pine and large picture windows that look out onto the Housatonic and the steep mountainside. Large fireplaces were built from rocks found on the property. A picnic terrace and swimming pool are additional features.

Mr. Armstrong also raises sheep. He owns a large flock of Corriedale sheep, a white-faced breed that was originally developed in New Zealand and is noted for its high-quality wool. Mr. Armstrong sells the wool to Knox Woolen Mills. One problem is easily solved by having the sheep—he never has to mow the grass. The sheep take care of this chore.

Another avocation is real estate. One of his friends urged him to go into the real estate business. Mr. Armstrong took his advice and put up his shingle. For nearly twelve years he served as tax chairman of the Kent Board of Assessors.

Besides teaching, farming, running his real estate business, and doing carpentry, cabinetmaking and stone masonry, he is a writer. One wonders how, with such a schedule, a man could also produce books for both children and adults. Perhaps his own comment on his work habits explains it. "I write every morning between 4:00 and 7:30 a.m. I develop a whole story while working on the farm before I start to write. It's amazing what getting up early does for your day. When other people are starting, you're way ahead of them because you've done half a day's work. It gives you a good feeling. All my classes at Kent are in the morning.

When I'm finished, I can almost say to myself, 'Well, you've done a full day's work and it's only noon.'

"It's a great feeling to watch the day dawn, and I'm in the right spot. Dawn comes up right over the hill."

Mr. Armstrong's farming interests stem from his childhood years. He was born on a farm in the Shenandoah Valley near Lexington, Virginia, on September 14, 1914. He obtained his B.A. degree at Hampden-Sydney College where he graduated *cum laude* in 1936; he also did graduate work at the University of Virginia. His facility in writing was always evident during his school years. He served as editor-in-chief on school publications and during his college years contributed a weekly column to his hometown newspaper, *The Lexington Gazette.*

Upon graduating he chose to enter the teaching profession rather than going into journalism. He taught at a high school in Roanoke, Virginia, and also at the Virginia Episcopal School in Lynchberg. He began teaching at Kent in 1945.

In 1953 his wife, Mary, died leaving him with three young children. This great loss led him to write an adult book, *Through Troubled Waters* (Harper, 1957): it deals with a father and three children who find their way via the legacy of faith that their wife and mother left to them. Before writing *Sounder* (Harper, 1969), his first novel for young readers, Mr. Armstrong had produced a number of books on education.

Sounder is a tale Mr. Armstrong heard as a boy growing up in Virginia. Charles Jones, a gray-haired Black man who taught in an all-Black one-room school, related the story to him. The man worked for Mr. Armstrong's father after school and during the summer months. Charles Jones and his story are included in the author's note to the book. The novel is a profoundly moving account of a Black sharecropper's life on a southern farm and of Sounder, a large coon dog. The volume won the 1970 Newbery Award.

The inspiration to write *Sounder* came to the author one moonlit night in autumn while he was walking along a quiet road beside the Housatonic River. Something recalled to his mind the faint, distant voice of Sounder, the dog. It might have been an owl's hoot or the rustling whooshes of the wind in the hemlocks. Whatever it was, the memory haunted him, and he determined to write the story. "So easy the thought on the night walk, so hard to write," commented Mr. Armstrong. "The winter was still long when *Sounder* was finished. Then it lay on the shelf till winter shortened. In the back pasture on March 18, while looking for the bluebirds that nest year after year in a hollow maple, so old that only half a tree is left, I saw my neighbor sawing wood across the fence. I climbed the fence, crossed the brook, and asked him if he'd read my manuscript. So this is how *Sounder* came to be."

In just several years the book has been translated

into seven languages and a dramatized recorded version has been produced by Miller-Brody Productions, Inc., in New York City. Of the recording Mr. Armstrong commented, *"Sounder* is presented with great dignity, wise selection of lines, and a background of feeling—lonely, yet not devoid of grace. It is beautiful, very, very well done. It is touching to listen to it."

In 1972 *Sounder* was produced as a motion picture by Robert B. Radnitz and Martin Ritt. Based on the book, the film received excellent reviews and several Academy Award nominations. The noted critic Judith Crist stated that the movie is "a missing chapter from *The Grapes of Wrath* and of equal stature." All of the major film critics gave raves to the sensitive performances of Paul Winfield and Cicely Tyson who portray the father and mother.

A year after *Sounder* was published, Mr. Armstrong's *Sour Land* (Harper), appeared. The main character in the story is Moses Waters, the boy in *Sounder*, now grown into manhood. Moses shares his love and knowledge of all living things with a White farmer and his three children who lost their mother.

Mr. Armstrong is not a man who talks much about himself. "I'm a loner," he stated, "and the pleasures I enjoy most in life are my flock of sheep, my three children, my land—ledge and all—my house and stone walls that I built myself, and my flowers and garden. I am not an instant writer. My stories and books have been with me a long time without my knowing they were good enough to be published. I've worked on a book about Abraham Lincoln for the past twelve years."

His three children are now grown. Christopher is pursuing a doctorate degree in criminology at the University of Pennsylvania; David is doing graduate work at the University of Indiana and is an artist of note; Mary has recently received a degree in fine arts from Boston University.

I asked Mr. Armstrong what his reaction was to winning the Newbery Award with his first attempt at a story for children. "I didn't know what it was, so there was no reaction!" he replied. "I reread the book two days afterward to see if I could figure out *why* it had won. I didn't even know *Sounder* was a children's book until it was published. As a matter of fact, I don't even believe there is such a thing as a children's books. My thirteen- and fourteen-year-old students get more fired up and excited about Herodotus and Thucydides than about anything else they read all year."

Also by Mr. Armstrong

Barefoot in the Grass: The Story of Grandma Moses (Doubleday, 1971).

Hadassah: Esther, the Orphan Queen (Doubleday, 1972).

To Price an April Field (Coward, 1972).

The MacLeod Place (Coward, 1972).

Natalie Babbitt

Among the things Natalie Babbitt enjoys in life are animals, (she has four cats and a dog), bad storms of every kind, (she finds them remarkably soothing), weird kinds of needlework, (at the time of this interview she had just spent a week making a mock turtle costume for her daughter), and doing crossword puzzles. She also is a joy to interview for she loves to answer lots of questions.

Ms. Babbitt is a young-looking forty year old. "As forty stares me in the face, I am just beginning to understand myself and to accept the things about me that I find disappointing," she commented. "I always intended to be dignified, but am not; serene, but am not; reserved, but am not."

Since her marriage to Samuel Fisher Babbitt, she has lived almost exclusively in the academic world. Mr. Babbit, an educator, is currently serving as President of Kirkland College. He accepted this position in 1968 and became the first president of this women's counterpart to Hamilton College for men in upstate New York.

The Babbitts have three children in their early teens. "My children are pretty much grown now, so my life is less complicated than it has been. I did not even try to begin my writing career until my youngest child was in kindergarten. But I am still a juggler, always having to make choices between my work and my more mundane duties. I try not to let my work suffer from this, but often it is inevitable. I am a strong supporter of women's liberation, but juggling can be very debilitating. I wouldn't want to be entirely independent. Family life is very dear to me, and I am entirely content living in this academic world," she stated.

Ms. Babbitt was born in Dayton, Ohio, in 1932 and grew up in towns all over Ohio. "I was the younger of two children, and our family was a tight, secure, protective unit. My mother was an artist of landscapes and portraits, though she never felt she had the time and/or the right to become a real professional. She gave me invaluable help. I had a very happy childhood in spite of numerous moves and spent most of my time reading and drawing. I read mostly fairy tales and Greek myths, but my mother would read aloud every night from a list she somehow came by of the children's classics, which included everything from *Penrod* to *The Water Babies. Alice in Wonderland* was read to me when I was nine; it has been my favorite book ever since."

While she was just about eight or nine years old, she made the decision to work in the field of children's books, but it was a long time before this decision bore results. The first book she worked on was her husband's *The 49th Magician* (Pantheon, 1966); she

illustrated the text. Their collaboration was inter-
rupted, however, because of Mr. Babbitt's academic
demands. With her husband pressed for time, she
turned to writing herself, creating two picture books
with stories in verse—*Dick Foote and the Shark*
(1967)* and *Phoebe's Revolt* (1968).

"I did not think originally of writing," she recalled,
"I wanted only to be an illustrator. If I have had the
courage to write, it is due entirely to the encouragement and support of my editor, Michael di Capua at
Farrar, Straus & Giroux. I don't think I would ever
have attempted to write prose without his urging. Now
I am far more interested in writing than in illustrating,
though I still enjoy the picture-making process very
much."

The Search for Delicious (1969), a prose fantasy
for middle-grade readers, marked a new direction in
her writing. "*Delicious* is to come out soon in Japanese—something I cannot wait to see!" she exclaimed.

The Search for Delicious was followed by *Kneeknock Rise* (1970), which was selected as a 1971
Newbery Honor Book. Ms. Babbitt told me about the
book's development: "*Kneeknock Rise* was a long
time in the hopper. I wanted at first to do a simple
picture book with the same title character as in *The
49th Magician*. In the beginning there was to be a
mountain, a symbol of life and accomplishment, which

---

* All titles mentioned have been published by Farrar, Straus.

everyone was in the constant process of climbing. The magician was to discover that most people stopped and settled down long before reaching the top; in other words, they were content with a good deal less than the whole bag! Then the magician evolved into a child, and I wondered what he might find at the top of the mountain. This led to the Kneeknock verse about the other side of the hill, and eventually around an undefinable psychic corner, to the Megrimum. It was to have been only a funny story, but it got away from me."

Following this book the author-illustrator produced *The Something* (1970), a picture book, and *Goody Hall* (1971), a skillfully wrought type of Gothic mystery.

While on the subject of *Kneeknock*'s development, I asked about her work habits in general. "I take my work very, very seriously and suspect that this is fatuous. With each new story, the pattern is much the same. It begins with a word or phrase that strikes some kind of sympathetic chord. (I have an inordinate fondness for words and the alphabet.) From this, a group of characters evolve. The characters assume more and more positive personalities, and the events that follow stem from the actions and reactions they might logically be expected to have. I never seem to begin by saying to myself that I want to write about superstition, for instance. *Goody Hall* really began with my sudden affinity for the word *smuggler*. All of the mulling over takes place before a single word is committed to paper, and there is usually a great deal of research and rewriting. I like to present my editor with as polished a first draft as I can. I never try out my ideas on children."

Kneeknock Rise is her favorite book so far. "For some reason the story almost seemed to form and write itself. I felt no constraint in the vocabulary I used nor in saying what I wanted to say; though for that matter, I seldom do. I am a firm believer in the perceptiveness and intelligence of children. The characters and the situation in *Kneeknock Rise* were very real to me well before I began to write. Perhaps this is because *Kneeknock Rise* has a very simple, straightforward message. Nevertheless, I thought then and still think that it is an odd sort of story, and its success has been a great surprise to me."

The Babbitts live in Clinton, New York, a country village nine miles southwest of Utica in the Mohawk Valley. Their house sits on a hillside just below a forest. "This is farming country with rolling hills, lots of sky, not very many people, and very dramatic weather," Ms. Babbitt commented. "Presently my greatest pleasures in life are evenings at home with my family with nowhere to go and nothing pressing to do (evenings like these are very rare during the academic year) and long telephone conferences with my editor. I am thoroughly unathletic, do not like cooking or housework, and have no special hobbies. I have no really strong feelings about possessions but am devoted to my workroom and all it contains from the most treasured book down to the last penpoint."

When Ms. Babbitt is not at the typewriter or drawing board, she is busy "homemaking". A great deal of time is spent as official hostess for Kirkland College where she also teaches classes in writing and illustrating. She frequently reviews children's books for the *New York Times* and contributes articles to educational journals.

* * * Harry Behn

Harry Behn (Bane), author, poet, anthologist, and screenwriter, was born on September 24, 1898, in Yavapai County, Arizona, just across Granite Creek from an Indian reservation. He reminisced: "I was born in McCabe, a mining camp I can no longer find even as a ghost town because Walt Disney or some such 'historian' bought it in its entirety and moved it to somewhere near Los Angeles for the edification of future students of my literature—at least so I modestly suspect!

"I grew up in Prescott, Arizona Territory, about

which I am now writing a novel for boys. It was a wonderful happy, and dangerous life. My parents were kind to me, but if I had been a baboon, I dare say they would have been quite as nice because they were very good-natured. The only near tragedy I remember was the sound of a trombone my father bought and practiced on one hour and twenty minutes for two days.

The turn of the century was an exciting era in the West, and Mr. Behn's childhood years certainly sound like a scenario for a Hollywood film. The Indians, who lived in wickiups on the reservations they were forced to live on greatly influenced him. He learned about nature from his Indian companions — plants and animals, weather and the seasons. He stalked antelope, stirred up quail, climbed canyons, and was chief of a homemade tribe who called themselves The Mount Vernon Avenue Alley Long Beargrass Tribe, named partly after the alley behind the street where most of the members lived and partly after a Yavapai boy named Charlie Long Beargrass.

Mr. Behn recalled going often to visit Charlie at the Indian camp, sitting around a campfire, and listening to Charlie's father tell of Indian lore.

Mr. Behn's father was a mining man, a trade that did not particularly appeal to the younger Behn, though he did occasionally pan a few grains of gold out of the creek. Cowboys and Indians — the real vintage — were as much a part of his life as television is to today's child. "Nothing has ever meant more to me than the lore I learned as a child from Indians," he declared.

After graduating from high school, he lived for a summer with the Blackfoot tribe. He might have stayed longer, but his parents "lured him into college."

In 1922 Mr. Behn received his Bachelor of Science degree from Harvard University; the following year he went to Sweden as an American-Scandinavian Fellow. From that time on his achievements in the arts have been manifold. He worked as a screenwriter for major motion picture studios, founded and managed the University of Arizona Radio Bureau, founded and edited the journal, *Arizona Quarterly,* founded the University of Arizona Press, edited *Anthropological Papers,* volumes one through four, and taught creative writing courses at the University of Arizona.

In 1947, at the age of forty-nine, he left Arizona to live in Connecticut where he settled down to write and travel. This move changed the course of his professional life; in 1949 his first book for children, *The Little Hill* (Harcourt), a book of poetry, was published.

"The book was written for my own children," he told me. The book's dedication reads "To Pamela, Prescott and Peter." Mr. Behn not only wrote the thirty poems in this volume, but supplied the picture-decorations as well. He thus chalked up three new vocations in one fell swoop—children's author, poet, and illustrator.

The following year *All Kinds of Time* (Harcourt, 1950) appeared, a poetic picture story describing the wonders of time for very young children. This unusual book has remained popular for over two decades. The first page of the slim volume gives a clue why and shows the poet's fresh use of words and imagery:

> I learned about clocks
> when I was quite little.
> I was half-past four.
> Now I'm five.

The book was designated as one of thirty classics selected by The New York Public Library and *Life* magazine.

Volumes of poetry for both younger and older girls and boys followed. Titles include *Windy Morning* (Harcourt, 1953), *The House Beyond the Meadow* (Pantheon, 1955), a book of seven long poems, *The Wizard in the Well* (Harcourt, 1956, 1959), and *The Golden Hive* (Harcourt, 1967), a book of poetry for older readers.

In 1962, Mr. Behn put on a new hat—translator of Japanese haiku poetry. For Peter Pauper Press he translated *300 Classic Haiku*. This book led to two more books published by Harcourt, his popular *Cricket Songs* (1964) and *More Cricket Songs* (1971). All three of his books of haiku are treasures to have: Haiku verse contains seventeen syllables broken into three lines of five, seven, and five syllables respectively. About this form the author stated: "It is made by speaking of something natural and suggesting simply spring, summer, autumn, or winter. There is no rhyme. Everything mentioned is just what it is, wonderful, here, but still beyond."

Both *Cricket Songs* and *More Cricket Songs* are

illustrated with handsome black and white photographs of paintings chosen from the works of Japanese
masters. They perfectly complement the texts.

Although best known for his poetry, this man of
many talents has also produced novels for older children. These include *The Faraway Lurs* (World, 1963),
a moving story set in Denmark during the Bronze Age
telling of the love between young people of warring
tribes; *The Two Uncles of Pablo* (Harcourt, 1959), a
tale set in Mexico; and *Omen of the Birds* (World,
1964), a book that received an Honor Award from the
Boys' Clubs of America.

I asked Mr. Behn if he had a favorite book among
the many he has produced. "To select from the many
books I did for children between the ages of three and
fifteen is like trying to choose a descendant to leave
my millions to," he answered. "The littlest ones are
my favorites, until I discover with amazement all sorts
of extraordinary touches of genius in some of those I
had scarcely noticed before. The book I am working on
is always my favorite."

Mr. Behn commented on the nature of children's
lives and the books that are produced for them. "Between writing my books, I am appalled by terrifying
books for and about children insulated from the earth
by asphalt, from the air by poisonous gases, and from
each other, parents, and decent life in general by television, radio, and a redundancy of propaganda horn-
ing in on one trend or another. I am not complaining
about books that are clearly illuminating."

Regarding his writing he told me: "All of my stories

and poems derive from dreams, which I believe are so ancient that they have not been items of gossip for fifty thousand years. I love to polish whole structures and sentences and verbal sounds almost as if they were music. As for formal writing training, I have endured much but seem able to forget all the rules."

Mr. Behn and his wife Alice live in Greenwich, Connecticut, in a house beside a lake. "What makes everyday a joyous event year round is the home of my wife, myself, visiting children, grandchildren, and friends. It is vividly beautiful here during every season. There are not many more lovely Japanese gardens or homes left in Japan. Care and nurture of my natural garden leaves me little time to be disturbed by unnatural, dire, and devious catastrophes about which I can do nothing.

"I am said to have a bland disposition but I can be roused to outrage by the private languages all special disciplines seem to think they must invent. The most repellant word to me today is *relevant.* To what or to whom is carefully unmentioned.

"My book *Chrysalis: Concerning Poetry and Children* (Harcourt, 1968) contains every important concept I live by; at least they are indicated therein."

Recently the author reread *Chrysalis* and "really enjoyed it. After two years of wondering just what it did say, I found that almost everything that matters to me is in there somewhere."

You can get to know Harry Behn better by reading *Chrysalis.* It is an important text that says a great deal about children, their growing-up years, their fresh awakenings, and their delight in sensing things for the very first time. Mr. Behn can be heard talking briefly about his life, reading twenty-four of his poems, and telling why he wrote some of them on the 33 1/3 rpm recording *Poetry Parade*, edited by Dr. Nancy Larrick and produced by Weston Woods Studios.

Also by Mr. Behn

The Painted Cave (Harcourt, 1957).

Timmy's Search (Seabury, 1958).

What a Beautiful Noise (World, 1970).

*
* **Michael Bond**
* *

United States readers have adopted and taken into their hearts some fine contemporary English authors and illustrators. For younger children there are the books of such talented people as Raymond Briggs, John Birmingham, Helen Oxenbury, and Brian Wildsmith; for older boys and girls library shelves are stocked with books by P. L. Travers, Leon Garfield, and the man who is the subject of this interview, Michael Bond, creator of the "Paddington" series.

Mr. Bond, his wife, and teen-age daughter live in a two-story house on the side of a hill in Haslemere, Surrey, a small town about forty-five miles from London in part of what is known as the "commuter belt." Theirs is a residential neighborhood surrounded with a wooded area and a great deal of National Trust land—land that cannot be built on.

"The best way to describe myself," stated Mr. Bond, "is this way: I once received a letter from a boy who had acquired a Dutch edition of *Paddington*. The book had a photograph on the back showing an early-Bond—tall, dark, and thick-haired. He wrote saying how surprised he was as 'he'd always pictured someone about forty-five years old, running to fat, and losing his hair.' All I could do was write back to the lad saying, 'I have news for you—you are so right!'"

Mr. Bond was born in Newbury, Berkshire, England, on January 13, 1926, and grew up in Reading, Berkshire. "I was an only child," he said. "I had very kind parents. After getting home from work in the evenings, my father used to play endless games of cricket with me in the local park, when he must have been longing to put his feet up. My mother read to me from an early age. My favorite reading matter then was a magazine called *The Magnet* about a school called Greyfriars and a character named Billy Bunter. I used to read it under the bed clothes by the light of a torch, until I knew it so well I could almost have written it myself. I had a dog called Binkie and three guinea pigs called Pip, Squeak, and Wilfred. I hated school, which I left at the earliest opportunity (fourteen in those days). I didn't pass my exams, but come to think of it—I didn't take any! I was mad-keen on anything electrical or mechanical and was always taking things to pieces. At the suggestion of my grandfather, who was a great tease, I once took a drum to pieces to see where the sound came from. I was also mad about puppets and built my own theatre with a revolving stage. I still love puppets."

Mr. Bond never thought of writing for children. He began writing in 1946 while serving in the army in Egypt. His first short story was published in a magazine, *London Opinion*. From then on he decided he wanted to be a writer. "I amassed a vast quantity of rejection slips but also had stories and articles published in various magazines and newspapers. I turned to writing radio plays, then television. At my agent's suggestion I turned one television play into a children's play and then began to write additional things for children."

His first book for children, *A Bear Called Paddington,* was published in England in 1958; that year marked two important births—Paddington and Mr. Bond's daughter, Karen. In 1960 Houghton Mifflin published the book in America and has continued to publish its sequels. (Titles in the series appear at the end of this interview.)

Mr. Bond recalled how the book came about: "I

bought a small toy bear one Christmas Eve. I saw it left on the shelf of a London store, felt sorry for it, and named it Paddington because we were living near Paddington Station at the time. I wrote some stories about the bear, more for fun than with an idea of having them published. After ten days I found I had a book on my hands. It wasn't written specifically *for* children, but I think I put into it the kinds of things I liked reading about when I was young."

Paddington *is* fun — he is a delightfully engaging bear who constantly gets himself in and out of unintentional mischief. Peggy Fortnum, illustrator of the series, has made the character even more endearing.

Mr. Bond's own personal favorite in the series is *Paddington Helps Out* (1961), "because this was the most fun to do."

The books have been translated into approximately ten major languages. "I am constantly surprised by all these translations, because I thought Paddington was essentially an English character. Obviously Paddington-type situations happen to people the world over."

In 1965, after producing several *Paddington* titles, Mr. Bond retired from his job as television cameraman with the British Broadcasting Corporation, a job he held for many years, to write full-time.

His writing habits are quite fixed: "I start at 8:30 sharp each morning and am a compulsive worker. I don't believe in sitting around waiting for inspiration. Ideas come by living life normally and developing a sense of observation. Everything that happens is material. I give a good deal of thought to ideas before starting work on them, partly because this is the fun part of writing and I hate the *act* of writing—putting the first words on paper and knowing in advance they are going to be wrong—but once I start, I like to work quickly. I don't do much reworking, except on *Paddington,* which these days often takes about twelve rewrites before I'm happy."

In 1971, a new character evolved from Mr. Bond's mind and pen—Olga da Polga, a guinea pig with extraordinary gifts and one who is as loveable as Master Paddington. Mr. Bond told how *The Tales of Olga da Polga* (Penguin, 1972; Macmillan, 1973) came into being: "Olga came about originally because I was asked to write a series of short, short stories for a local magazine and Olga was—is—a pet guinea pig. Olga first came into our lives in August 1965. She was a birthday present for our daughter and came from Basingstoke. It all took place much as I've told it. Some of the stories in the book actually happened—like the time she fell out of her house and nearly had to be put to sleep; others are figments of Olga's imagination. I'm not too sure which are which any more."

The author is fond of this book because Olga is an important part of his family and because he feels it's his best work to date.

A mouse called Thursday is the main character in another of his series. One of the titles, *Thursday in*

Paris (Lothrop, 1969), was set in France, a country which he loves and where one day he would like to live. *"Thursday in Paris* was great fun to do," he commented, "because it meant going to my favorite city to do the research, and I could legitimately claim the trip as an expense, though the tax authorities took some convincing." (Tax authorities are the same everywhere in the world!)

Mr. Bond is a compulsive collector of catalogs, books, magazines, and bits of paper. But sometimes he revolts against all this "as there is a nomad inside me trying to get out, and I am romantically envious of people who don't own very much." He hates sports but enjoys building and making things. He also likes to travel and enjoys cities: "I like exploring back streets."

He loves the theatre and been involved in it via television for which he created forty-five puppet episodes for the BBC—one series entitled *The Herbs,* another *The Adventures of Parsley.* Parsley is a lion, and all the characters have herbal names: Dill, the dog, Constable Knapweed, Sage, the owl, Sir Basil, and Lady Rosemary. All of these characters will soon find their way into a series of children's books.

"My first ambition in life was to be a scene-shifter because I once went to the theatre and when the curtain went up, I saw one who had been caught onstage. I have never lost the kick of the contrast between the red plush of the theatre and life backstage."

His current obsession? An idea for an adult comic strip.

Also by Mr. Bond

"The Paddington Series"
(All published by Houghton Mifflin)

Paddington Helps Out (1961).

More About Paddington (1962).

Paddington at Large (1963).

Paddington Marches on (1965).

Paddington Takes the Air (1971).

Paddington Abroad (1972).

"The Thursday Series"
(All published by Lothrop)

Here Comes Thursday (1967).

Thursday Ahoy (1969).

Thursday Rides Again (1969).

** *
* * Frank Bonham
*

Sam Stone

"I had been writing twenty years when I discovered children's books. I was astonished and delighted to learn that almost any subject was a good one for children's stories, and after backing into the field, continued to write mysteries, television scripts, and westerns, I

decided the real satisfaction was in writing adventure books for young people," declared Frank Bonham.

His first book for young readers was *Burma Rifles* (T. Y. Crowell, 1960), a story of the Niseis (Japanese-Americans) with Merrill's Marauders in World War Two. Since then he has written over a dozen books for children in the middle grades as well as short stories, novels, and novellettes for adults. He has also produced television scripts for such series as "Wells Fargo," "Shotgun Slade," and "Death Valley Days."

Mr. Bonham commented on his childhood: "I was born on February 25, 1914, in Los Angeles, California, and I was raised there before smog and freeways. My father was born there also and his mother before him, in 1853. We moved around a little, trying to find a place where an asthmatic child—me—could breathe. Asthma was one of the big realities of my childhood. It never quite killed me, but it ended my college career, and I moved to a mountain cabin where I started writing. Indirectly I owe a lot to ill health. It kept me from becoming a third-rate newspaperman and forced me into a profession I love and for which I am suited. And because I had to take care of myself, I am now in good shape. I run two miles a day. My family life as a child was unremarkable, although my grandfather was a gold camp judge, and both he and my mother were poets. I started writing for pleasure when I was about fourteen. I think I wrote out my dissatisfactions—just as a canary sings out of loneliness."

He described himself as "a shy, self-effacing little

man who lives a sort of Walter Mitty existence. I get most of my kicks inside my skull. Yet aware that there is some fun going on out there, I force myself into activities such as skin diving, working out at the Y every night, working as a volunteer at a parolee house in San Diego, researching subjects for stories—dolphins, tuna boats, juvenile delinquency, racial problems, and police work. The necessity to do field research has brought me much pleasure—and a little wisdom.

"I am a hard-core unemployable; I have never held a job. Sometimes I think one should start in some other occupation and then become a writer, if only to value and appreciate one's freedom in the profession. Everyone envies me my freedom, except around bill-paying time. There is no floor or ceiling on a free-lancer's finances."

Mr. Bonham lives with his wife, Gloria, a schoolteacher, in La Jolla, California, in a quiet, middle-class neighborhood. "We were on the outskirts of the city until a few years ago and used to feed foxes in our backyard. Then houses began to spring up, and the foxes seldom come anymore. I imagine they are as sad about this as we are," he sighed.

The Bonhams have three children, all boys. The youngest is now in college. Two of their children are handicapped. "I am sure that my boys have shaped much of my feeling for the underdog. I have learned much from them. I think we learn a lot more from unhappiness than from happiness, but there are limits to what human beings can absorb in this way. The gods should use more judgement in the matter! But I do know that if everything had gone swimmingly well, I would be a lousy, shallow writer. My oldest son is married, and I have three delightful, little grand-daughters."

Writing for Mr. Bonham is a continuing educational process, and he loves it. When he wrote western stories, he owned a horse and rode. When he wrote stories about submarines, he took a trip on a submarine, rode a sub tender, and had endless conversations with "old submariners" in the process. He also learned to skin dive with a snorkel and fins. When he wrote a story about boys and their racing cars, he spent many hours riding in midget racers and talking with the mechanics and drivers. Realism and fact are to him the basis of any good story.

Commenting on his work habits Mr. Bonham told me: "Ideas come to me from my reading and living, and in the early development of my stories, I rely heavily on my sub- or unconscious. A fragmentary idea dropped into one's unconscious will rise again, if it is a worthy idea, as a hint of a story. Then there is a lot of hard, conscious work in developing the ghostly outline into a story-line. I rework my stories as I go along and after I finish. For *Durango Street* (1965)* I had nearly two thousand pages of rough draft, out of

*Unless otherwise noted, all titles mentioned were published by Dutton.

which came two hundred pages of finished manuscript."

Durango Street is a strong, dramatic story about Rufus Henry, a seventeen-year-old, whose only method of survival is as a gang member engaged in gang warfare.

"The book started out as a story about White kids in a gang. But I soon learned that gang activity is largely just another aspect of racial discrimination. So to tell a story, a true story about what it was like to be born poor and Black, I changed the original concept. White kids, at first, did not show much interest in knowing these things. However Blacks immediately took the book to their hearts. I did research for about a year and a half on the background before beginning to write. Then I realized with panic that I had no plot. As soon as I turned on the faucet, the outline of the story emerged. Ten months of hard work went into writing this book. It has given me great satisfaction to know that the kids who are living the lives I describe in the book, or something close to them, are reading it and saying, 'That's true!' " The novel embodies his beliefs about many aspects of our society.

Since *Durango Street,* Mr. Bonham has written other books for and about minority youngsters, including *The Nitty Gritty* (1968), *Mystery of the Fat Cat* (1971), and *Viva Chicano* (1971).

His favorite book is *The Vagabundos* (1969) for "it expresses more of what I feel about the human condition. It is an escape book—a father fleeing his family, a son trying to find him and bring him back." The book is also a favorite because it is set in Baja, California, where he spends time skin diving and beachcombing.

Mr. Bonham recently resumed studying French "after many years off," in order to read Georges Simenon, the contemporary mystery-adventure writer. He likes exercising and running "because I know it keeps my mind more alive." He collects first editions of favorite authors' works, has a random collection of beach-worn shells, which he gazes at now and then "for modified escape purposes," and enjoys yard work, which he wouldn't really call gardening.

His mysteries, popular among children, depict many of his life interests. They include *Mystery of the Red Tide* (1966) and *Mystery in Little Tokyo* (1966). I asked Mr. Bonham why he felt mysteries have such appeal to youngsters. "I think mysteries lift all of us out of the rut," he replied. "We try to see mystery in everything—we want to believe something extraordinary has happened or is about to happen. And in mysteries the right things usually happen, after many a close call; this leaves the reader satisfied. Kids love to fantasize, and mysteries take these mental adventures a step further for them. Children want to believe in the unusual—don't we all?

He said of his work habits: "I studied composition in school and took journalism, but I don't think one can study writing as such. It's a matter of discovering one has a liking and a talent for working with words and developing it by hard work. A woman once asked Robert Frost when he decided to become a poet. He replied, 'When did you decide to become a beautiful woman?' It just happens, but you can help the process a little.

"I run my business the way a businessman runs his —going to work at 8:30 a.m., quitting at 4:30 p.m. But it's not that simple. Magic either happens or doesn't happen. There are traps in writing for young people, and one of these is the temptation to preach. I hope that I do not suffer from this disease in its severest form; I feel sure that I do not, since there are few things of which I myself feel certain and not many topics on which I could care to write a sermon."

The Bonhams recently bought one hundred acres of fir woods in Oregon where they hope to spend part of the year one day. "Azaleas, rhododendron, daffodils, and many other plants grow there. And coyotes, foxes, elk, deer, and a million birds live among the trees and plants. I promise not to build houses or supermarkets on the land!" he exclaimed.

Also by Mr. Bonham

All published by Dutton
The Ghost Front (1968).
Chief (1971).
Hey, Big Spender (1972).

✳ Arna Bontemps✳

I first came to know Arna Bontemps (Bon-tamp) while working on an anthology, *Don't You Turn Back: Poems by Langston Hughes* (Knopf, 1969). Virginie Fowler, my editor, had asked Mr. Bontemps to prepare an introduction to the collection. No one else could have written such an introduction, for Mr. Bontemps and the late poet, Langston Hughes, were life-long friends. Mr. Bontemps is now an executor of the Langston Hughes estate.

Mr. Bontemps was born in Alexandria, Louisiana, on October 13, 1902. In 1906 his family moved to California. He grew up in Los Angeles and its suburbs —Glendale, Watts, and San Fernando. He attended college in northern California, graduating with a B. A. degree from Pacific Union College in 1923. The following year his first poem appeared in *The Crisis,* the official magazine of the National Association for the Advancement of Colored People. At the time, Dr. W. E. B. DuBois was the editor. Mr. Bontemps' poetry continued to be published, and he became a prominent literary figure in New York's Harlem.

---

*Mr. Bontemps died at his home in Nashville on June 4, 1973.

Among other things, the 1920s marked the era of the Harlem Renaissance, a period of important cultural accomplishment for Blacks. This creative movement ended when the Great Depression began in the early 1930s.

During Mr. Bontemps seven years in New York, he was an active participant in this renaissance and won awards and prizes for his poems and short stories. His first book, *God Sends Sunday* (AMS, 1931) was a novel for adults. After leaving New York, he spent three years in Alabama and then returned to California. Here he wrote his second adult book, *Black Thunder,* a historical novel based on the slave insurrection of Gabriel Prosser. It has recently been re-issued in paperback by Beacon Press, some thirty years after its first publication.

His first book for children was *Popo and Fifina* (out of print), written in collaboration with Langston Hughes. "Langston had the story and told it to me; I had the children! So we worked together," he recalled.

He again left California, this time to do graduate work at the University of Chicago where he received an M.A. degree in 1943 and to serve on the staff of the director of the Illinois Writers Project. During this time he began writing books for young people. His first was *Sad-Faced Boy* (Houghton Mifflin, 1937), a story about Slumber, a boy who never smiled. The text was illustrated by the late Caldecott Award-winning artist, Virginia Lee Burton; it was her first book, too! At that time few books portrayed Blacks realistically, and unfortunately the illustrations were usually stereotypes, far from what would be considered acceptable in the 1970s.

I asked Mr. Bontemps why he decided to write for young people. "For two reasons," he replied. "As a child I read a great deal and never forgot the books I had enjoyed most, and secondly, by the time I started writing as a man, I had children of my own and wanted them to read *my* books—as well as other people's, of course!"

In 1941 a small classical volume of poetry appeared, *Golden Slippers: An Anthology of Negro Poetry for Young Readers* (Harper), compiled by Mr. Bontemps. This was the first effort to gather into one volume a collection of Black poetry suitable for young people. Some thirty years later the volume remains a treasury of Black poetry and contains the works of such greats as Paul Laurence Dunbar, Countee Cullen, Claude McKay, and, of course, Langston Hughes. But again the drawings by Henrietta Bruce Sharon depicted stereotyped Blacks.

In 1948 Bontemps' *Story of the Negro* (Knopf) was cited by the American Library Association as a Newbery Honor Book. In 1955 *Lonesome Boy* (Houghton Mifflin) appeared, a slim, twenty-nine page book that is still quite popular with middle-grade readers. It tells the story of Bubber, a New Orleans boy who loved his trumpet so much that he felt lonesome if he walked without it. The text was illustrated by the Polish-born painter, Feliks Topolski, whose portraits of George Bernard Shaw, Sir Winston

Churchill, Jawaharlal Nehru, and Queen Elizabeth II are as well known as his murals in Buckingham Palace. It was the first juvenile Mr. Topolski illustrated.

An important contribution to literature, *Hold Fast to Dreams: Poems Old and New* (Follett) appeared in 1969. This is the anthology the *Horn Book* magazine described as "a varied feast of poetry and a wonderful representation of poets." Mr. Bontemps said of it: "Sometime during my childhood I heard it said that old-time bakers would save a little of the dough they mixed each day. The following day they would mix a little of the dough saved from yesterday with today's dough and then bake them together. I asked my old great uncle about this. He was a retired baker in my school days, and he assured me that this was right. I liked the idea of mixing a little of the old with the new in this way. So when I became a teacher in Chicago, an editor at Follett, Ms. Bertha Jenkinson, asked me if I had in the back of my mind some book that I had always wanted to do. I told her that I would like to collect a book of poems old and new that seemed to go well together. I said I thought all poems could be divided two ways—the poems we remember and the ones we forget. Mine would be a collection of the poems I remembered well, and some would be old, some new. The result was *Hold Fast to Dreams.*"

"What is poetry?" I asked Mr. Bontemps. He replied: "If you have to ask, there is no need trying to tell you! The old folks down home used to say when talking about singing or preaching or the old-time religion, 'You will shout when it hits you.' You may not shout when you remember poems you have read or learned, but you will know from your toes to your head that something has hit you."

Presently Mr. Bontemps lives on a hilltop overlooking Nashville, Tennessee. He is married to "the same beautiful girl" he married in 1926. "All night we can see, but not hear, cars and trucks on a highway, half a mile away. A sea of lights keeps the sky bright down below us."

The Bontemps have six children and ten grandchildren. He has been a teacher, librarian, and author, dividing his time equally between the three professions. For more than twenty years he served as librarian at Fisk University in Nashville. He has lectured widely throughout the United States and has visited most parts of the world. His interest in sports led him to write *Famous Negro Athletes* (Dodd, Mead, 1964).

Commenting on his diverse writing interests, he said: "I have never had to worry about ideas. My problem is finding enough time to write them down. So many things happened while I was growing up, and I have seen and participated in so many activities; I keep a full storeroom of ideas."

As a final question I asked Mr. Bontemps his opinion of the many current books of prose and poetry written by children—many emanating from Black areas and expressing Black experiences of the 1960s and 1970s —and if he thought of this phenomenon as perhaps a second Harlem Renaissance. "The Harlem Renaissance was a lodestar and as such has been most influential," he answered. "But I see a difference between the Black experience then and now. They were alike in that each was centered around very young people. The young people of the Harlem Renaissance are remembered for inspired self-expression in the arts. The young people of the Civil Rights Movement will long be remembered for inspired *action*. I think this is the essential difference. Those children who are just now in grade school may be said to represent still another wave, a second generation. Since children are often more like their grandparents than their parents, these may, a few years hence, produce a second Harlem Renaissance."

Also by Mr. Bontemps

The Fast Sooner Hound (with Jack Conroy; Houghton Mifflin, 1942).

✳ ✳ Carol Ryrie Brink ✳

If you know of a child in the upper-elementary grades who has never read *Caddie Wood-lawn* (Macmillan, 1935), steer him or her to the nearest public library or bookstore to pick up a copy. The book depicts pioneer days in the Wisconsin wilderness during the 1860s, but the story is about Caddie Woodlawn, a spunky, eleven-year-old girl, and her life during the Civil War era.

The book has received many well-deserved awards and honors, including the coveted John Newbery Award in 1936 and a Lewis Carroll Shelf Award in 1959 as a book "worthy enough to sit on the shelf with *Alice in Wonderland.*" Charlotte S. Huck and Doris Young Kuhn in their *Children's Literature in the Elementary School* (Holt, 1968) state that the episodes and adventures of Caddie Woodlawn read like a pioneer *Tom Sawyer.*

I encountered the book during my own childhood days. Growing up in Newark, New Jersey, was as different from rural Wisconsin as the planet Mars; however, this book took hold of me, and Caddie has been a friend throughout my life.

Part of Carol Ryrie Brink's own life is responsible for this modern classic. She was born on December 28, 1895, in Moscow, Idaho. But let her tell about her family life as a child:

"I grew up in Moscow, a small university town in a region of rolling wheat fields and blue mountains. I lost my father when I was five, my mother when I was eight, and I went to live with a very wonderful grandmother and a loving and indulgent aunt. Much of my childhood was lonely, but it was not unhappy—just enough unhappiness to make me think and appreciate. Because I was lonely, I learned a most valuable thing —how to make my own amusements by reading, writing, drawing, making things with my hands, and spending many happy hours on horseback. I always had animal friends—dogs, cats, and pet chickens. My grandmother and aunt were both great storytellers, and I lived vicariously the exciting childhood that my grandmother had lived on the Wisconsin frontier. Her stories were one of the delights of my earlier years."

If Ms. Brink had not been an orphan, *Caddie Woodlawn* might never have been written, since the episodes of her grandmother's life were the natural background for the book.

Ms. Brink entered into the writing world via poetry. Very soon after graduating from the University of Idaho in 1917, she married Raymond W. Brink. "I always wanted to write books, and at first I wrote and published some poetry. I have written poetry all my life but after I began writing prose, I no longer tried to publish the poems. When my two children, David and Nora, were small, they brought home Sunday school papers for me to read aloud. As I read the stories, I said to myself, 'If I can't do better than that, it is too bad.' So I sent my first children's stories to the Sunday school papers, and they were kindly received by friendly editors. I learned more in this humble field than I ever learned from creative writing courses in college.

"One year when we were in France, my husband, small son, and I bought a small motor boat and drove it up the Seine and Yonne rivers from Neuilly to Sens. We had intended to go much further, but the river locks took time, the weather turned cold, and motor trouble developed. But it was a great adventure, and I fictionalized this trip for children in my first book, *Anything Can Happen on the River* (Macmillan, 1934)."

Caddie Woodlawn was her second book. To get the authentic detail and reality for her text, Ms. Brink wrote back and forth to her grandmother, Gram, asking question after question. And Gram always answered. When the book was published the real Caddie, Gram—Caroline Woodhouse—was eighty-two years old and quite amazed at the life her granddaughter had recreated. Ever since the book's publication individual citizens and groups in Wisconsin have wanted a park to commemorate the ideals expressed and implied within its covers. It wasn't until 1968, however, that a specific goal was set. Money was raised for the site in numerous ways, from selling buttons and having square dances to presenting a Caddie Woodlawn play that the author wrote.

In the summer of 1970 the Dunn County Historical Society of Menomonie, Wisconsin, dedicated the Caddie Woodlawn Memorial Park on a corner of what was once Ms. Brink's grandfather's farm. The old house where Caddie, Tom, and Warren Woodlawn (really Woodhouse) lived has been restored and may be visited. The book has been translated into at least ten languages including Japanese, Chinese, and Afri-caans; the play has been produced by children's theatre groups all over the United States and six or eight performances are now given annually in July at the Mabel Tainter Memorial Theatre in Menomonie.

I asked the author how it feels to know *Caddie* is a classic—a book that will be read by generations of children to come. She replied: "Once at a P. T. A. book fair, I sat at a table that displayed my books and a poster giving my name. A very bored and dutiful husband and father sauntered by, but at the sight of my name, his face lit up and his boredom vanished. 'My God,' he said, 'Are you still around? My sister used to read your books when I was a child. I thought that you were just like Louisa May Alcott!'

"It's gratifying to be classed with Ms. Alcott, even though I hope it may still be some years before I go to join her.

"Of my juvenile books I suppose that *Caddie* is my favorite. It is my grandmother's story, and I loved hearing it as a child. I find that children are always delighted to know that the story is true. Also, *Caddie* has made me so many friends all over the world that I must always be grateful to it—to her. Winning the Newbery Award made me very proud and happy, and it has certainly done much to make the book well-known and popular. The medal is one of my prized possessions, and I shall always be thankful for it."

Other later books include several adult novels and juveniles such as *Family Grandstand* (Viking, 1952) and *Family Sabbatical* (Viking, 1956), two novels sparked by her own family life, and *Two Is Better Than One* (Macmillan, 1968), an "almost all true story" of a short period in her childhood. "Of all my twenty-four books," she declared, *"Snow in the River* (Macmillan, 1964; an adult novel) is my favorite. Although it is freely fictionalized, it is probably as near to an autobiography as I shall ever write. I put great feeling into it."

Ms. Brink commented on her work habits: "I like to start with something that I know—a place, a person, an experience—something from which I have had an emotional reaction. Then I enjoy fictionalizing to various degrees and try to recreate my feelings for my readers. I write in the mornings and usually I can put things down in fairly final shape at the first writing. This is because much of the preliminary work has been done in my head as I do other tasks. I used to try out my stories on my own children, particularly my daughter who was a good little critic. Now, after many years experience, I know pretty well what children will like. Perhaps I am still something of a child myself and if I please myself, the children are likely to be pleased.

"But I am first a housewife and homemaker. My husband, a professor of mathematics and writer and editor of college math texts, has always been very helpful and understanding of my writing career. We have the same work habits; all we need are a couple of desks, plenty of paper and sharp pencils, and free time to be happily content. The only advantage he has over me is that he can read and criticize what I write. His writing is as incomprehensible to me as Greek!"

The Brinks live in La Jolla, California. They have a

fairly large house on two levels with a lovely garden on the lower level. A lemon tree, an orange tree, a fig tree, an avocado tree, and a persimmon tree grow in the garden; it also contains lots of roses, camellias, hibiscus, and poinsettias at Christmas time, and many hummingbirds. A bedroom window looks over the ocean, although trees have blotted it out from most of the other windows in the house. The Brinks' favorite possessions are their books; Ms. Brink is also fond of the Caroline table—a small colonial table made by one of her ancestors for his wife Caroline. Ms. Brink told me that, "The table has come down to the many Carolines of the family, including my grandmother, Caroline Augusta Woodhouse. It will go to my daughter, Nora Caroline Hunter."

When asked to describe herself, she replied: "I think that I am probably what you would call a nice, old lady with grey hair, grey eyes, slightly overweight, and reasonably wholesome and harmless. I have a happy disposition and enjoy my life. I like people, almost all kinds, and I like animals. I belong to the Humane Society because I feel that I owe animals a great debt. My husband and I have traveled and lived abroad a good deal. We have a very primitive cabin on a lake in northern Wisconsin where we go in the summer; we enjoy nature and the outdoors. Knowing the wild flowers and trees has been a hobby of mine. For many years I also collected old children's books. I am still an amateur painter."

The Brinks also enjoy their family. Their son is a

lawyer in Minnesota; their daughter a housewife in Whittier, California. "Each of my children has four children of their own and, naturally," the author boasts, "we think that the eight grandchildren possess all possible charms, talents, and delights."

Also by Ms. Brink

Andy Buckram's Tin Men (Viking, 1966).

Winter Cottage (Macmillan, 1968).

The Bad Times of Irma Baumelin (Macmillan, 1972).

✳ ✳ ✳ Robert Burch

*"If you didn't know me, Lee, I'd certainly cheat both you and your readers and describe myself as dark, extremely handsome, and muscular. I might even throw in curly hair and magnificent blue eyes. But it would all be a lie, because I'm rather mousy in looks and disposition. It's very sad," lamented Robert Burch. But it isn't sad at all. I have known Mr. Burch for

years. In 1966, when his book *Queenie Peavy* (1966)*
was awarded the Child Study Association Award,
which is granted to "a book for young people which
deals realistically with problems in a contemporary
world," I was teaching in Fair Lawn, New Jersey. I
attended the luncheon in New York City where Mr.
Burch made his acceptance speech. Several years
later I met him again at an American Library Association conference and through the years have been
fortunate to become well acquainted with the man and
his works.

Mr. Burch is of average height, has a light complexion, and is somewhat taciturn with new acquaintances. But, oh, the inward beauty (there's
plenty of outward beauty, too, to the people who know
him) and the rare insight he has about children and
their growing-up problems, which he describes so
well with his sensitive pen.

Mr. Burch explained how he drifted into the children's book field: "I had not been interested in writing of any sort until I was thirty, when I began taking
writing courses for the fun of it. One course led to
another, and it was in workshops conducted by Dr.
William Lipkind, the Will of the Will and Nicolas picture
book team, that I became serious about juvenile fiction.
I have been fortunate throughout my career with the
tremendous help received from many people—editors,
librarians, educators, friends. But my greatest debt is

*All titles mentioned have been published by Viking.

to Dr. Lipkind. He taught me a healthy respect for children and their books, and his interest and encouragement prompted me to write for a number of years before producing publishable material. I'm delighted that at last I have discovered what I hope never to drift away from."

His first book for children in the middle grades was *Tyler, Wilkin, and Skee* (1963). Prior to this he had written several shorter books, including the picture book, *A Funny Place to Live* (1962). *Tyler, Wilkin, and Skee* tells the story of one year in the life of a Georgian farm family. In creating the book, the author drew upon his own boyhood memories and discovered "the real pleasure in writing books for young people."

In 1964 *Skinny* was introduced to readers. Skinny is a character whom the late Ruth Hill Viguers described in the *Horn Book* (August 1966, p. 443) as "one of the most appealing young illiterates of fiction." The story is about a boy who was orphaned when his father, an alcoholic, died. Wonderfully amusing and touching things happen to Skinny, an unforgettable boy whose adventures are presented in simple and natural prose. The book was awarded the 1969 Georgia Children's Book Award.

Mr. Burch said of *Skinny:* "I wanted to do a character study of someone who was more or less a victim of the cruel sharecropping system of farming that was prevalent at the time in which the story was set. I also wanted to develop a character who would be so self-reliant that neither he nor the reader would really feel defeated by the downbeat ending that was the only honest one for the story. I would have failed myself and the characters in the book if I had contrived a happier solution.''

Two years later *Queenie Peavy* came into the literary scene—a poignant, realistic story set in rural Georgia during the Depression. Queenie is another unforgettable character. She is a defiant eighth-grader who can hit any target with a rock, chew tobacco, and fight hard—all to prove she is just as good as any child, despite the fact that her father is in prison. I asked Mr. Burch if he could tell how he developed this character.

"I wanted to do a character study of a type of person I've known, adult as well as child, who covers up deep-seated hurt with outrageous behavior. Such 'chip-on-the-shoulder' individuals have always interested me. However, Queenie was not based on a real person. I might have used a boy as the central character, but a certain amount of the behavior would then have been dismissed by the adults in the story as 'boys will be boys.' ''

Besides being honored by the Child Study Association of America, the novel has received many other awards since its publication.

Other books by Mr. Burch have been set in rural Georgia, including *D. J.'s Worst Enemy* (1965), a brief sequel, *Renfroe's Christmas* (1968), *Simon and the Game of Chance* (1971), and *Doodle and the Go-Cart* (1972).

Discussing his work further, Mr. Burch said: "I never base characters in my stories on real people. Some of them may be composites of people I have known, but I could never trace one of my characters back to a real person. Nor am I any of the characters myself, although often the setting and the economic circumstances of my stories are what I have known firsthand. Usually I begin a story by thinking of central characters. After I know them so well that they are real to me, I consider plot, wanting it to grow as naturally as possible out of character development and the circumstances of the time and place in which the story is set. Then I rush through the first writing, trying to get the story on paper as quickly as possible. You can be sure that my first drafts are drafty indeed; I can't always make sense of them myself! However, at that stage the real work has just begun. I spend months, sometimes years, rewriting, never entirely satisfied with a manuscript. I eventually reach a point at which I feel that I've done the best I can. It's time then to submit the story and take a few days off for a fishing trip before settling back to work again."

Georgia is home territory to Mr. Burch. He was born there on June 26, 1925, in Fayetteville. "I was the seventh of eight children, six boys and two girls. Although I was a child of the Depression, I did not feel depressed. After all, everybody else was broke too. I learned early that material wealth really isn't important anyway, and we children had ourselves a pretty good time. We also had work to do. Fayetteville in those days was a village, each family having its own live-stock, and I made the mistake of learning to milk when I was in the fourth grade. The following year, when an older brother went away to college, I inherited his duties as the family's milkman, a job I held until I finished high school. Perhaps the work was good for me, but" he confessed, "I'm awfully glad that today my milk comes from a case in the supermarket instead of from a cow.

"As a boy I planned to be a farmer. Possibly this was due more to my love of farm animals than a desire to earn a living from the soil. Even my college training was in agriculture."

Prior to making writing his career, he lived in various parts of the world; while in the United States Army he served in New Guinea, Australia, and Japan. "At one time," he recalled, "I circled the globe, a highlight of the experience being a freighter jaunt from the Orient to Europe. I still enjoy seeing new places and meeting new people, but I'm less of a gypsy now than in years past. In fact I've stayed so close to home in recent years that I've acquired a cat—one of Joey's cat's kittens." (*Joey's Cat* (1969) is a picture book written by Mr. Burch and illustrated by Don Freeman.)

At present Mr. Burch lives in the house in which he grew up; it was built by his great grandfather around 1850. In back of it now are two modern banks and a post office, yet the oldest courthouse in Georgia is only a block away. Old houses stand across the street, but nearby is a new apartment complex. The neighborhood is a mixture of the old and the new in a curious blending of residential and business buildings.

Among his favorite possessions are drawings and prints given to him by illustrator friends and books written and/or illustrated by friends. "At the moment my 'treasure' is a new, electric typewriter. To understand what this means to me," he continued, "you must realize that the machine on which I had been typing was so worn out that the trade-in allowance was only $2.50!"

He leads a quiet life. "A dozen nieces and nephews provide pleasure and at times exasperation. I worry that some of them do not read very much, when I should be worrying that neither do I. I enjoy reading, however, and in addition to adult offerings, I like to read children's books—new ones and the ones I missed while growing up. I regret that I was not a reader as a child.

"My social life consists chiefly of visits with friends at informal gatherings, trips to nearby Atlanta for dinner and a show, and every now and then a card game. Few things are more relaxing for me than a real cutthroat game of cards. I'm not a good player but I'm lucky. I go to New York occasionally for editorial conferences and a reunion with friends. I love the big city but by the end of a sojourn in it, I'm usually saying, 'New York isn't the same any more.' However, no sooner am I on a plane leaving it than I begin planning my next trip back.

"Here at home I especially enjoy a wooded tract that I bought because of its rich variety of native plants, including wild azaleas. I'm frustrated if a day passes without my spending some portion of it in the woods. I am attempting to tame only a bit of it, the site on which I hope to build a lake, studio, and bog garden. These things are a long way into the future, but like Skee, I like to plan ahead.

"One of my hobbies during eight years I spent in New York was clay sculpture. I had just become a Greenwich House potter when I returned to Georgia to live. Sculpture remains an interest with me, but whenever I get my hands in clay nowadays, it is more likely to be in connection with a gardening activity."

At the conclusion of our interview, Mr. Burch commented: "I'm pleased by any attention paid to my work and am delighted when one of my stories is singled out for special recognition, whether by adult selection committees or by children themselves. As a fond parent is happy when a son or daughter has made the honor roll, I'm naturally pleased when one of my books, in effect, has made good grades. But I'm equally proud of the ones who haven't, seeing them as the good-natured kids who will never make an A+ in their lives but who may be more fun to know and more comfortable to be around than their brighter siblings."

**Betsy Byars *

Betsy Byars is a charming woman, filled with vitality — one whose effervescence is catching. I first met her in Dallas, Texas, on June 21, 1971, the evening she made her Newbery Award acceptance speech for her book, *The Summer of the Swans* (1970).*

The previous days had been hectic ones for her; she had to leave her home in West Virginia to fly to Dallas, deliver a speech to hundreds of fans at an annual banquet, meet a host of people at almost round-the-clock breakfasts, lunches, dinners, and cocktail parties, autographing copies continuously. The schedule became a weary one, yet Ms. Byars remained nervously calm.

In a profile article, "Betsy Byars" (*Horn Book, September, 1971, pp. 359–62*), her husband, Edward, a professor of engineering at West Virginia University, described his wife as: " . . . a typical American housewife with four normal, healthy kids . . . a reasonably respectable husband, and a suburban home complete with mortgage . . . Physically attractive she is personally rather shy, certainly not extrovertive or pretentious in the least."

---

* All titles mentioned have been published by Viking.

This "typical American housewife" lives in Morgantown, West Virginia, in a modest, two-story house. West Virginia-made patchwork quilts cover the beds, wicker furniture sits on a screened porch, a swing dangles expectantly on the front porch waiting for someone to sit on it.

Two of the Byars daughters are in college; a third daughter and their only son attend high school.

Ms. Byars was born in Charlotte, North Carolina, on August 7, 1928, and grew up there. "I was a happy, busy child," she told me. "I started sewing when I was very young because my father worked for a cotton mill and we got free cloth. I was making my own clothes by the second grade, although I have a vague recollection of not being allowed to wear them out of the yard. I could make a gathered skirt in fifteen minutes. I sewed fast, without patterns, and with great hope and determination, and that is approximately the same way that I write.

"When I was young, I was mainly interested in having as much fun as possible. Adults were always saying to me, 'If only you would take your piano lessons seriously.' (I had to play "The Spinning Song" three years in a row at my recital!) Or, 'If only you would take your math seriously—or your English.' Or whatever! Enjoying things was just more important to me than taking things seriously.

"I went to Furman University for two years and then transferred to Queens College in Charlotte," she continued, "and graduated in 1950. I was an English major. Right after graduation I married Ed, who was then a professor at Clemson University."

She began writing magazine articles to fill long hours while her husband attended graduate school at the University of Illinois. This was in 1956. Her articles were published in popular magazines including *Saturday Evening Post, Look,* and *TV Guide.*

"My goal was to write mystery stories. I never developed the ability to sustain a mystery, however, and would inevitably give the whole thing away on the second page. As my children grew. I became interested in books for children. My first was published in 1962, *Clementine.* Since then writing has been my main interest."

The Midnight Fox was published in 1968. The central character of this novel is Tom who is sent to stay for two months on his aunt and uncle's farm. A fox becomes the focus of his life.

"This is my favorite book," she asserted, "because it is very personal. A great deal of my own children and their activities went into it, and a great deal of myself. It came closer to what I was trying to do than any of my other books."

The Summer of the Swans, like most of her books, grew from real life experiences. The book is set in present-day America and tells of teen-age Sara who finds life in general rather dull, until Charlie, her retarded brother, disappears in the middle of the night. Ms. Byars reminisced on the development of the story: "Several years ago I was asked to join a volunteer program to tutor some mentally retarded children.

The novel came out of this experience. Although the character, Charlie, is not one of the children I tutored —he is purely a fictitious character—he was an outgrowth of the experience, and the book would never have been written if I had not come to know the children I was tutoring.

"The idea for the swans in the story came from an article in my college alumni magazine about the swans at Furman University in Greenville, South Carolina, who persist in leaving their beautiful lake and flying away to less desirable ponds. I took the liberty of moving the swans to West Virginia and the story began.

"Winning the Newbery Award was a startling experience. One Tuesday morning I got up as usual, got the children off to school, my husband off to work, threw some clothes in the washing machine, and got ready to leave for class. (Ever since we were married we have lived near one university or another, and I have taken courses or sat in on classes that interest me.) As I was leaving the house, the telephone rang. When I learned I had won the Newbery, I couldn't think of anything to say. At that point in life I was not what you would think of as a professional-type writer. I knew very little about the publishing business; I had never been in an editor's office. I didn't even know any other writers. So this seemed the most astonishing thing that had ever happened."

I asked Ms. Byars about her work habits. "Talking about my writing is difficult because I have no set rules rules for working. There is nothing I always do, nothing I try especially to avoid. Each book has a different experience. Sometimes I write a first draft straight through. Sometimes I write one chapter and work on it awhile before I continue. I particularly enjoy writing books about boys and girls in the world today because we are living in an exciting and lively period, and young people are very bright, very individualistic. In the past few years writing has become easier for me, more of a pleasure than work, so much so that I half expect someone to tap me on the shoulder and say, 'Now if you could just take your writing *seriously!*' Two recent books are *The House of Wings* (1972), a poignant story of a frustrated and angry boy who gradually comes to terms with his grandfather through sharing his concern for a wounded crane, and *The Eighteenth Emergency* (1973) about Benjie who enrages Marv Hammerman, the toughest boy in school.

The one hobby she shares with her husband is not the kind you might expect from a typical American housewife. Betsy Byars flies!

"My husband's real love is flying, and so we have always done a lot of it. We used to have very old planes, and when we stopped at airports for gas, people would come out and stare at us. It was disquieting. Once someone asked if we were on our way to an antique air show. But now our plane is more modern, and my husband has a glider, which I help assemble and disassemble. This means putting the plane together, taking it apart, holding a fifty-pound wing tip over my head for long periods of time, polishing the wings and taping the joints. I drive the trailer around the countryside and pick Ed up after flights. He once had a four hundred eighty-five mile flight in Texas so there is a lot of driving! Gliding makes up a big part of our spring and summer activities."

As you can see, Betsy Byars does most of her writing during the winter months when there is time — and strength left.

Also by Ms. Byars

(All published by Viking)

Dancing Camel (1965).

Rama, the Gypsy Cat (1966).

Trouble River (1969).

Go and Hush the Baby (1971).

✳ ✳ ✳ Natalie Savage Carlson

Coit Studio

*During the winter months Nata-*lie Savage Carlson, her husband, Daniel, and their pet dog, Mr. Maclee, live in a mobile home in Clearwater, Florida. She hasn't been going to Florida for too long, but, she declared, "I already have Spanish moss hanging on me!"

As winter ends and spring comes, the Carlsons return home to their estate in Newport, Rhode Island. They live at Periwinkle in a house that was built in 1851. The house has a long literary past; it was the home of Henry Wordsworth Longfellow's Perry relatives. It is said that Mr. Longfellow proofread his famous narrative poem "Hiawatha" under the Carlsons' old cherry tree.

Ms. Carlson was born on October 3, 1906 in Winchester, Virginia. Her childhood years were spent in Weaverton, Maryland, and she grew up in Long Beach, California. "We were a family of seven girls and one boy," she told me. "My brother was the youngest. I have loved animals ever since I was a child. When we lived in Maryland, my greatest enjoyment was horseback riding. I had pet pigeons; I yearned for a muskrat since there were muskrats at our pond, but I was never able to catch a young one. I brought home a pair of wild doves to tame once, but they eventually died. Now I satisfy myself with a dog. As a child I also loved to read and write. I began writing for the children's page of the *Sunday Baltimore Sun* when I was eight years old. I have told about this in my autobiographical book, *The Half-Sisters* (1971)."*

Having an interest in newspaper journalism she worked as a reporter on the *Long Beach Morning Sun* for three years. In 1929 she met and married Mr. Carl-

*All titles mentioned were published by Harper.

son, a naval officer. As a service wife she traveled to and lived in many states, Mexico, and Canada. France was her home for three years and is the setting for many of her books, including her personal favorites —*The Family under the Bridge* (1958) and the "Orpheline" series. (Orphelines are what the French call girl orphans.)

"These are my favorite books because I wrote them when I lived in France and enjoyed the sights and customs of that country so much. My mother being of French-Canadian extraction may have influenced in me my love for anything French.

"My first book, *The Talking Cat and Other Stories of French Canada* (1952), is a retelling of stories told to me by my mother who had heard them from her French-Canadian great-uncle when she was a child in Detroit, Michigan."

I asked Ms. Carlson how the popular *The Family under the Bridge* (1958), a 1959 Newbery Honor Book, developed. She replied: "When I lived in Paris, I was interested in a newspaper account of a Christmas Eve party for the tramps of Paris that was to be held under one of the bridges. I went to the party on my way to midnight mass at St. Etienne-du-Mont but was given the bum's rush by the tramps because I looked too prosperous. At that time I was with a group helping the poor people in Abbe Pierre's shanty town, just outside Paris. Three red-headed children there attracted me, so I combined them with a tramp. Also I was impressed by the number of gypsies in France. Once two gypsy children came to my door selling pins, and I chatted with them about their life. (One of the little girls is Tinka in the book.) I found Christmas preparations in France so fascinating that I used them as the background to the story."

This gay and tender novel has been translated into many languages including Japanese, Persian, and English. "The English edition is one which *misspells* the words," Ms. Carlson laughed.

Book after book have flowed from her pen, including such popular titles as *The Empty Schoolhouse* (1965), winner of the Child Study Association of America Award, *Ann Aurelia and Dorothy* (1968), and *Befana's Gift* (1969). In 1966 Ms. Carlson was nominated as the United States candidate for the Hans Christian Andersen Award.

Regarding her writing she told me: "I took a writing course at night school in San Diego High School one year when my husband's ship was away in Hawaii. I learned much from a splendid teacher. The course cost me one dollar!

"I'm an old-fashioned writer; I only write when I'm inspired. I do, however, spend much time thinking out ideas. I go over my work and revise innumerable times. I don't find it valuable to try out ideas on children because the personal contact and interest prejudice them."

Answering letters from children is as much a part of her life as writing books for them. And she receives many! "I try to answer children's letters as fast as they come in, otherwise I'd be snowed under. Many of the writers want a sequel to some book. They often ask if the story is true; one little girl wanted to correspond with Brigette, the orpheline.

"The letter I liked best began: 'I don't know whether to call you Miss or Mrs. because I don't know if you're married, but for your sake I hope you are.' " (Today children can be saved from this inquiry by addressing the envelope *Ms.*)

She is married, of course. The Carlsons have two daughters, Stephanie and Julie. Stephanie Sullivan is married to an army officer and has four children. The elder, Julie McAlpine has a doctorate degree and teaches children's literature and language arts at the University of Connecticut; her husband teaches non-English-speaking children in Newport.

Ms. Carlson is five-feet two-inches tall. "And I'm one hundred twenty pounds," she added, "but find it a strain to stay there." She loves to cook and invent dishes. "I make the best spaghetti sauce I've ever tasted and also good French pancakes. But my beef roasts are failures."

She collects figurines of children, interesting toys, and postcards. "If we ever decide to live in Florida permanently," she said, "I'm going to have to get rid of some of them." She also enjoys traveling, sightseeing, and "buying stuff in tourist traps; I like dog and rodeo shows, too."

This interview gives a brief glimpse into the life of Natalie Savage Carlson—a woman of charm and wit. The whole story can be found in her two autobiographical novels—the aforementioned *The Half-*

Sisters and *Luvvy and the Girls* (1971). *The Half-Sisters* will soon be published in England. "I don't know *what* the English will call half-sisters," she mused.

Read both books and come to know this author even better.

Also by Ms. Carlson

(All published by Harper)

The Happy Orpheline (1957).

A Brother for the Orphelines (1959).

A Pet for the Orphelines (1962).

The Orphelines in the Enchanted Castle (1964).

Luigi of the Streets (1967).

* **Matt Christopher**
* *

Children in the middle grades, especially sports-minded boys and girls, take to Matt Christopher's books as they take to the annual World Series. Baseball has always been Mr. Christopher's prime interest next to writing. At one time he seriously considered baseball as a career and was offered an athletic scholarship to Cornell University. However, he lacked credit for a required course in mathematics, and since he was the oldest of nine children (seven boys and two girls), he decided to take a job to help bolster the family income.

Mr. Christopher was born in Bath, Pennsylvania, on August 6, 1917, and grew up in Portland Point, New York, near Ithaca. "My mother came from Hungary, my father from Italy," he told me. "I can remember building miniature electric poles, roads, and steam shovels out of wooden boxes when I was still of pre-school age. Later, after moving from Bath to Portland Point, my interests became more sophisticated. I built model airplanes and model ships. My father worked at a cement plant, drawing wages barely sufficient to keep our large family in food and clothing. For a time we weren't able to afford a car. We had to ask neighbors to cart us to the doctor, about a ten-mile drive, whenever one of us became so ill that it worried our parents. We raised pigs and chickens, which helped supplement out meat supply, and in summers we had a garden, the pride and joy of my parents and grandfather, who lived with us. We played the usual games kids did at that time—Annie-over, lost turkey, duck-on-the-rock, and, of course, baseball, which we played with a tennis ball and broom handle."

At the age of fourteen, Mr. Christopher began writing poems and short stories. "I wrote airplane and detective stories just for the fun of it during study periods in high school," he recalled.

In 1937 he entered a national short story writing contest and won a prize. "This proved to be the fatal bite of the bug!" he exclaimed. At fifteen he began to play semi-professional baseball. This was followed by professional playing in the Canadian-American League. He also played in an exhibition game against the New York Giants; on another occasion he was selected the Freeville-Dryden baseball team's most valuable player of the year and was honored by a Matt Christopher Day.

He continued writing and selling humorous verse, one-act plays, teen-age stories, and serials. In 1952 an adult mystery, *Look for the Body,* was published by Phoenix Press. After writing a total of about eighty pieces, he considered writing a baseball book for young people. "Frankly, I couldn't find one I really liked, or thought young people in the fourth or fifth grades would really like, so I tried doing one," he explained.

This was *The Lucky Baseball Bat* (1954).* Other titles about baseball, basketball, and football followed. In all his books the author not only gives a clear account of the game about which he is writing but in each develops a main character and a problem theme. Remembering his first book for children, Mr. Christopher remarked: "In his wish to play baseball, Marvin, the hero, thinks that the bat given to him by a

---

*Unless otherwise noted, all titles mentioned have been published by Little, Brown.

friend is the only bat with which he can hit a baseball. He is unaware of the fact that he is naturally athletic and that baseball is a game that came to him much easier than it has to other boys. When something happens to the bat, his hopes sink, because he thinks the bat was responsible for his good playing, not believing it was himself.

"Having played baseball many years myself, I have seen boys react very much the same way as Marvin did toward their bats. The book has plenty of baseball in it. Marvin's sister, his mother, and dad, are drawn into the story too, which makes me believe, at least hope, that girls would like the book also.

"I tried to accomplish a few things in the book: Marvin's courage in striving on to play the game he loves best in spite of obstacles, his obedience to his family, and his learning that one cannot always succeed at the first try. I wanted to show too, that at his age, he was still susceptible to tears when everything seemed to have gone against him—even as it does sometimes with adults. I wanted this to be not only a baseball story, but also a story of Marvin, a boy to be remembered. I hope I succeeded."

Mr. Christopher then talked about his work habits and how his story ideas are developed: "First, I decide what kind of story I plan to write—baseball, football, or some other sport. Then I decide on a nucleus, the main character's problem. The next step is to devise scenes applicable to the story, select names of my characters, write a plot outline, and then compose from it on my typewriter. After the first draft is written, I go over it about three to four times, polishing it, tightening it, making the story as suspenseful as I can, as plausible as I can. I am the main character in that story. I suffer and laugh with him. I have witnessed incidences in baseball that I have used in my novels. The boy getting hit on the head by a pitched ball, for example, in *The Catcher with a Glass Arm* (1964) was based on an incident that had happened to my nephew."

Mr. Christopher lives with his wife, Cay, and their teen-age son, Duane, in Ithaca, New York. "On a clear day we can see Cayuga Lake. I'm pretty much a father around the house. I enjoy doing carpentry work, repairing appliances—simple ones, that is—and always enjoyed playing with our children and now our grand-children." The Christophers' other children are Martin, Dale, and Pamela.

Mr. Christopher stands five feet ten-and-a-half inches tall and weighs one hundred seventy pounds. He remarked: "I'm quite modest, I think, and more sensitive than I'd like to be. I'm a much better listener than a talker, and I've found that I can adapt myself to most people in any walk of life."

He is an active man. He has taken flying lessons so that he could write airplane stories authentically and has sailed and boated for the same reason. He enjoys swimming, good movies, the television series "Mission: Impossible," the theatre, and traveling. Having played baseball, football, and basketball, he naturally still has an avid interest in these sports, "Although I can only *watch* now!" he conceded.

I asked Mr. Christopher if he had a favorite amongst his books. "My favorite," he replied, "is usually the last one. But this time I'm quite certain about it, for it's the first time I can recall laughing with tears in my eyes while reading the galleys for *The Kid Who Only Hit Homers* (1972). It's my thirty-eighth book!"

Also by Mr. Christopher

All published by Little, Brown

The Year Mom Won the Pennant (1968).

The Basket Counts (1968).

Tough to Tackle (1971).

Face-Off (1972).

Mystery Coach (1973).

✱ Ann Nolan Clark

The temperature in Las Vegas, Nevada, during Thanksgiving 1971, was in the high 70s. A modernistic Santa Claus graced the entrance to the Flamingo Hotel where Ann Nolan Clark was to deliver a speech at the National Council of Teachers of English annual Children's Book Luncheon.

Ms. Clark sat on the dais wearing a lei of white and purple flowers. Behind her hung seven large murals created by children depicting scenes from her books. Several hundred people gathered in the ballroom to hear her presentation. After the luncheon Ms. Clark and I had a chance to talk, prior to our exchange of letters during the following year.

Ms. Clark was born and grew up in the western frontier town of Las Vegas, New Mexico, at the turn of the century. "I had a good and happy childhood," she told me. "I was a child who grew up with and knowing people of four diverse cultures—Indians, French trappers, Spaniards, and a variety of individuals from all over the United States, all of whom lived in my small home town."

In her autobiography, *Journey to the People* (1969, p. 107)*, she stated: "It was the days of early Las Vegas that set the pattern for my thinking. It set the pattern for my acceptance of people and folkways and traditions. It set the pattern which the years have deepened."

She attended school in Las Vegas and later graduated from Highlands University; after this she taught for a short period in two nearby mining communities, before marrying Thomas Patrick Nolan. She did not return to teaching until some years later after her husband died and she had the responsibility of raising their son, Patrick, and then she taught the Indians

---

*Unless otherwise noted, all titles were published by Viking.

in the area. In 1923, she began working with the Bureau of Indian Affairs where she taught and supervised the teaching of Indian children until her retirement in 1962.

Early in her career she endured primitive conditions. She reminisced about one situation where she taught in a one-room schoolhouse with a dirt floor in a pueblo. "The Indian Council would come in and sit around. I was frightened to death of them but soon came to realize they were my friends." She also ran into many "educational insanities." She recalled an incident where she was told that one of the first things one did as a teacher was to teach spelling. *"I* couldn't spell," she exlaimed, "but was told that's what one did." She also remembered teaching the Indian children on Columbus Day all about Columbus and how *he* discovered *them!* "I was always caught between God and John Dewey," she sighed.

In 1940 her work with the Bureau of Indian Affairs changed from teaching to writing. She was assigned to write a series of "Indian Life Readers." The series, all published in the 1940s, were issued in paperbound editions and included titles about the Sioux, Navajo, and Pueblo Indians; they were published in English, Sioux, Navajo, and/or Spanish. (The books are available through Publication Services, Haskell Indian Junior College, Lawrence, Kansas 66044.) The texts far excelled other readers of this era and are distinguished by fine writing telling delightful stories of familiar everyday Indian life and containing simple, informative material. At this time Ms. Clark established a monthly magazine for middle-grade Indian children throughout the country.

When World War II came, however, appropriations were cut and so were the funds for further publishing ventures. Ms. Clark was asked to join a team working with relocated Japanese-Americans to help them establish their own educational programs. During the war her son, an Army Air Force pilot, was killed on a flying mission.

The year 1941 marked a turning point in her life and career. She wrote *In My Mother's House,* a beginning geography book for third-grade Pueblos. The book's exquisite prose and the design and illustrations by Velino Herrera were heralded by critics and designated a Caldecott Honor Book. Three books followed *In My Mother's House;* her fifth, *Secret of the Andes* (1952), won the coveted John Newbery Medal in 1953. "The book had been a gradual piling up of all that I had learned, and of all that I believed," she commented. The story tells of Cusi, an Inca boy who lives in a hidden valley high in the mountains of Peru, with Chuto, an old llama herder. Unknown to Cusi, he is of royal blood and is the "chosen one." "The theme of the book—I guess you'd call it that—is based on an historical fact," she confided.

From 1953 to the present Ms. Clark has written over twenty books for children of various age levels and brought readers her rich, life-long involvement with Indian culture. I asked her if she had a favorite among her books. She replied: "My favorite is always the one I'm now writing—never the one that was just published."

Currently Ms. Clark lives in Cortara, Arizona, a desert town nearby Tucson. "I only have one close neighbor here. As for favorite possessions, all my possessions are favorite ones. If they don't mean something to me, I don't keep them. I have no hobbies. I don't have time for them." She has one grandson, two great-grandchildren.

Further information on the life and philosophy of Ann Nolan Clark are given in the previously mentioned autobiography, *Journey to the People.* Much of her philosophy was also stated in her Newbery acceptance speech (*Horn Book,* September 1953, pp. 251+), when she commented:

All children need understanding, but children of segregated racial groups need even more. All children need someone to make a bridge from their world to the world of the adults who surround them. Indian children need this; they have the child problems of growing up, but also they have racial problems, the problems of conflicting interracial patterns between groups, and the conflicts of changing racial patterns within the group. Anyway you look at it, it's rugged to be a child. Often I think more of us did not survive the experiences than meets the eye.

Also by Ms. Clark

Santiago (Viking, 1955).

The Desert People (Viking, 1962).

Along Sandy Trails (Viking, 1969).

Circle of Seasons (Farrar, Straus, 1970).

Hoofprint on the World (Viking, 1972).

✳ ✳ Beverly Cleary
✳ ✳

Beverly Cleary's first book, Henry Huggins,* was published in 1950. Henry, a very healthy, natural, normal boy is constantly involved in some sort of extravagantly funny predicament. On page seven we learn a bit about this likeable character: "Except for having his tonsils out when he was six and breaking his arm falling out of a cherry tree when he was seven, nothing much happened to Henry." In this first of a series of Henry stories, the problem centers on a hungry, stray dog, Ribsy, and Henry's efforts to keep him.

Within the last two decades, Ms. Cleary has intro-

---

*All titles mentioned were published by William R. Morrow.

duced a host of delightfully amusing characters and situations to middle-grade readers. Beatrice, known to fans as Beezus, a girl whom Henry Huggins finds the least obnoxious of all girls, shares some wild adventures with him in *Henry and Beezus* (1952); Ribsy returned in 1954 in *Henry and Ribsy* and again in 1964 in *Ribsy,* where the plot emphasizes the dog rather than his owner. *Beezus and Ramona* (1955) involves an hilarious romp between the two sisters. Ramona also has center stage in *Ramona, the Pest* (1968), a tale in which adult-child relationships are perceptively handled by the author's comic style. And in 1973 *Socks,* her newest character, a tabby cat who suffers from jealousy and anxiety when a new baby arrives, was introduced.

The above characters are only a few of the ones Ms. Cleary has created. From 1950 to the present she has produced over twenty books for readers of many ages — from pre-schoolers to teens.

Ms. Cleary, an only child, was born on April 12, 1916, in McMinnville, Oregon, and grew up in Yamhill and Portland. "Reading meant so much to me as a child. I was also fortunate in having a teacher-librarian who suggested that I should write for children when I grew up. This seemed like such a good idea that I decided writing for children was what I wanted to do. Making this decision while still a child was most fortunate, because I began to read critically while I was still reading from a child's point of view.

"Unless you count an essay I wrote when I was ten years old, (I won two dollars, because no one else entered the contest), *Henry Huggins* was my first attempt at writing for children.''

After finishing high school, Ms. Cleary attended Chaffee Junior College in Ontario, California, and the University of California at Berkeley, graduating with a B. A. degree in English. She then entered the School of Librarianship at the University of Washington in Seattle, specializing in library work with children. She was children's librarian in Yakima, Washington, until 1940 when she married Clarence T. Cleary and moved to Oakland, California. Here she served as post librarian at the Oakland State Hospital during World War II.

When the Clearys moved to Berkeley, she found a pile of typing paper in the linen closet of the house and remarked that now she could write a book. "Only we never had any sharp pencils," she recalled. The next day her husband brought home a pencil sharpener; the result has been a host of books that have amused and entertained millions of readers.

The Clearys now live in Carmel, California. They are the parents of twins, Marianne and Malcolm, and the owner of a cat named George, who was left to starve in a park when he was a kitten. Their house is located a short distance from the ocean. "We can hear the breakers crashing and the seals barking. If the seals were dogs," she laughed, "the neighbors would probably complain about their barking, but since they are seals, everyone smiles and says, 'Just listen to the seals!' "

The streets surrounding the house are lined with

cypress trees and flowers that bloom with unusual brilliance because they are so close to the sea. During the wintertime a host of monarch butterflies flit about.

I asked Ms. Cleary how life has been with twins in the house and whether or not their growing-up adventures spilled into any of her stories. She replied: "Life with twins? It's busy! *Mitch and Amy* (1967) came out of their experiences and the experiences of their friends when they were in fourth grade."

Another of the author's popular titles is *The Mouse and the Motorcycle* (1965), a fantasy about a mouse named Ralph and Keith, a young boy who teaches Ralph how to ride his toy motorcycle. Ms. Cleary told me about the book's origin: "This book came about after several years of wondering how I could write a book about motorcycles that eight-year-old boys would enjoy. One night in England, our son got a sudden fever; we were staying in a spooky, old hotel and did not have an aspirin and could not buy any at night. The next day, along with the aspirin tablets, we bought him some miniature cars and a miniature motorcycle for him to play with. When we returned home, a neighbor showed me a mouse that had fallen into a bucket in her garden. The thought crossed my mind that the mouse was the right size to ride the little motorcycle my son had brought home. That was the beginning of the book."

Commenting on her work habits, she said: "I sit at my desk twirling around on a swivel chair, staring out the window and hoping some strange new bird will light on the plum tree so I will have an excuse to look it up in *Field Guide to Western Birds.* Some parts of stories come out right the first time; others I rewrite several times. I wouldn't dream of trying out my ideas on children or anyone else. A book should be the work of an author's imagination—not the work of a committee. If I start a book and do not like it, I just don't finish it. I don't try to be funny. Because of some lucky quirk in my personality, my stories turn out to be humorous. In my books, I write for the child within myself. Writing is a pleasure, and I feel that if I did not enjoy writing, no one would enjoy reading my books. If my books are popular with children, it is because my childhood was bounded by the experiences of an average American child, and I have been fortunate enough to make stories out of the ingredients such a childhood provides.

"I have many occupations in addition to writing— marketing, cooking, chauffeuring my daughter's cello, loading the washing machine, sewing, and trying to keep up with my mail."

She receives hundreds of letters and answers them all. One ten-year-old girl from Wichita, Kansas, wrote her a six-page description of her family. The contents were so vivid, Ms. Cleary felt as if she could sit right down and write a book from it. Another girl wrote, "I have a jumping feeling in my heart that you mean what you say in your books."

The most touching letter ever written to her came

from a little girl in a big city who said, "I love to read your books, because they make me feel so safe." Ms. Cleary remarked, "I often think about that letter and wonder about the life of the child who wrote it."

When there are spare moments, she does handicrafts. "I always have a table filled with sewing projects," she said.

Ms. Cleary told me that people often state that she looks exactly the way they think the author of *Henry Huggins* should look. "Once when I thought I looked quite dashing, in a new dress and hat, a young male teacher said to me, 'This is a wonderful opportunity for children to learn that an author looks like someone they might meet in a supermarket' "

Ms. Cleary has received many awards for her books — mainly awards given by teachers, librarians, and children. In 1958, she received the Dorothy Canfield Fisher Children's Book Award offered by the P. T. A. and Vermont Free Library Commission for the book that is most popular with boys and girls in grades four through eight in the Vermont schools for her novel *Fifteen* (1956); it is about a girl who emerges from the agonizing awkwardness of adolescence. In 1968 she received the William Allen White Children's Book Award chosen by an annual vote of Kansas schoolchildren in grades four through seven for *The Mouse and the Motorcycle*. Three of her titles were chosen as Nene Award winning books, an award given by the children of Hawaii and sponsored by the Children's

Section of the Hawaii Library Association. The Nene Award was given to *Ribsy* in 1968, to *The Mouse and the Motorcycle* in 1969, and to *Ramona, the Pest* in 1971. *Ramona, the Pest* also received the Second Annual Georgia Children's Book Award in 1970.

"These awards are most meaningful to me, because they all have come from the votes of children. I am deeply touched that so many girls and boys, when given the opportunity to express a preference, have voted for my books. Knowing that one's books really reach young readers is the most rewarding experience that can come to a writer of children's books."

Also by Ms. Cleary

(All published by Morrow)

For younger readers

The Real Hole (1966).

Two Dog Biscuits (1961).

For middle grades

Otis Spofford (1953).

Ellen Tebbits (1951).

Emily's Runaway Imagination (1961).

Runaway Ralph (1970).

For older readers

Jean and Johnny (1959).

✳ ✳Elizabeth Coatsworth ✳

Robert Prampton

A bibliography of works by Elizabeth Coatsworth could easily fill several pages; she has been writing and publishing stories, poems, and books for children and adults since 1923. Her descriptive style portraying life in early America and in other countries has gained her international recognition. She was an American candidate for the Hans Christian Andersen Medal in 1968 and one of the final runners-up. She has also received many other awards and honors, including honorary doctorate degrees from the University of Maine in 1955 and New England College in 1958.

Ms. Coatsworth was born on May 31, 1893, in Buffalo, New York. She grew up there spending summers on the Canadian shore of Lake Erie where her family owned a grain elevator. Freighters unloaded their cargo there prior to shipment down the Erie Canal and the Hudson River to New York. In her late teens she entered Vassar College and completed a bachelor of arts degree in 1915; she earned a master of science degree from Columbia University in 1916 and later took courses at Radcliffe College.

Her initial interest was writing poetry. Among her

first publications were three volumes of poetry for adult audiences: *Fox Footprints* (Knopf, 1923), *Atlas and Beyond* (Harper, 1924), and *Compass Rose* (Coward, 1929). In 1927 her first book for children, *The Cat and the Captain* (Macmillan), appeared. This resulted from a prod from Louise Seaman, a former Macmillan juvenile editor. "Louise was one of my Vassar classmates and friends," Ms. Coatsworth recalled. "She became the first editor exclusively of children's books in the world. I used to stay with Louise when I came into New York City, and we discussed the books she was publishing. One day while I was commenting and criticizing one of her little library books, she challenged me, 'Write a better one then,' she said. And I did! I wrote *The Cat and the Captain,* writing one small chapter each night, usually after returning from the theatre. And I have been writing children's books ever since."

Her fifth book for children was another cat story, *The Cat Who Went to Heaven* (Macmillan, 1930), which won the 1931 Newbery Medal. Ms. Coatsworth discussed the tale's origin with me: "In 1916–1917 my mother, sister, and I spent a month in Kyoto, Japan. In one of the old temples we were shown a picture of the death of the Buddha, which included one of the attendant animals, a cat. 'This is very unusual' said the monk guide. 'The cat is usually not shown because of its lack of humility.' Later we were in Java and visited the old Buddhist temples. Carved letters included the animal incarnations of the Buddha. These things lay unnoticed in my mind for ten years until the winter before my marriage. I was staying in California when they began to take form. In a week I had written the book, illustrated it, and typed it. My drawings served as a basis for Lynd Ward's final artwork."

Although the book remains among her most popular, it is not her favorite. "Perhaps *The Cave* (Viking, 1958) or *Door to the North* (Holt, 1950) or *The Enchanted: An Incredible Tale* (Pantheon, 1951) or *Jon, the Unlucky* (Holt, 1964) are my favorites. Why? Because these books, I hope are written in a style clear as glass so that the writing never comes between the reader and the subject."

A characteristic of Ms. Coatsworth's style is the inclusion of poetry in several of her works of fiction. For example, the songs of the housekeeper in *The Cat Who Went to Heaven* continue the story and express the deep meanings of life; in *Away Goes Sally* (Macmillan, 1934) poems tie the chapters together. Within this volume is one of her finest and probably best known poems, "Swift Things Are Beautiful," a poem that might have been written just yesterday as an ode to ecology. This poem and many others appear in countless numbers of anthologies for girls and boys.

I asked Ms. Coatsworth to define poetry for me. "Poetry is thoughts whose intensity makes the heart beat faster. The words follow the rhythm of the heart. Often, climaxes in prose writing turn into poetry," she replied.

"I love to write," she said, "but like any other craft,

there are hours of correcting, polishing, and rewriting that a writer must be ready to put in, as well as the wonderful hours of writing, when the pen seems to be running away with the story. Notice I say pen and not typewriter, for I am an old fashioned writer and prefer the silence of the pen to the mechanical sounds of the typewriter."

Her Sally stories, all historical fiction, were written in this manner.

Ms. Coatsworth lives with a housekeeper on Chimney Farm in Nobleboro, Maine. Built in 1835, the house looks down hay fields to a twelve-mile lake. It is set on a dead end back road. On one hillside a few gravestones are reminders of those who once lived on this land. In April, 1968, Ms. Coatsworth's husband, Henry Beston, an author and naturalist, passed away and was buried in this graveyard at the top of the fields.

Ms. Coatsworth said: "I am quite old now, white-haired, and lazy. Since Henry died, I am learning to live alone with a housekeeper and a big, black poodle puppy—but not liking it."

One of her greatest pleasures in life is having her family visit with her. "My older daughter, Margaret —Meg—and her husband and four children live in Anchorage, Alaska, but they expect to be here for a month next summer. My younger daughter, Catherine —Kate—also has four children; her oldest daughter, Elizabeth, writes very good poetry, like her mother. It's better than mine!

"When all of us were younger, we used to spend many happy hours making new trails in our woods, canoeing in summer, and snowshoeing in winter; these were the things that we enjoyed, next to the pleasure of talking with our friends. And, of course, reading. I enjoy looking at the sun now and watching the changes of its light. Few cars pass by here. But after a life of travel throughout the world, I am content to live this quiet life.

"I like animals, almost every kind, though many I don't want to own. We feed four or five raccoons and a family of skunks every summer; they eat off the same dishes."

Perhaps the poet-author's lifelong likes and her memories can best be described through her poem:

*Such Things I Praise**

Some sing of seas and some of skies,
some sing eternity and death;
I sing the dewdrop on the grass,
    holding my breath.

The quiet and domestic home,
sun-shining on a flower-filled vase,
the household stir, the moving pen,
    such things I praise.

I hear my daughter's running feet,
my husband's finger on the keys—
hush, do not stir lest you should brush
    such light as these!

Poems by Elizabeth Coatsworth, Macmillan, 1957.

Also by Ms. Coatsworth

The Children Come Running (Golden, 1960).

Lucky Ones: Five Journeys toward a Home
(Macmillan, 1968).

Indian Mound Farm (Macmillan, 1969).

Under the Green Willow (Macmillan, 1970).

The Wanderers (Four Winds Press, 1972).

Daisy (Macmillan, 1973).

*** Hila Colman**

Robert Gumpper

"I was born and raised in New York City, where I lead the over protected life of a well-to-do, middle-class Jewish family; my mother was the hard-working designer of children's dresses for the family's manufacturing business in the garment center. She was a forerunner for women's liberation, strong in her belief of independence—financial as well as every other way— for women and knocked that concept into the heads of her two daughters. Both my sister and I went right to work after college and have been at it ever since," stated Hila Colman.

Ms. Colman attended Radcliffe College for two years. After leaving school, she did publicity and promotion work for the National War Relief Agency and later served as executive director for the Labor Book Club. In 1949 she began a free-lance writing career while raising a family.

"Writing for children and young people grew out of my interest in the fabulous teen-age years and the struggles, both good and bad, of my own teen-age years with no help from anyone. Maybe someone else can benefit by my own, now more mature, conclusions," she commented.

Her first book for children, *The Big Step* (Morrow), was published in 1957. "The idea for this book came from a family I knew. A man with two teen-age daughters married a woman with one teen-age girl; suddenly the three girls were thrown into one household together. While my book has little to do with that particular family, the situation intrigued me."

Ms. Colman continued to write books for the pre- and adolescent reader because of her interest with today's teens. "I'm fascinated with their hair, their clothes, the social awareness, and the search for beauty and relevancy that the kids today possess. I'm also impressed with their articulateness and their zany humor. I truly feel that my contemporaries and I have produced a marvelous generation. I am on their side, and I expect great things of them; I do not believe I will be disappointed."

Ms. Colman is a small, dark-haired woman who

usually wears a large hat, which makes me think of her as the Bella Abzug of children's literature. Besides the hats she loves to get involved in a wide variety of things. "I'm restless, politically-minded, very curious, and often impatient," she told me. This perhaps accounts for the potpourri of topics she has written about, from *Beauty, Brains and Glamour: A Career in Magazine Publishing* (World, 1968; under the pseudonym Teresa Crayder) to *Making Movies* (Morrow, 1969). She has written numerous articles and short stories for leading magazines such as *McCalls, Redbook,* and the *Saturday Evening Post.* Her love of cooking— "for the right people"—led her to co-author *The Country Week-End Cookbook* (Barrows, 1961) with her husband, Louis, who is a medical writer.

Commenting on this diversity she declared: "I really *like* to write and I really like writing fiction. I find, however, that nonfiction research is stimulating and takes me out to meet and talk with different kinds of people. I do a great deal of rapping with young people, and whenever I am asked to speak at a school, I say yes. I find that my audience is my pipeline to ideas. I don't think you can write for young people, if you don't have a pretty steady line of communication with them."

Claudia, Where Are You? (Morrow, 1969) is her own personal favorite and is considered by many adult critics to be her most effectively written book. The theme deals with the generation gap, and the chapters alternate, written first by Claudia, then from the viewpoint of her mother. "I had a good time with my younger son and his friends researching that book in the East Village. I enjoyed writing from the point of view of the mother as well as from that of the daughter. I was pleased with the way the book turned out and has been read and received.

"All my nonfiction has been journalistic in form, based on interviews with various people in different fields. That part of the work is fun—but the sitting down at home and writing each book is the hard part and more of a chore than writing fiction.

"I am a rather disciplined writer and, except for vacations and weekends, I find myself rather uneasy if I haven't spent some time during the day in my study. My study is an absolute refuge for me. I would feel only half a person without it."

Another of Ms. Colman's popular titles is *The Girl from Puerto Rico* (Morrow, 1961), which describes the problems of newly arrived Puerto Ricans in the United States. It was awarded the Child Study Association of America Children's Book Award in 1962. Ms. Colman said of the book: "I was living in New York City at the time in what is called a 'mixed neighborhood.' With that exposure, it would seem to me almost impossible for a writer not to become involved in the plight of the Puerto Rican families coming North in search of 'the good life.' A book about this situation seemed a natural to me." In the novel the author depicts the problems the girl confronts, including cultural differences, poor housing conditions, and discrimination.

The Colmans live in Bridgewater, Connecticut.

Their house is surrounded by beautiful woods and gentle, rolling hills. Now that their two sons, Jonathan and James, are both married, the only other family member residing in "the house that's grown over the years," is Max, a big, black standard poodle who is "enchanting."

But life is far from quiet in the Connecticut residence. One son lives in nearby Hartford with his wife and five children, which include a set of twins; the other son lives in Amherst, Massachusetts. "We visit each other often, and while I still don't have any gray hair yet, I love being a grandmother," she confessed.

When leisure time is available, Ms. Colman enjoys traveling, sunshine, tennis—when she has the energy —and likes to do a great deal of walking. Concluding our interview Ms. Colman remarked, "I guess my main quality is enjoying myself. I have a very good time in life."

Also by Ms. Colman

Classmates by Request (Morrow, 1964).

Car Crazy Girl (Morrow, 1967).

A Career in Medical Research (World, 1968).

Cleopatra (Coward-McCann, 1969).

End of the Game (World, 1971).

The Family and the Fugitive (Morrow, 1972).

Diary of a Frantic Kid Sister (Crown, 1973).

Benny the Misfit (T. Y. Crowell, 1973).

Chicano Girl (Morrow, 1973).

* *Julia Cunningham *

"When I am working on a book, I make a valiant effort to sit down at my typewriter at the same time each morning, usually nine o'clock. I am only able to concentrate effectively for about an hour and a half and am lucky to come up with a page a day. The ideas come from anywhere—a conversation, a turn of someone's head, a fragrance, or simply a character walking into my imaginary life and taking over. I am not able to do much rewriting, at least not successfully, and am mostly an intuitive worker. The first draft must always be completely right.

"I never had any formal training in writing. I just began at about the age of nine and continued; I did have a wonderful English teacher in high school who did not interfere but encouraged me," related Julia Cunningham.

Her first book, *The Vision of François, the Fox* was published by Houghton Mifflin in 1960 (reprinted by Pantheon).* The work evolved during a visit Ms. Cunningham made to France in the autumn of 1950.

---

*Unless otherwise noted, all titles have been published by Pantheon.

"I found a room and a welcome with a French family where affection and friendship were communicated without words; it was a rather lonely time at the beginning, so I took solitary trips. I found a silent and direct appeal in the twelfth century. The winter rose I stole one snowy day from the gardens at Chenonceau was mine, just as certainly as another rose was once François' when he was around to pick it."

During the fall of her second year in France, Ms. Cunningham borrowed her French family's attic. "I set up my typewriter on an old trunk bound in brass and invited François, the fox, to tell his story. He told it not for me or even for himself, but as a kind of giving back for all I had been given. This book, as well as many of my books, represent a very deep love for that country and its people."

Other books set in France include *Viollet* (1966), a suspenseful tale of a thrush set against the mellow background of southern France at vintage time; *Burnish Me Bright* (1970), set in a French village infested by prejudice and suspicion; and *Far in the Day* (1972), a sequel.

Ms. Cunningham was born in Spokane, Washington, "though in my case that doesn't mean much as I left there a year later. I grew up in a variety of places, mostly New York City, then New Jersey, California, Pennsylvania, Virginia, and at eighteen, back to New York to earn a living.

"I had two brothers and a mother who was a violinist. It seems to me now, looking back, that we all shared a very creative life—giving plays every evening with improvised sets, scripts, and costumes, going to concerts, dance recitals, marionette shows, and the like, and, of course, we were encouraged to practice what we could in art, music, and writing."

I asked her why she decided to write books for children. "I don't write for children, though I am very proud indeed when they like my books because, being truly honest, they constitute the best of audiences. It is a puzzle how to reply to the next natural query —then who do you write for? I've come to believe that the only true answer is for myself. This is not, God forbid, ego—but truth."

Her second book, *Dear Rat* (Houghton Mifflin, 1961), remains her favorite. "Why? Perhaps because Andrew, the rat, was and is such a good friend. He makes me smile!"

Other books followed: *Macaroon* (1962), an engaging story of a raccoon who adopts an "impossible child" for the winter months; *Candle Tales* (1964), a touching book about six animals who each tell a story to Mr. Minikin, an old man, in exchange for a candle. The candles are collected by the animals to give a surprise birthday party for Mr. Minikin who never had a birthday party in his life.

Dorp Dead (1965) is a first person narrative by a young boy, Gilly Ground, who leaves an orphanage to serve as an apprentice to a laddermaker who is an eccentric bachelor. Life in his house is ordered and disquieting, but before long Gilly recognizes its sinis-

ter undercurrent. Blood-chilling incidents occur at the
end of the novel as Gilly plans an escape. This book
is considered controversial by many critics. For example, Charlotte S. Huck and Doris Young Kuhn in
their text, *Children's Literature in the Elementary
School* (Holt, 1968), state: "Viewed as realistic fiction
this story seems too evil and unbelievable. Seen as an
allegory, (it) becomes an exceptional book."

Ms. Cunningham commented on the book's de-
velopement and the controversy sparked by its publication: "I remember talking to a friend, saying 'I
feel ready to write another book, but what shall it be
about?' She replied with 'How about a story about an
orphan who has absolutely nothing?' I asked, 'What
is his name?' She answered, 'Gilly, of course.' And
from there Gilly began to become so real, I had to sit
down and record his story.

"I never have any idea how a story will say what it
says. It just arrives. Oh, I make an outline before
launching on the wide seas of uncertainty, but I allow
that mysterious need to communicate take the reins.
There are many ways to describe this happening, but
none of them is truly accurate. To me *Dorp Dead*
wasn't controversial. It merely told the story. And I
still believe that the story is possible. Much more horrible things have taken place in this world."

Ms. Cunningham is a sensitive person "through
both interest and necessity. My adult life is on the
whole a happy one. There is so much to learn and enjoy and wonder about and be joyful for. I am quite

consistently of an even temperment, prefering harmony to turmoil (except in my stories), and I like to laugh.

"I enjoy cooking and listening to the world and what's in it. I am constantly curious about what is over the next hill, especially in France. I've never owned any animals but have them as friends in my books. I like crafts and painting in an amateur way; I am not a gardener but am fascinated by the communion some have with plants. I once played the piano and would have chosen to be a musician if it had been financially possible, which it wasn't."

Ms. Cunningham lives in Santa Barbara, California, in a small apartment over a garage. The neighborhood has many trees and much grass. The walls of her apartment are lined with prints of paintings and drawings. Favorite possessions include her phonograph and the broad table that is her desk. There are windows on three sides of the apartment; the sunlight and shadows that enter are vital to her, along with the stars.

She works as an assistant to the owner of the Tecolate Book Shop where she sells books and is a children's book buyer. Past jobs include saleswoman in the book and art shop at the Metropolitan Museum of Art in New York City and as associate editor of *Screen Stories* magazine.

As a final question I asked Ms. Cunningham if there was anything else she felt a child reading her books would want to know about her. Her succinct answer was, "Not really, except that I regard them as people."

Also by Ms. Cunningham

Onion Journey (Pantheon, 1967).

*∗*Roald Dahl

Philip Spalding

"I spent at least twenty years of my life writing nothing but short stories for adults, but then our first child came along. When she was old enough to have stories told to her at bedtime, I made a point of making up a story every single night. It became a routine that continued when our second child came along. Of course, many of the stories I made up did not hold their attention — they became restless or their minds wandered. It was very rare to hit upon something that really made them sit up and sparkle. Had I not had children of my own, I would have never written books for children, nor would I have been capable of doing so," declared Roald Dahl (Roo-all Doll).

One of the books that grew out of these nightly storytellings was *James and the Giant Peach* (1961)∗

*Unless otherwise noted, all titles have been published by Knopf.

"The plot somehow seemed to capture the children's imaginations and hold them. So I enlarged on it and eventually had a go at writing it down," he recalled. *James and the Giant Peach* came along eighteen years after his first published story. "The Gremlins" appeared in 1943. In between he created many adult short stories, which appeared in leading magazines including *New Yorker, Playboy, Saturday Evening Post, Esquire,* and *Harper's.*

His popular novels for children that followed *James and the Giant Peach* include *Charlie and the Chocolate Factory* (1964), *Fantastic Mr. Fox* (1970), and the sequel to *Charlie and the Chocolate Factory—Charlie and the Great Glass Elevator: The Further Adventures of Charlie Bucket and Willie Wonka, the Chocolate-maker Extraordinaire* (1972).

All his books are popular fantasies that are filled with mad adventures and wildly curious characters from Aunt Sponge and Aunt Spiker, two wicked aunts (in *James and the Giant Peach*), to Boggis, an enormously fat and mean man, and Bunce, a pot-bellied, nasty dwarf (in *Fantastic Mr. Fox*).

The plights of such characters are as curious as the characters themselves. *James and the Giant Peach,* for example, begins with James' parents being suddenly eaten up while shopping in London—"in full daylight, mind you, and on a crowded street by an enormous angry rhinoceros which had escaped from the London Zoo." Soon James finds a huge peach that he enters, finding strange new friends and having madcap adventures.

Charlie and the Chocolate Factory was also tested out on the Dahl children. More than five hundred plots were tried before the final Charlie was created. The book has sparked some controversy in recent years because of the Black stereotype. To combat this criticism, the book is being issued in a new edition with new art and some textual changes. The novel has fast become a modern children's classic. It has been translated into many foreign languages, has sold hundreds of thousands of copies, and in 1970 was made into the motion picture *Willy Wonka and the Chocolate Factory* for which Mr. Dahl wrote the screenplay.

Mr. Dahl said of this story: *"Charlie* is the most dangerous kind of book to try to write. It's a book with a moral, and children don't like being corrected. It also contains violence in a muted fashion. Children love violence—they are naturally aggressive. It baffles me that many adults do not realize this."

Mr. Dahl has been married to the Academy Award-winning actress, Patricia Neal, since 1953. Ms. Neal gave birth to their fifth child, Lucy, in 1965 following a serious illness that attracted worldwide attention. Their other children are Tessa, Theo, and Ophelia. Their daughter, Olivia, died of measles at the age of seven. A biography of the couple, *Pat and Roald* by Barry Farrell, was published in 1969 by Random House.

The Dahls live in Buckinghamshire, England, a small village of about three thousand inhabitants, midway between London and Oxford. Surrounding their painted-white house is a garden and five acres of apple orchards. "My hobby now, which I am crazy about, is growing one type of orchid called phalaenopsis in a greenhouse," Mr. Dahl told me.

Mr. Dahl's life and life experiences have been varied. He was born on September 13, 1916, in Llandaff, South Wales, to Norwegian parents. His father was a shipbroker, painter, and horticulturist; he died when his son was four years old. As a youngster Roald attended boarding school in England. From 1932–1939 he was a free-lance writer for the Shell Oil Company of East Africa working in Dar es Salaam, Tanzania. Following this, from 1939–1945, he served in the Royal Air Force as a fighter pilot, later becoming a Wing Commander.

"I joined a fighter squadron in the western desert of Libya in 1940," he reminisced, "and was promptly shot down by the Italians. I spent six months in a hospital in Alexandria and rejoined my squadron in Greece flying Hurricanes. When the Germans kicked us out of Greece, we flew against the Vichy French in Syria. Then my old injuries caught up with me, and I was invalided home to England. In 1942 I was sent to Washington, D. C. as an Assistant Air Attache and that was when I started writing."

It is little wonder that from his many personal adventures—and misadventures—he was well equipped to write the screenplay for the James Bond movie *You Only Live Twice,* produced by United Artists in 1967.

"Working on the film was enormous fun. It is, in fact, the only film that I have really enjoyed working on. We spent three months in Japan on this film and went to all sorts of crazy places, mostly by private plane or helicopter."

Mr. Dahl is in his late fifties. He has a crisp, distinctive British accent. When not writing or caring for his phalaenopsis, he cleans and restores old paintings, collects antiques, and gambles. "My faults and foibles are legion," he confessed. "I become easily bored in the company of adults. I drink too much whiskey and wine in the evenings. I eat far too much chocolate. I smoke too many cigarettes. I am bad tempered when my back hurts. I do not always clean my fingernails. I no longer tell my children long, long stories at bedtime. I bet on horses and lose money that way. I dislike Mother's Day and Father's Day and all the other days and all the cards that people buy and send out. I hate my own birthday. I am going bald. I hope all this is enough for you!"

Reluctantly I agreed to "enough." However after writing this interview, methinks I will journey down to New York's Central Park where an alleged giant peach stone sits. If I'm lucky, perhaps James Henry Trotter, the lad who found the peach, will welcome me and fill me in even further on the fact and fantasy world of his creator—Roald Dahl.

Also by Mr. Dahl

The Magic Finger (Harper, 1966).

✳✳Marguerite Lofft de Angeli ✳

Marguerite Lofft de Angeli (An-jel-ee) is certainly one of the most famous names in the field of children's literature. Her writings for every level of childhood have been praised throughout the world.

In 1971 Ms. De Angeli's autobiography, *Butter at the Old Price** was published. Within the forty-three chapters she tells of her life-long work as a writer-illustrator, of the development of her books—how they came to be, the trials and tribulations of doing them —and warmly relates anecdote after anecdote of her late husband, children, grandchildren, and great-grandchildren.

Ms. de Angeli was born on March 14, 1889, in the small town of Lapeer, Michigan. At the age of thirteen, her family moved to Philadelphia, Pennsylvania. There she studied with a voice teacher who encouraged her to develop her talents as a singer. She took her singing seriously. At nineteen, she was offered a part in an opera by Oscar Hammerstein. "After one rehearsal and the prospect of going with the company to London, my parents persuaded me that by marrying the young man to whom I was engaged, I would

---

*All titles mentioned have been published by Doubleday.

lead a much happier and more satisfying life than that of an opera singer. I listened and never regretted it," she asserted.

She continued singing in a church choir until 1910, when she married John de Angeli and started raising a family. While the children were small, she began to take drawing lessons and soon devoted her spare time to illustrating.

"The need to draw and write kept popping up, but children did too," she exclaimed. "When the children numbered three, I met Maurice Bower, then a well known illustrator, who gave me help and criticism. After a year of working on several subjects, I was given a story to do for Westminster Press. It just went on from there. After fifteen years of illustrating for magazines and books, Helen Ferris suggested that I write the text as well for a book for six-year-olds. I did!"

The book, *Ted and Nina Go to the Grocery Store* (1935), was based on the activities of two of her five children. Over the years her family has grown to include many grandchildren and great-grandchildren —at last count there were thirteen. Many of the children have served as models for her books.

After her first book, Ms. de Angeli produced a stream of titles—books dealing with family experiences, books about the Philadelphia area where she grew up and still lives, historical novels, Bible stories, and books dealing with minority groups.

In 1950 her first work of historical fiction, *The Door*

in the Wall (1949) was awarded the Newbery Medal. The book relates the story of young Robin de Bureford, a crippled boy from a noble family who lived in thirteenth century England. Robin's story is based on the childhood experience of Harmon Robinson, a lame neighbor and dear friend of the de Angelis. The title came from a belief Ms. de Angeli passed along to her own children: "When you come to a stone wall, if you look hard enough, you will find a door in it."

To illustrate the text authentically, Ms. de Angeli visited England to sketch the exteriors and interiors of the churches, castles, and inns that had stood in Robin's day. Many black and white drawings appear in the text as well as three color illustrations, attesting to the fact that her art is as beautifully detailed as her writing.

The Door in the Wall has received much acclaim in addition to the Newbery Award; in 1961 it was cited as a Lewis Carroll Shelf Award as a book "worthy enough to sit on the shelf with *Alice in Wonderland;*" it has been adapted into a play, produced as a sound filmstrip by Miller-Brody Productions, Inc., and translated into many foreign languages.

A trip to Scotland provided the material for *Black Fox of Lorne* (1956), the story of two young Norsemen, twin brothers, who are shipwrecked off the coast of Scotland.

Between these two books Ms. de Angeli found the time to produce her magnificent volume *The Book of Nursery and Mother Goose Rhymes* (1954) which contains over three hundred rhymes and jingles and many, many pictures. The book took her three-and-one-half years to complete.

A list of honors that have been bestowed upon Ms. de Angeli could fill pages. I asked her which, of all the awards she has been given, was the most meaningful. She replied: "Of course the Newbery was immensely exciting because it was the most important one up to that time. Besides, when the news came, my husband and I had just arrived at Nina and Alf's (her daughter and son-in-law). I read the announcement to them, and we all cried with joy.

"The Regina Medal (awarded her in 1968. This medal is presented annually by the Catholic Library Association for a lifetime dedication to the highest standards of children's literature.) was very exciting too. Then there was a citation from the Governor of Pennsylvania and in May 1972, a long citation from the Governor of Michigan and a whole week of celebration in honor of *Butter at the Old Price*."

Ms. de Angeli's homey Philadelphia apartment is filled with books, tokens from friends, manuscripts, and drawings. She enjoys people, books, work, and cooking.

"I am an old lady of eighty-four," she told me. I am homely and have white hair, which I like more than the brown, mousy color it was before! I have blue eyes, still good to see with, and I talk and walk very straight for one of my age. I am happy here in Philadelphia and very fortunate to have many friends. I also have a little house in the country among my four sons' families where I go in the summer. Besides, twice a year or so I visit my daughter and her family in Cincinnati, Ohio. I miss my dear husband, but we were married almost sixty years before he died.

"I don't have a favorite among my many books because each one means a whole collection of new friends and new scenes. I hope that as time has passed I have improved in writing and drawing. I still have echoes from even my earliest books especially *Henner's Lydia* (1936) and *Yonie Wondernose*(1944; both titles deal with Pennsylvania Dutch families and their customs).

"Perhaps a child would like to know that I love my grandchildren and my greats. I have just been to Boston to meet the latest great, Melora Kuhn, who is several months old, lively, crowing, laughing, and perfectly well and happy. Her daddy is my daughter Nina's son, David."

The one thing I could quarrel about with Ms. de Angeli is her remark about being homely. With her snow-white hair, cheery voice, smile, and glasses, she reminds one of a typical grandmother.

Children across the land cannot cuddle up in her lap as her own grandchildren and greats can, but cuddling up with her stories is certainly within the realm of possibility. They can catch her warmth, vitality, and sensitivity—and you can, too!

Also by Ms. de Angeli

Published by Doubleday

Skippack School (1938).

Thee, Hannah! (1940).

Bright April (1946).

The Ted and Nina Storybook (containing *Ted and Nina Go to the Grocery Store* (1935), *A Summer Day with Ted and Nina* (1940), and *Ted and Nina Have a Happy Rainy Day* (1936), published in 1965.

Published by Westminster Press

Turkey for Christmas (1944).

The Empty Barn (1966).

✳ ✳ **Meindert DeJong** ✳ ✳

Marvin Lanninga

Meindert DeJong (Mine dert De Yung) is the first American to win the Hans Christian Andersen Medal (1962), which is given by the International Board on Books for Young People to an author whose works are an outstanding contribution to children's literature. But that's not the only award he's won. Four of his books are Newbery Honor Books: *Along Came a Dog* (1958),* *The House of Sixty Fathers* (1956), *Hurry Home, Candy* (1953), and *Shadrach* (1953); *The Wheel on the School* (1954) received the 1955 Newbery Medal, and *Journey from Peppermint Street* (1968) won the first National Book Award for Children's Literature in 1969.

There have been other awards too, but the man who has created such a body of fine books is even more interesting than his list of prizes.

On March 4, 1906, Mr. DeJong was born in the village of Weirom in the province of Friesland in The Netherlands. His parents were descended from French Huguenot families who fled to Friesland during the persecutions of their Protestant religion. When he was eight, his family came to the United States and settled in Grand Rapids, Michigan. Mr. DeJong and his three brothers spent their first few days in their new country searching for a dike!

"Father was busy earning a living; mother was so homesick that she refused to learn English or even allow it spoken in our home. School life was unhappy because of language problems. Add this to the loss of beloved grandparents, and it added up to a lonely childhood."

Educated at local religious schools maintained by Dutch Calvinists, Mr. DeJong received his B. A. degree from John Calvin College in Michigan where he ma-

---

*All titles were published by Harper.

jored in English. He also studied at the University of Chicago for a short time. At Calvin College he contributed to *The Young Calvinist,* a youth magazine started by the Christian Reformed Group.

During the Depression he went to work on the farm his father had bought when his business failed. In the evenings, after a sixteen-hour work day, he wrote short stories for magazines that kept going out of business before they could pay him for his efforts. Mr. DeJong sold eggs to the Grand Rapids Public Library, and when the children's librarian there heard of his tales of a pet goose and a duck, she insisted that he write out the story. This led to his first book, *The Big Goose and the Little White Duck,* a picture book published in 1938 and reissued in 1963 with new illustrations by Nancy Ekholm Burkert.

"I never decided to write for children," he explained. "A librarian, a goose, and a duck decided it for me. I owned the goose and duck; they were wonderful pets."

During World War II, Mr. DeJong spent three years in the general area of Chungking, China, in the little village of Peishiyi as official historian for Chennault's 14th Air Force, an experience on which *The House of Sixty Fathers* is based. He recalls some amusing encounters with the Chinese who were fascinated by his blond hair and persistently wanted to feel it, though women often ran from him in fright. Because of the color of his hair, he was treated in some villages as one of the venerable old men and was invited to sip tea with them.

The House of Sixty Fathers, a vividly realistic story, is set in China during the early days of the Japanese occupation. Tien Po, the novel's main character, is a small Chinese boy who is separated from his family when their sampan breaks loose from its moorings and is swept back into the enemy territory from which his family had just escaped. The book presents a grim portrait of the personal horrors of war. "Possibly, this book is my favorite, since the experience was real to me," he declared.

The experiences described in his other books are real, too. His characters are alive and vital. Perhaps his ability to write so convincingly is best explained in his Newbery acceptance speech for *The Wheel on the School:*

> To get back to (the essence of childhood) you can only go down. You can only go in — deep in. Down through all the deep, mystic, intuitive layers of the subconscious back into your own childhood. And if you go deep enough, get basic enough, become again the child you were, it seems reasonable that by the way of the subconscious you have come into what must be the universal child. Then, and then only, do you write for the child.

The Wheel on the School tells of an event in the lives of the people in Shora, a small Dutch fishing village, and how a teacher encourages storks to nest on the rooftops of the schoolhouse. The reader finds himself living each moment of the story and becoming as concerned over the storks' fate as are the characters.

At least seven of Mr. DeJong's books have been illustrated by the Caldecott Award-winning artist, Maurice Sendak. I asked Mr. DeJong if he would comment on Mr. Sendak's interpretations of his characters and episodes. He replied: "I love the guy and know him well from mutual suffering on the speechmaking circuit. I love his work. I only wish my editors could afford him for everything I write."

Until 1954 Mr. DeJong held a variety of jobs ranging from professor to mason, tinner, installer of warm air furnaces, bricklayer, church janitor, and grave digger. "In any of these trades, I can promise you a good job," he declared. He finds manual labor conducive to writing. "Manual work is fine; cerebral work interferes with my writing."

When working on a book he spends the morning in his study. "At a later stage the work takes over, and I spend the whole day writing. Still later I read it aloud, bit by bit, using my wife as a sounding board. I revise and revise."

Mr. DeJong is five-feet ten-inches tall, has blue eyes, and sports an unruly mop of whitened hair. "I'm a typical Frieslander," he told me. He and his wife Beatrice live in Chapel Hill, North Carolina, five miles outside the small town where the University of North Carolina is located. Their home is on five acres of woods.

"My favorite possession? I'll give them to you in order. First there's my wife. I'm very happily married.

Along with my second wife, I painlessly acquired a step-daughter, three step-sons, and eight grandchildren, all of whom I enjoy greatly." ("And they all adore him," added Ms. DeJong.)

"Next there are my cats and dogs, a few paintings, and a few books."

He enjoys animals. Several of his books reflect this love—*Along Came a Dog* tells of a little red hen that lost its toes and a homeless dog who protected it; *Hurry Home, Candy* is about a lost dog; *Smoke Above the Lane* (1951) depicts a relationship between a skunk and a tramp who become friends during a terrible journey in a boxcar. Other titles also have animal characters.

"In the letters I get from children, they always want to know if I have a pet. Well, yes I do—several. Mine are Lisa, a Great Dane, Ian and Angus, collies and brothers, Tien Kai and Kismet, Siamese cats, Sieba, an Abyssinian cat, Ah-So, a Burmese cat, Principe and Rosita, half Siamese cats, and Alexander the Great, a Maine coon cat. During the six years we lived in Mexico, we had for a time a burro. I bought and liberated several foxes, an ocelot, and a couple of coyotes which were intended for sale to tourists." In short, he is an animal lover!

I began this interview citing several of the numerous awards Mr. DeJong has won. I couldn't let him go without asking which award has been most meaningful to him and his career.

"Let's say for pride, security, and self-belief, the

Newbery Award. But perhaps the most meaningful was the Aurianne Award given for books that help develop humane attitudes toward animals. This was given in warmth and for animal love. And it required no speech!''

Also by Mr. DeJong

(All published by Harper & Row)

The Tower by the Sea (1950).

Far out the Long Canal (1964).

✳ ✳ Elizabeth Borton de Treviño
✳ ✳

Carla Kenny

On November 28, 1970, the New York Times carried a story on its front page bearing the headline ''A Velázquez Brings $5.54 Million.'' Dated London, the article stated that ''A Velázquez portrait was sold to the Widenstein Gallery of New York for $5,544,000, a world record auction price.''

Again in the *New York Times* on May 13, 1971, a front-page story carried the headline ''Metropolitan

Was Buyer of $5.5-million Velázquez." In this report, John Canaday, the noted art critic reported, "The Metropolitan Museum announced yesterday the acquisition of Velázquez's portrait of his Moorish assistant, Juan de Pareja, which set an auction record last November when it was knocked down to Wildenstein & Co. at Christie's in London for $5,544,000."

I, Juan de Pareja (Farrar, Straus, 1965) by Elizabeth Borton de Treviño, (dā Trə vē´ nyō), tells the unusual story of Velázquez and the Moorish slave who became his indispensable assistant, companion, and life-long friend. Ms. de Treviño told me about the circumstances behind her book: "It was my son Luis, who, while studying painting, learned the true story of Juan de Pareja and told it to me. I loved the story; when I went to Spain some years later, I tried to find out all I could about him. When I saw a reproduction of the portrait Velázquez painted of Juan, I was determined to write about him, for his face seemed to me to be that of a dignified, noble, and proud person whose story should be told.

"I looked for information in many books—all I could find. All my sources were in Spanish, and they were at variance on many points. But the main outline was clear: a slave had secretly taught himself to paint, had confessed this to his master, and had been freed and elevated to the position of 'assistant' by Velázquez.

"Whenever the stories differed, I chose the version that most closely fitted my conception of the characters of Juan and his master. In no book telling of Juan and

Velázquez did I find a word to throw doubt on the fact that these two men loved and respected each other. They started out as master and slave, continued through life as companions, and ended as equals and friends."

In her afterword to the book, she further explains:

My story about Juan de Pareja will, I hope, be forgiven the liberties I have taken with known facts and the incidents I have invented. It will appeal, I hope, to young people of both White and Negro races because the story of Juan de Pareja and Velázquez foreshadows, in the lifetime of the two men, what we hope to achieve a millionfold today. (pp. 179–80).

The novel won the John Newbery Award in 1966 —one of five biographies ever to win the Medal. I asked Ms. de Treviño if winning the award changed her life in any way. "It has reaffirmed for me a deep sense of professional responsibility," she answered.

Long before Ms. de Treviño wrote this award-winning book, she was a reporter on the performing arts for the *Boston Herald* in Boston, Massachusetts, a job she held for seven years.

She was born on September 2, 1904, in Bakersfield, California. "I had an unusually happy childhood. My father, a lawyer, always took us on weekend picnics; I spent my summers with a beloved grandmother at Monterey on the coast. Our family was close; we were read to in the winter in front of the fireplace, and my mother and grandmother taught my sister and me how to sew, knit, crochet, and tat. We had much loved pets—dogs, cats, and even once a donkey. I am still fortunate in having friends from my childhood to this very day.

"I studied English literature in high school and at Stanford University, but I have written since I was eight years old." (Her first published verse appeared in the *Monterey Peninsula Herald* at this ripe age of eight!) "I always had severe but helpful critics in my parents and teachers," she continued. "My work as a reporter provided excellent training. I have always loved books and stories, and so far as I can determine, the story is the thing in all writing for children. Children don't want or expect problems, tragedy, troubles, or tracts, and I feel freer to indulge my imagination since I remember that my own childhood was made rich by many imagined people and events.

"My first book was a commissioned novel for the late Eleanor Parker's "Pollyanna" series; it was titled *Pollyanna in Hollywood.* I had been reporting from Hollywood for the *Boston Herald* for several seasons. Page and Company offered me this commission. I took it—gratefully."

Four other Pollyanna books followed. In 1934, while on a newspaper assignment in Mexico, she was met at the border by young Luis Treviño Gomez, who had been sent from the Monterrey Chamber of Commerce to escort her and act as interpreter. The American writer went home engaged to Luis, and a year later returned to Monterrey as his wife. An account of her young married life and her Mexican in-laws appears in her adult book, *My Heart Lies South* (T. Y. Crowell, 1953); her story is continued in *Where the Heart Is* (Doubleday, 1962).

Ms. de Treviño has remained a legal resident of Mexico but retains her American citizenship. Currently her home is in Cuernavaca, Mexico. "I live in a very simple Mexican ranch-style home in the midst of a large garden with tall trees, only two blocks from the big city market. I hear footsteps all day long, passing on the sidewalk outside my high stone walls. Cuernavaca is a small enough town so that every trip to the post office means I will see two or three friends. This is delightful. My social life is rich in friends who love the same things I do. We exchange books; we play bridge occasionally, I play violin and piano sonatas every week and quartets a few times a year. The whole town joins in much charitable work. Cuernavaca is beautifully ecumenical, which makes me proud to live here. I love my friends, and I love making chamber music. I adore all sorts of animals and birds. I do some handiwork. I read all the time.

"My favorite possessions are my violins, my carved Spanish furniture, and many hand-knitted and hand-made articles, especially needlepoint, made for me by my mother, and knitted garments made by my sister. I also treasure an antique Chinese cloisonné teapot and an assortment of other tea pots. I drink lots of tea, you see.

"I am a typical American in appearance—fair, somewhat plump, graying blond hair. Thank God I am reasonably active and have not lost any of my faculties."

One of the books she is most fond of is *Nacar, the White Deer* (Farrar, Straus, 1963), published two years before *I, Juan de Pareja.* This also has an historical background and is set in the seventeenth century. But even more it is a warm, appealing story evolving around a peasant boy's love of a deer and his journey with it through Mexico.

"I generally get story ideas from some true event or moment in history that fires my imagination," she commented. "All of my books contain a little kernel of truth, something that really happened. *Nacar* enlarges upon a note I found in the history of the "Manila" galleon, the Spanish vessel that plied between the Orient and Acapulco, New Spain (now Mexico). According to that note, at one time the great ship carried across the Pacific a beautiful albino deer, which was reshipped from Veracruz to Spain as a gift for the king."

Other books by Ms. de Treviño include *Casilda of the Rising Moon* (Farrar, Straus, 1967), which recounts the story of a young Moorish princess in Spain in the eleventh century who became a Christian convert and a saint, and *Turi's Poppa* (Farrar, Straus, 1968), the tale of a small boy and his father who walked halfway across Europe so that the father could take up a position as a violin-maker in Cremona, Italy.

Each of her stories requires travel, research, and study; each attempts to paint a true picture of the countryside and of the century in which the characters live.
ive.

"At the same time," Ms. de Treviño remarked, each of my stories tries to show some phase of love, that powerful emotion that makes the world go round. *Casilda of the Rising Moon* is a study of the way in which the love of God may express itself in compassion for all living things. And *Turi's Poppa* tells of the love between a boy and his father and of a man for the craft he has learned."

When she is at work writing a book, she tries to discipline herself to producing a fixed number of words a day. "I rewrite only after the first draft is down on paper. I try out my ideas on friends, especially friends with children."

I asked her if she receives many letters from girls and boys. "Many children write to me," she replied. "Mostly they want to know how I get my ideas for stories. But one practical child wrote to ask how long it took me to write a book and how much money I made. I am always delighted to hear from my readers and to answer any questions if I can. I hope that my stories may be read over often and read aloud and shared."

This interview cannot end without mention of Ms. de Treviño's two sons of whom she is very proud. "Both are single," she stated. "Luis is a painter who has had several professional shows in Mexico City and Europe. And Enrique is a teacher and lawyer."

Also by Ms. de Treviño

A Carpet of Flowers (T. Y. Crowell, 1955).

The Greek of Toledo (T. Y. Crowell, 1959).

House of Bitterness Street (Doubleday, 1970).

Here Is Mexico (Farrar, Straus, 1970).

Lavinia Dobler

Scholastic Magazines and Book Services is a complex organization. One of the busiest places in the company's editorial offices in New York City is the library. It is a special library containing all sorts of reference materials needed by the writers and editors. Overseeing this vast collection of books and magazines is Lavinia Dobler, known better as "Vee" to friends and colleagues.

Besides being head librarian at Scholastic, Ms. Dobler is the author of more than twenty books and fifty short stories.

Ms. Dobler was born in Riverton, Wyoming, and grew up there as well as in Long Beach, California. "Mother, who had graduated from Cornell College in Iowa and had taught in Iowa, came out to this new land in Wyoming to homestead," she told me. "Daddy, who had just finished his law degree, also came out to homestead on the land opened up by the government. They were founders of this new town on the prairies, in sight of the snow-capped Wind River Mountains. My sister and I were the first twins born in Riverton and the third babies. We had a wonderful childhood. My twin, Virginia, and I were close companions; she's still my best friend. We fished in the irrigation ditch, we spent some time on the two homesteads in the summer, and we went to a Camp Fire Girl camp in August near the historic gold rush town called Atlantic City. We lived in the largest house in Riverton.

"Daddy was a member of the Wyoming legislature, and the family went with him to Cheyenne. In 1916 the Dobler twins were given the privileges of the House—we were permitted to roller skate on the marble floor under the capitol's dome, the only time this has ever been allowed to my knowledge. We knew many of the pioneers who settled Wyoming. The only sadness was that our younger sister, Frances, was very ill most of the time we were children."

Ms. Dobler was educated at the University of California at Berkeley; additional work was completed at the University of Southern California, Columbia University, and New York University. She has been both a teacher and a supervisor of teachers teaching English in Puerto Rican schools.

"I decided to write for children when I was a teacher. I realized that there was much material but not the right kinds of books for children," she recalled. "My first book was *Glass House at Jamestown* (Dodd, Mead 1957), a historic novel that tells about the first boys who came over to America with the English who settled Jamestown in 1607. I used the real names of these boys. I had found their names listed on the ship's log while I was doing research. This book remains one of my favorites.

"I consider writing a skill just as much as practicing law or medicine, but one needs guidance and training, especially in learning how to plot. I get my ideas from all kinds of sources, but mostly from my own experiences. My goal is to write only one sentence a day. I write this on the bus on my way to work. I usually find that I write more than just one sentence, but the important point is that I have accomplished the goal I set by 9:00 a. m."

Ms. Dobler is best known for her nonfiction works, which require a great deal of research. Among her popular titles are *Great Rulers of the African Past* (co-authored with William A. Brown, Doubleday, 1965) and *Pioneers and Patriots: The Lives of Six Negroes of the Revolutionary Era* co-authored with Edgar A. Toppin, (Doubleday, 1965). Both these titles are part of the acclaimed "Zenith Book" series, which presents the history of minority groups in the

United States and their participation in the growth and development of the country.

Great Rulers of the African Past contains five biographical studies of leaders who lived between the thirteenth and seventeenth centuries. *Pioneers and Patriots* includes the lives of Benjamin Banneker, Paul Cuffe, Phillis Wheatley, Peter Salem, Jean Baptiste Point de Sable, and John Chavis.

Two other fine reference books for children in the upper grades are *Customs and Holidays Around the World* (Fleet, 1962), which presents the origins of holidays, and *National Holidays Around the World* (Fleet, 1968), a fiesta trip through each month of the year giving capsule information on holidays celebrated in many places from Israel to the Maldive Islands.

"Because of my full-time job, I can only do research in the evenings. I try to do about sixteen hours of writing each weekend. When I am into a book I am willing to give up all kinds of social life," she told me.

"One of the pluses my writing has given me is that I have been able to donate about $25,000 to the new college in Riverton, The Central Wyoming College. The College is located on my father's former homestead. There is a gracious room adjoining the library with a huge fireplace made of semi-precious stones. It is called the Dobler Room and was given in memory of my pioneer parents."

Ms. Dobler is an energetic woman who rarely sits still. She moves quickly, thinks and talks fast and is one tiny bundle of energy-plus. Her home in New York

ind some eight or
e with our white
in Boonville. I had
ng in the moonlit
e playing the stair
als in the story, in-
coon, and the bear,
other; their actions
servation. Even the
l printed out for me
ng, as was the final
't take place in our

bery Medal for *The*
life in any way. He
stroke of luck, and

t man. Digging into
Newbery was not the
: *Hound Dog Moses*
ead, 1954) was given
; he has also received
College, Rutgers Uni-
Harvard University
6.

ts, Mr. Edmonds said:
ces—old newspapers,
almost never rewrite,
em to let a paragraph

City is a cooperative in an old brownstone close to the United Nations. "But my favorite place is my home on Candlewood Lake in New Milford, Connecticut," she declared. This house was purchased when Ms. Dobler received the Dodd, Mead National Librarian Award in in 1957 for *A Business of Their Own* (Dodd, Mead, 1957); she used the prize money as a down payment.

Favorite possessions include books written by author friends. "I also love pictures of mountains —rugged, snow-capped mountains, which are part of my Western heritage, for I am a Westerner at heart. I sometimes think I am only free when I am at the top of a high mountain. My favorite color is the blue of the clear sky. Swimming is my favorite sport, but I like water skiing and surfing, too. I adore cats and dogs. But people are more important to me than anything else—not just my friends but strangers I might meet in the park or on a trip to Africa, South America, or any- where. I like to hear their different opinions about life, and I often try to photograph strong, beautiful faces."

Ms. Dobler spends a great deal of time with her twin's family and enjoys her nephew and niece, Jim and Beverly; she makes a point to be with them for every special holiday and occasion.

Ms. Dobler's life philosophy is really what she is all about. "I have an optimistic attitude toward life. I keep an open mind and try to absorb what is going on in the world. This is important if one is going to write for children. I find I learn something new and wonderful each day—one never stops learning."

*Walter D. Edı

To be able to do fo
one's own way was
which first brought so
to this land. There
people who confuse
coming rich, but mo
the American dream a
has been. Money can
of anything you cho
a man's life is made of courage, independe
cency, and self-respect he learns to use.

The above quotation is from Walter Dum
monds' foreward to *Two Logs Crossing: Jo*
kell's Story (Dodd, Mead, 1943), an account (
teen-year-old boy who faced up to the loss
results of his first year's fur trapping. The qu
also sums up the philosophy Mr. Edmonds lives

plained: "This book began in my r
nine years ago when I was alor
Labrador at Northlands, the place
put the dog out and was standi
hall, when I saw two house mic
game. They and all the other anim
cluding the Rockendollar rats, the
I saw face-to-face at one time or a
in the story are all based on ob:
escape from Reagan Ready was a
in the snow one October mornir
toilet paper scene—though it didn
house."

I asked him if winning the New
Matchlock Gun had changed his
answered, "No change. It was a
the only prize I ever won."

But Mr. Edmonds is a mode:
literary records, I found that the
only prize he had been awarded
and the Promised Land (Dodd, M
the Boys' Club of America awar(
honorary degrees from Union (
versity, Colgate University, an
where he received his B. A. in 19

Commenting on his work hab
"I get ideas from all sorts of sou
books, or letters from readers.
except as I go along. I can't se
go until I think it is all right."

During the winter months he and his second wife live in Concord, Massachusetts. "I still spend summers on the place in Boonville. I sleep in the room in which I was born. I no longer farm the land though."

Spare time is spent gardening, mainly vegetables, and fly fishing. He has three children and his second wife has three. "Between us we have eighteen grandchildren," he boasts, "but I expect this may not be the end yet!"

Also by Mr. Edmonds

They Had a Horse (Dodd, Mead, 1962).

✳✳Julie Edwards✳✳

Dominic

Julie Edwards is better known to millions of fans as Julie Andrews. But it is Julie Edwards' first book, Mandy (Harper, 1971), that introduced her into the circle of author of children's books.

Ms. Edwards was born Julia Elizabeth Wells on October 1, 1935, at Walton-on-Thames in Surry, England, a town eighteen miles south of London. Her father was a teacher of metalcraft and woodworking; her mother a pianist. While Ms. Edwards was still young, her parents were divorced. Her mother later married Edward Andrews, a music hall singer. Julia became Julie, and she took her stepfather's surname.

During the Nazi blitz of London in World War II, Ms. Edwards' distinctive voice was discovered. During an air raid the family gathered in a London underground shelter. Bombers were flying overhead. To booster morale, her stepfather led the family and friends in community singing. Julie's voice soared above the crowd.

"Life as a child was somewhat haphazard," she told me. "My mother and stepfather, with whom I lived, were in the vaudeville side of show business. I toured with them a great deal. My attendance at various schools was very sporadic until the age of twelve, when my family moved to Walton-on-Thames; I spent my teen-age years there and received schooling from a private tutor. At the age of twelve I also made my professional singing debut."

The debut took place at London's Hippodrome Theatre where Ms. Edwards sang an aria from *Mignon*. In 1953 she appeared at the London Palladium in the title role of *Cinderella*. There she was seen by Vida Hope, director of the London production of *The Boy Friend*, who brought her to New York's Broadway. The show opened in New York on September 30, 1954. The production and nineteen-year-old Julie Andrews were hailed by the critics.

On March 15, 1956, theatre history was made and a star was born. On this date *My Fair Lady,* the musical comedy based on George Bernard Shaw's *Pygmalion,* opened at New York's Mark Hellinger Theatre. In Shaw's stage directions for *Pygmalion* he described Eliza Doolittle, the Cockney flower girl, as "perhaps eighteen, perhaps twenty, hardly older." Lynn Fontaine was thirty-nine when she portrayed Eliza in 1926; Gertrude Lawrence was forty-seven when she performed the role in 1945. At twenty-one, Julie Andrews became the stage's youngest Eliza.

Following her stage success, the actress moved on to the film world and starred in such major motion pictures as *Mary Poppins,* based on the book by P. L. Travers, for which she won the Academy Award, and Rodgers' and Hammerstein's, *The Sound of Music.*

One might well wonder how, with a busy stage, film, and TV career and raising a family, the actress found time to even think about writing a novel for children. I wondered too! But Ms. Edwards told how: "I have two stepchildren; Jennifer, for whom the book was written, is now fifteen years old, Geoffrey is thirteen, and my own daughter, Emma, will be ten in November. While on location in Paris for the film *Darling Lili,* life was very chaotic because we had been traveling for a good many months with a rather large entourage. The children went beserk for there was no one to keep an eye on them.

"I tried to establish some sense of order for the

children by making a game out of certain rules. For example, a failure to put away laundry or to brush teeth would result in a forfeit of some kind. Jennifer, being a smart eleven-year-old at the time, suggested that I play the game too and that I stop swearing. Needless to say, I lost the game within the first hour, and my forfeit to Jenny was to write her a story — hence *Mandy.* At first I was going to write a short thing, but it turned out to be longer than I thought it would be."

Her husband, producer-director Blake Edwards, gave her great encouragement, and she finally started writing things down. "I wrote it all in longhand at first," she recalled. "I began in the summer of 1968 and finished in time for Jenny's birthday in March, 1970. The book was written in many parts of the world — Switzerland, Paris, Ireland, and Beverly Hills."

The story turned into a book. Ms. Edwards had a few copies typed up, had them bound, and gave one to each of her children. Her agent read it and submitted it to Harper & Row who bought it immediately.

The heroine of this sensitive novel is Mandy, an enterprising ten-year-old who lives in an orphanage on the outskirts of St. Martin's Green, a country village. Mandy is one of thirty children in the orphanage. The plot revolves around her discovery of a tiny, deserted cottage in the woods just beyond the home. Mandy makes the cottage her own. She works hard to fix up the place; she saves her money to buy seeds and flowers to enhance the garden; she steals implements from the orphanage; she lies to Matron Bridie and her best friend, Sue, to conceal the cottage—the one thing in life that truly belongs to her.

The day comes, however, when Mandy's secret is discovered. The terrible consequences that take place at first are compensated for by a happy ending when Mandy is adopted by "a secret admirer" and his wife.

Mandy is not a maudlin story. It is filled with adventure combined with tenderness, and portrays a child's struggles against loneliness and her yearning for a real family life. Mandy is a real child—one whom young readers will enjoy meeting and getting to know.

I asked Ms. Edwards if any parts of the book were autobiographical. "Not particularly," she answered. "My small knowledge of the countryside was definitely influenced by my father teaching me about it when I was young. Jake, the gardener in the book, is very much like my great-uncle Harry who worked for us as our gardener when I was a child. That's about it."

I also asked if she felt her career as an actress helped in forming characters or dialogue. She replied: "Not really, though perhaps it did help in creating certain scenes."

At the time of this interview Ms. Edwards had received a contract with Harper & Row for a second book, which is tentatively titled *The Last of the Great Whangdoodles.* "A 'whangdoodle,' according to my

Random House dictionary, is a humorous mythical creature. Hopefully, the book will be an unusual and interesting adventure story," she remarked.

The Edwardses live in a pleasant Mediterranean-style home in Beverly Hills, California. Along with the children there are two dogs, two cats, assorted goldfish, one hamster, one canary, one finch, "and there is a tortoise *somewhere* in the garden!" Some of the pleasures she enjoys most in life are "being Ms. Blake Edwards and collecting paintings and sculpture. Blake and I are the proud owners of one or two special paintings and some good sculpture. I also enjoy strolling through my garden, reading, holidays with the family, listening to good music, and writing stories for children."

It seems a bit ridiculous to describe Julie Edwards. I doubt if there's an adult in the world who wouldn't recognize her. She has a flawless milk-like complexion, light brown hair, is five-feet seven inches tall and weighs in at about one hundred thirty pounds. Her life is as magical as the Cinderella she once played, as unpredictable as Mary Poppins.

As a final question I asked if there was something special that she felt a child might like to know about her. "Yes!" she exclaimed. "I can fly. But not without my umbrella—and I do have to practice *very* hard."

She might be jesting. I didn't see her do it, but I wouldn't be surprised if she really, truly could fly.

* * * Eleanor Estes

Jim Theologos

In September 1941, a new family was introduced to children—the Moffat family. It was introduced via the pen of Eleanor Estes (Eś-tease) in her book *The Moffats.** The family reappears in two sequels, *The Middle Moffat* (1942) and *Rufus M.* (1943). Set in the New England town of Cranbury just before and during World War I, the adventures evolve around a poor family. The main characters are Mama, a widowed dressmaker, and her four children, Sylvia, Joey, Jane, and Rufus. Each of the books was illustrated by the Caldecott Award winning artist Louis Slobodkin. Each is filled with warm and humorous family adventures, and each consists of a series of episodes, many deriving from Ms. Estes' own life.

Ms. Estes recalled her childhood for me: "I was born in West Haven, Connecticut, on May 9, 1906. (West Haven is the Cranbury of my early books.) It was a small town then, ideal for children, having open fields, woods, brooks, and hills and also lovely little beaches along the shore of the New Haven harbor, excellent

---

*All titles have been published by Harcourt Brace Jovanovich.

for swimming, clamming, or taking off in a rowboat or a canoe. Now West Haven is a big, sprawling suburb of New Haven, and the brooks and fields are all gone. The Green, however, is still as it was, and the church, which figures in the Moffat books and in *Ginger Pye* (1951), is as lovely as ever.

My family life as a child can be sensed from reading most of my books, which drew largely on memories, though embellished by my wayward imaginings, which took me anywhere.

"I never really decided to write for children. It just happened that I did. I always wanted to become a writer, and I suppose it was because of my long association with children in various public libraries that I unconsciously directed my stories to them, to amuse, to entertain, and to make them laugh or cry."

Upon graduating from high school, Ms. Estes went to work in the children's department of the New Haven Free Public Library. In 1928 she was made head of the department. Three years later she was awarded the Caroline M. Hewins scholarship for children's librarians. She then went to New York to study at the Pratt Institute School of Library Science.

Lucky was the day she entered Pratt, for it was here that she met and married a fellow student, Rice Estes. She worked in various children's rooms of the New York Public Library system until 1940—the time when *The Moffats,* her first book, was accepted for publication. "I left," she said, "because I became a writer— at last!" Writing had always been her true goal.

The Moffats, although a typical American family, have crossed international boundaries. The books have been translated into many foreign languages.

In 1944 *The Hundred Dresses* appeared. This classic story tells of Wanda Petronski, a Polish girl from a poor, motherless family. Wanda's story of the hundred dresses she "owns" has become a staple in the field of children's literature. Not only is the book must reading for children of any background, it is one that should be required reading in teacher-training programs. Tender and compassionate, it well deserves the many kudos bestowed upon it.

In 1947 Ms. Estes turned away briefly from children's books to write her first novel for adults, *The Echoing Green,* a recollection of her childhood and growing-up years. But it wasn't long before she returned to writing and illustrating children's books.

1951 marked the publication of *Ginger Pye,* a novel about the Pye family's adventures and of Ginger, their "intellectual" dog; it won the 1952 Newbery Medal. I asked Ms. Estes how this story developed; her answer made it seem quite easy: "I just wanted to write a book about a smart dog, one my brothers and I had had as children. His name was Ginger. He did get lost on Thanksgiving Day as a puppy and came back in May—grown up. Originally I had thought the story would be a fourth Moffat book, but for various reasons I changed my mind and invented the Pyes. Of course the locale, Cranbury, is the same as that of *The Moffats.*

"I felt it was an honor to win the Newbery Award. I don't know whether it changed my life in any way, because I don't know what my life would have been like otherwise. I was grateful for the award, and I cherish it."

Like the Moffats, the Pyes came back in *Pinky Pye* (1958). In this book the Pyes are vacationing on Fire Island, and Pinky is an abandoned kitten. Pinky isn't as intellectual a cat as Ginger is a dog—still she is astonishing for she can type!

For many years the Estes lived in Brooklyn in a little faculty house on the campus of Pratt Institute where Mr. Estes was director of the Pratt Institute Library. Both the house and the neighborhood are described in two books, *The Alley* (1964), about a burglary, and *The Tunnel of Hugsy Goode* (1972). The Estes recently moved to New Haven, Connecticut, near the scene of Ms. Estes early books.
moved to New Haven, Connecticut, near the scene of Ms. Estes early books.

Regarding her writing habits she told me: "I try to work a couple of hours each morning on a book and hopefully another hour or so in the afternoon. Sometimes I am able to follow this schedule!

"I don't know where I get my ideas. They come from childhood remembrances mainly. Frequently, in the middle of the night, I may remember something someone may have said or done which sparks my imagination. I revise my books again and again, trying to improve them all the way along through to the final proofs. I feel quite lost when a book is finished and immediately start a new one. Occasionally when a manuscript is finished, I try out a chapter I've enjoyed on Rice. I love it when he laughs or says, 'This is good!' I don't know what I would have done without his encouragement and appreciation, for Rice has always given me the finest criticism and kind analysis of my work. The few times I have sent a manuscript off without his reading it, I've been very frightened. When our daughter Helena grew old enough to read my manuscripts, she, too, read them; she also loved to read the work in galleys.

"I really don't have a favorite among my books. Sometimes I like one better than another but this varies. Long after I've written a book, one like *The Moffats,* I begin to enjoy them. It's as though someone else had written them, and I laugh at the funny parts. When writing, I simply try to make the book I'm working on as good as it can possibly be; years may go by before I open its covers again."

Ms. Estes relishes "many of the joys in life with the exception of sports which, aside from baseball, don't interest me a great deal. I like to be with people, all kinds and ages, and most especially with children. I like to travel, especially once I'm back home safe and sound again. The places in the country I like most are Rockport on Cape Ann because I love the ocean, seashore, rocks, and gulls. I love New York City because of the theatre, opera, concerts, movies, and museums.

"We've always had pets; they're in all my books.

I'm afraid of horses and equally afraid of chickens when they flap their wings. I especially like to cook. It's possible that I use cooking to put off getting on with my work. I like to do *nothing* but have little time to develop this hobby!

"Our daughter Helena, who is in a number of my books under various names, married recently and is working in a public library on Long Island and attending library school. The stories in *The Witch Family* (1960) are based on stories I told her long ago. Her husband is working toward his Ph.D. degree in the field of psychology, so they are very busy people."

Eleanor Estes' books have been widely acclaimed. The town of Cranbury, where first the Moffat family and then the Pyes lived, has been a very special place for children for over thirty years. Frances Clark Sayers, also a children's author, has said that the books are "destined to become part of the glad heritage which parents share with children, remembered from childhood, through adulthood, and returned to childhood again through one's children, and their children's children." One reviewer called Ms. Estes "the Proust of children's literature." She thought that was very complimentary. Another once said, "An Estes is an Estes is an Estes." She rather liked that, too!

Also by Ms. Estes

(All published by Harcourt Brace)
The Sun and the Wind and Mr. Todd (1943).
The Sleeping Giant and Other Stories (1948).

Miranda the Great (1967).

The Lollipop Princess (1968).

✳ Walter Farley

Hank Cohen

Readers meet The Black on page six of Walter Farley's *The Black Stallion:** "He was a giant of a horse, glistening black—too big to be pure Arabian. . . The head was that of the wildest of all wild creatures—a stallion born wild— and it was beautiful, savage, splendid." And once one meets him, he never forgets him! The Black was created in 1941 by Walter Farley, a man who was born in Syracuse, New York, and grew up in New York City—a place where one rarely sees a horse nowadays, except perhaps at a nearby racetrack or in Central Park.

But let Mr. Farley tell how his own childhood sparked his book: "I lived in midtown Manhattan at the Hotel Roosevelt where my father worked as an assistant manager. I commuted by subway to Erasmus

---

*All titles have been published by Random House.

Hall High School in Brooklyn, because the school had a good track team. I loved New York City for all its year-round opportunities for sports and other activities; it was a great place for a kid in those days and perhaps still is, providing kids take advantage of what is there. Like most kids, I was very interested in sports and was able to play tennis, ride, run, and ice skate most of the year. And there were plenty of horses — in Central Park, Squadron A with its indoor polo, Long Island, Connecticut, and Westchester trails, and the race tracks at Belmont, Jamaica, and Aqueduct where I spent many, many days. Later I moved to Flushing where several of my friends had horses stabled in lots now occupied by apartment buildings. And it was there I set the locale for *The Black Stallion* as I rode on trails through Kissena Park and along the Long Island Expressway.

"I enjoyed writing as much as I did reading or participating in sports or anything else. I enjoyed writing stories on the typewriter, any kind of story at all, at the ages of fourteen, fifteen, and sixteen. I read a great deal, but there were few books about horses — at least only a couple that I knew of. There was Anna Sewell's *Black Beauty* (Dodd, Mead, 1877, 1941) and Will James' *Smoky, the Cow Horse* (Scribner, 1926, 1965), but these were not enough to satisfy me; I honestly thought, even at that age, about the thousands of horse lovers like me who wanted more books about horses. So I had fun writing my story for them and for myself. I became absorbed in *The Black Stallion* by becoming Alec, of course, a boy from New York City who brought a horse like The Black to my Flushing barn. I remember well devoting two and three nights a week writing it."

The Black Stallion was begun while Mr. Farley was still a student at Erasmus Hall High School (the school one of today's stellar celebrities, Barbra Streisand, also attended). He continued writing the book while studying at Mercersburg Academy in Pennsylvania; it was published while he was an undergraduate at Columbia University. Mr. Farley used his first advance to go traveling. Shortly after the book was published, World War II began, and Mr. Farley joined the United States Army, where he spent four years, 1942–1946. Most of that time he was assigned to *Yank,* an army weekly magazine.

He continued writing for children, however, and two other books appeared during these years, *Larry and the Underseas Raider* (1942) and the first sequel, *Black Stallion Returns* (1945). In all Mr. Farley has created close to thirty others.

Mr. Farley and his wife, Rosemary, spend part of each year in Florida and part in Pennsylvania. In Florida they live in a house on the beach located a little south of Venice. He works in a small office away from the main house and looking over the water. "It's good for my eyes to look up from the typewriter to the horizon. There's been lots of close work through the years," he sighed. "And I love water. We have a small Boston whaler and a thirty-four-foot Rhodesdesigned sloop. We sail a lot, race a little, and skin dive as much as possible. There are beautiful islands to the south of us. I also do lots of riding, mostly on Arabians.''

In Pennsylvania the Farleys have a home in Powder Mill Valley, an eighty-acre tract of woods and lush farmland near Boyertown in the southeastern part of the state. Many of his books were created in a converted chicken coop.

Commenting on his work habits he told me: "I get up very early, usually just before dawn. When in Florida I jog on the beach; at the Pennsylvania farm I jog around the pond, always accompanied by a great dane—I've always had one for some twenty years. Thor is the present dog, and there's a book about him, *The Great Dane Thor* (1966), which is my only non-horse story to date. We swim after running, then I work at my writing until about 1:00 p.m. After that I'm off riding, sailing, swimming, or doing some other outdoor activity; I truly need the exercise after a long stint at the typewriter.

"I have no occupation other than writing. The only income I've ever had has come from writing books. I do raise race horses and Arabians occasionally and sell them, but there's really little money in it. Writing for me is fun. All my books are completely different from one another; otherwise I could never have stayed with the same characters who are used as springboards into whatever it is I want to write about. Kids know how different my books are; most adults don't. I've written fantasy and science fiction, *The Black Stallion's Ghost* (1969) is a horror story of the supernatural; *Man O' War* (1962), the story of one of America's mightiest thoroughbred racing horses, is a fictional biography —authentic but seen through the eyes of a fictitious stableboy."

The "author's foreword" to *Man O' War* gives further evidence of his love of horses. Here he recounts the time his father took him to Faraway Farms to see "the greatest horse that ever lived."

Mr. Farley compares the creation of his books to having a baby: "Conception. Initial thrill at its development. Drudgery as the months wear on. And post-birth blues."

The Farleys have three children, Alice, Steve, and Tim. Several years ago their oldest daughter, Pam, just twenty, was killed in an automobile accident crossing the Austrian Alps during her junior year at college. Following her untimely death, her father wrote *The Black Stallion and the Girl* (1971), featuring the only female character ever to appear in his books as a central figure.

Mr. Farley believes strongly in encouraging both his own and other children to pursue their interests. "Kids are so apt to think something that is fun and comes easy to them is not important. I was no different. When I go to book fairs, I always make a point of encouraging kids to develop the talent that comes easy and naturally. You ought to pursue your hobby—not become a lawyer so you can spend your spare time pursuing your hobby. If you can't make a living water skiing, then take up something related to it—sell the equipment or edit a magazine about it," he tells girls and boys.

The author is convinced that children's reading tastes have not changed greatly in the past thirty years. "Children still ask the same questions now as they did then—whether they write to me from France, England, or Finland," he said. (His books have sold over nine million copies in the United States and in fifteen other countries including Saudi Arabia, Czechoslovakia, India, and Malaya.)

"Children's letters are very, very important to me," he continued. "I don't really know how many hundreds of thousands of letters I've received over the years, but I've read them all between books. And it might interest your readers to know that I've saved them all; they're in an appropriate place, stored in my tack room at the farm above stalls and horses. I can't destroy them and sometimes wonder if there isn't someone who would like to make a study of them for they span such a long period of time. And how different are kids in their love for horses now than they were in the 1940s? I think little. Many kids would rather ride on the back of a horse at twenty to twenty-five miles per hour than pilot a spaceship to the moon!"

Also by Mr. Farley

(All published by Random House)

For young readers
Little Black: A Pony (1961).
Little Black Goes to the Circus (1963).
For older readers
The Island Stallion (1948).
The Island Stallion's Fury (1951).
The Black Stallion and Flame (1960).

✳ ✳ ✳ Leonard Everett Fisher

The art of Leonard Everett Fisher has received many kudos: The *New York Times* has called it "powerful, impressive;" The *Chicago Daily News,* "monumental;" The *Cleveland Press,* "dynamic;" and the *Saturday Review,* "striking." One needs only to look at a book illustrated by Mr. Fisher to see why critics have hailed him.

A series widely used in classrooms throughout the country is "The Colonial Americans" series published by Franklin Watts. It includes over fifteen titles that focus on the crafts, trades, and extraordinary products

colonial Americans created with the tools and tech-
niques of their era. Children entering this world of the
past meet and learn to appreciate such talented people as *The Hatters* (1965), *The Printers* (1965), *The
Wigmakers* (1965), *The Weavers* (1966), *The School-
masters* (1967), *The Limners: America's Earliest
Portrait Painters* (1969), and *The Potters* (1969).

These books, originally geared to fifth-grade audiences, have become highly regarded in the fields of
art and the social sciences. One can find the volumes
not only in public schools, but on the shelves of such
technical libraries as The Institute of Fine Arts and New
York University. They also appear in the book stalls of
the Detroit Institute of Fine Arts and New York's Metropolitan Museum of Art.

Mr. Fisher did the linoleum-like cut illustrations for
this series on *British* scrapeboard. "Isn't that an interesting historical coincidence with respect to "The
Colonial Americans" series?" he joked.

The books took years to produce; they required
much specialized research, writing, and, of course, the
execution of the illustrations.

One might well think what a fifth-grade child thought
while perusing the fifteen-plus titles: "This author just
has to be a couple of hundred years old to know all
this," he mused.

But of course Mr. Fisher isn't that old. He was born
on June 24, 1924, in New York City and grew up in
the Sea Gate area of Brooklyn, New York. "My young
life was warm, free, adventurous, boisterous, some-

what intellectual, and memorable. We all indulged as money would allow, but that wasn't too often; we were never pampered. While my younger sister and I were my parents' only children, the rest of the family was enormous, close, and always about. Sometimes I think we had a prototype commune. And while the afterglow still burns brightly, it has left a certain mark.''

His father, a marine engineer and amateur artist, steadily directed his son's career from the time he was four years old. Mr. Fisher's formal training began at Manhattan's Heckscher Foundation in 1932; he completed his master degree studies at Yale University's School of Fine Arts in 1950. While concluding his studies he was awarded the Joseph Pulitzer Fellowship in Art, which gave him the opportunity to travel widely throughout Europe. During the thirties and forties he was involved in numerous activities and won a variety of prizes, fellowships, and honors.

During World War II he served with the United States Army Corps of Engineers as a map specialist. One of his assignments was a highly classified position with the Operations Section of the 30th Engineer Topographic Battalion, where he participated in the cartographic planning of the Battle of Northern Italy, the invasions of Southern France, Austria, Germany, and Okinawa, and the unrequired, but planned, assault on the Japanese home islands. In 1944, while in North Africa, he executed a mural at the direction of the United States Army Special Services, but it was destroyed before completion. In 1945 he was one of several artists commissioned by the American Red Cross to decorate the recreation facility of the 219th Military Hospital at Schofield Barracks in Oahu, Hawaii. The entire building was demolished after the war; the whereabouts of the panel, if removed prior to demolition, is unknown.

After returning from Europe in 1951, he worked as an assistant to Auriel Bessemer, a muralist, before being appointed Dean of the Whitney School of Art in New Haven, Connecticut, becoming the youngest such professional school officer in the United States at that time.

In 1952 he married; a year later he resigned from his administrative post at Whitney to give his entire time to painting and working in the field of children's literature. The first book he illustrated was Geoffrey Household's *The Exploits of Xenophon* (Random House, 1954). Since then he has provided illustrations for over two hundred books for children, many of which he has also written.

Besides illustrating children's books he finds time to paint. His work is in many private collections and in such permanent public institutions as the Library of Congress, the Norton Gallery of Fine Art, the Free Public Libaray of Philadelphia, and the Milwaukee Public Library. In 1970 Mr. Fisher completed a fourteen-panel wall, "Stations of the Cross," for St. Patrick's Church in Armonk, New York. This job was finished right after he had an accident that nearly ended his career. Mr. Fisher explained: "I'm busy. Always busy. And I love every minute of it. But sometimes I get too involved and don't know when to stop. I had just completed an exhausting speaking tour and came home. I thought I'd mow the lawn to unwind. My hand almost got chopped off in the mower."

He is busy. He never stops. "I have a hell of a memory, and I work all the time—even when I'm not working," he told me. "I'm artistically driven."

Driven indeed! In addition to all the above works, he recently (1972) designed and executed a block of four first class United States postage stamps to commemorate the American Bicentennial. The stamps, depicting colonial American craftsmen, were commissioned by the United States Postal Service. This does not mean he'll find time to lick any of them!

Among the author-illustrator's favorite things in life are his wife, his three teen-age children, Julie Anne, Susan Abby, and James Albert, his dog, his piano, and an occasional sip of Jack Daniel's sour mash. He also enjoys traveling, sailing, "and every simple gift, trinket, and card my wife and children have given to me." He resists great crowds, physically and artistically. "Mostly artistically!" he exclaimed.

He never reworks his illustrations or paintings but does rework his texts. "I have no idea where my many ideas come from," he declared. "Many different things pop into my head—and out again. I work on whatever feels comfortable, interesting, and challenging. I pursue all my work to a conclusion or eventually discard the whole lot."

His home and studio in Westport, Connecticut, reflect his love of art. He owns several art treasures including a 1470 Veronese, an 1869 Robert, an illuminated German dictionary done by a fourteenth century pope, several visual efforts done by his children, and some drawings of his late father. Among his own personal favorite books are *Pumpers, Bailers, Hooks, and Ladders* (Dial, 1961) — "It's open and vigorous and the first book written, illustrated, and designed by me" — *A Jungle Jumble* (Putnam, 1966) — "Because of the jaguar on pages nine and thirteen" — and *Death of Evening Star* (Doubleday, 1972) — "Because it was an exciting thing to write and illustrate. It's my first piece of full-blown fiction."

I could write on and on about this bundle of creativity but here I shall end with one bit of advice: For those of you who do not know his works, rush to your public library and look up the work of Leonard Everett Fisher. Once you see it, you'll surely like it.

Also illustrated by Mr. Fisher

Suranay, Enrico. *The Golden Frog* (Putnam, 1963).

————. *Ride the Cold Wind* (Putnam, 1964).

Thayer, Ernest L. *Casey at the Bat* (Watts, 1964).

Irving, Washington. *Rip Van Winkle* (Watts, 1966).

* *Genevieve Foster
*

When I was a college student and later a teacher of children, I personally welcomed Genevieve Foster's contributions to the world of children's literature. Her histories not only helped me to understand what was going on when and where, but they clarified the interrelationships of people who lived during the same era.

Children find it difficult to develop a sense of time and of chronological relationships. Young children, for example, are often amazed to learn that Abraham Lincoln *read* about George Washington and Benjamin Franklin. "Didn't Abe *know* George Washington?" is a question I've often been asked, since many girls and boys think George Washington was the first president and Abe the second!

I welcomed meeting and talking with Ms. Foster for she is a vibrant, energetic, and engaging eighty-year-old. She met me at the door of her penthouse apartment on New York's East 38th Street. Before I got down to the fundamentals of her writing life, I told her a startling fact I had uncovered while doing some preliminary research—we were both born on April 13th! When I told Ms. Foster this, she laughed heartily, "but you're young enough to be my grandson."

Spending an afternoon with her was like listening to a grandmother telling stories—one could just sit and listen for hours on end.

Ms. Foster was born in 1893 in Oswego, New York. A year after she was born, her father died, and her mother returned to her old home in Whitewater, Wisconsin. Three years later her grandfather passed away, leaving four females—her mother, grandmother, aunt, and herself—to fill a house with twenty-odd rooms.

"Both grandmother and her house had great influences on me," she recalled. "Growing up among all the memories of four generations gave me a great sense of stability, of deep roots, and of a feeling for the continuity of past and present. Two large rooms on the fourth floor were filled with fascinating old things. On one wall were crossed swords used by an uncle in the Civil War. There was a walnut box of surveying instruments belonging to my grandfather who had helped bring the first railroad to Chicago in 1839, just after he graduated from Union College in New York State. There were piles of an early fashion magazine, bouquets of waxed fruits and flowers under huge glass domes made by a great aunt, beautiful anatomical drawings by my father who had been a science professor, boxes of daguerreotypes, and many family portraits. Stowed away in what was known as the trunk room were some of the costumes some of the ladies had had their portraits painted in—tiny bodices and huge skirts of wonderfully heavy plaid silk, shirred bonnets, and hoop skirts.

"Among the chests and trunks, some of which were brass studded and covered with hair cloth, was a round bonnet trunk, which had been used by great-grandmother when she came to visit her son, making the trip from New York State by way of the Erie Canal and the Great Lakes. The trunk was round, about two feet high, decorated with the scene of an old Dutch town, and had actually been made from a hollowed-out trunk of a tree. This, I learned, was why chests came to be called *trunks* in the United States.

"There were boxes of old letters written and sent before there were postage stamps. The oldest thing of all was an account book with a heavy cowhide cover used by Hendrick Schermerhorn, my grandfather's grandfather, in 1736—forty years before the American Revolution.

"To live history vicariously in this way made it seem very real to me. History in school was dreadful. I loathed it. It was a complete mess. You memorized what the teachers said, gave it back to them, and bingo bango, you received a good grade if you were right, and then forgot the whole terrible experience."

Ms. Foster's distaste for schoolbook history was what sparked her to "do history my way." Her first writing venture was *George Washington's World** (1941), which was selected as a 1942 Newbery Honor

---

*All titles were published by Scribner.

Book. Similar texts followed, including *Abraham Lincoln's World* (1944), a 1945 Newbery Honor Book, *Augustus Caesar's World* (1947), *The World of Captain John Smith, 1580–1631* (1960), and *The World of Columbus and Sons* (1965).

"Her way" is a sensible one. In each of her books she gives a broad, panoramic, horizontal view of individuals and the period in which they lived. "History had always been sliced vertically for me," she commented. "There must have been teachers who saw the story as a whole, but none happened to come my way. The history of each nation, isolated from the others, was presented from beginning to end, with only the barest reference to what was taking place in the rest of the world at any given time. The result was lifeless and confusing to me.

"I had an idea to write a history showing not only what was going on in the United States, but all over the world, and how events in the various nations were related. The idea possessed me. I determined to try it, visualizing it as a multiple history, one in which scientists, artists, musicians, writers, and explorers would be included as well as kings, presidents, and generals. I wanted to show how their lives fitted together and what part each played in the great adventure story of history. It is natural, I thought, for all of us to correlate world events in point of time with events in our own lives."

One need only pick up a volume of Ms. Foster's "World" books to appreciate the vast amount of information she has presented. Each book is filled with drawings, maps, and time-lines, all prepared by the author, to further instruct and "un-confuse" young readers.

"Illustrations, maps, and charts play an important part in the books. I plan and sketch them as I write the text. I try never to duplicate in a drawing what I have described in words. Illustrations often destroy the pictures a reader forms in his own mind. Interfering with the image created by words destroys part of the joy of reading. I try always to remember the old adage that one drawing is better than one thousand words."

At the time of this interview Ms. Foster was completing *The World of William Penn* (1973). We sat looking over the complete dummy of the text and discussed the great amount of research that went into it. "It takes about three years to do each book," she told me. "There is much research to be done, much writing, much rewriting, and then I allow about six months to complete the artwork.

"Research is time-consuming but fascinating. I read encyclopedia accounts, general histories, and several outstanding biographies written about the person I'm concentrating on. Of course I read skimmingly or I'd never get through the mountains of material. I do all this to see where people's lives cross and how patterns fit together. I also use Will Durant's *The Story of Civilization* as a basic reference tool.

"The people I'm writing about become friends to me. I often ponder why a certain individual did something and have to look hard and long to find answers to my own many questions."

Despite the mass of material she uses for each volume, her work space in her apartment is quite small, neat, and uncluttered. "I can't bear disorder—either in history or in my own life!" she exclaimed. And her desk and apartment certainly show this to be true.

Ms. Foster told me how she chose Scribner's as a publisher. "I did most of *George Washington's World* in Illinois where I lived with my husband and two children. I chose Washington because his name and the colonial period were familiar to all elementary school children. One day I decided to go to New York to see a publisher about my work. It was during the Depression and money was quite scarce, so I set out on a bus to New York City with very little money. Upon arriving I made appointments to see three publishers. The first one I visited was Scribner's. The editor, Alice Dalgleish, took an immediate interest in my approach and my work. She was somewhat startled to see me for she was going to contact me to illustrate a children's book. I had done illustrations for children's stories in *Child Life* and other magazines.

"I told her that I didn't want to illustrate a manuscript. I wanted to illustrate my own book. I saw two other editors at publishers' offices that day but returned to Alice. She was the brightest woman I met."

With the exception of one book, now out-of-print, all of Ms. Foster's titles have been published by Scribner's.

In 1949, Ms. Foster's "Initial Biographies" were introduced to younger readers. This is an easy-to-read series geared to children in grades four and up and are outgrowths of the "World" books. The first of this series, *George Washington* (1949) was selected as a 1950 Newbery Honor Book. When complete, the series will include six or seven presidents and will cover high spots in American history.

Her "Year" books came about in 1969. Several include *Year of Columbus, 1492* (1969), *Year of the Pilgrims, 1620* (1969), and *Year of Lincoln, 1861* (1970). Ms. Foster remarked: "Needless to say, these short, condensed volumes demand as much research as longer ones. In fact, a more thorough digesting of the material is necessary to reduce it to its essentials."

Other books include a two-volume series, "Birthdays of Freedom" (1952), which were also chosen as Newbery Honor Books in 1953.

When not working and writing, Ms. Foster enjoys going to the theatre, playing Scrabble, sewing, knitting, and gardening. She also likes game shows on television "though I'm not fast on remembering specific dates and events at a snap of a finger!"

Her two children, Orrington and Joanna, are both married. Joanna is a writer of books for children and adults as well as a film producer for Connecticut Films in Westport. Her company recently produced a thirteen-minute, color, 16mm film entitled *Genevieve Fosters's World*. Ms. Foster's husband, Orrington, died in 1945.

Over a glass of sherry, Ms. Foster autographed my copy of *Year of Independence, 1776* (1970). My 1972 birthday, which was only a few weeks away, will always be a special one: Ms. Foster's inscription read: *For Lee—my new co-Aries friend, Happy Birthday to us—April 13th. G. F.*

∗
∗ **Jean Fritz**
∗

"If you want to locate me in a crowd, look for a middle-aged, non-violent type, size fourteen, probably wearing hoop earrings and sandal-style shoes, among other things. I may be fishing in my pocketbook for one of my three pairs of glasses or I may be simply staring into middle space. In this case, it means that I am eavesdropping, which I do regularly and do well. Don't disturb me then," declared Jean Fritz.

When not in a crowd, she can be found at home in Dobbs Ferry, New York. She and her husband, Michael, live in a Dutch colonial house on an old maple tree-lined street; the setting is reminiscent of an old *Saturday Evening Post* cover. "With its numerous children, dogs, bicycles, and balls, the street has a nostalgic, small-town air that I appreciate less now than I did twenty years ago when we moved here. But America and I were both younger then. Our children are grown now and away from home. My husband and I sometimes talk of a house on the ocean, in the woods, or on a hilltop; still we are happy here. The big maple on the terrace that we share with bluejays is an old friend; the house and furnishings, particularly the Chinese pieces that have survived from my childhood, are at home together. I think I could probably be content in any home that had my two Chinese rugs that have been in every house I have lived in."

Ms. Fritz was born in Hankow, China, where her parents were missionaries. Remembering her childhood years, she told me: "I lived in the French concession, attended a British school, played with two German girls, and spent my entire childhood fighting a private revolutionary war in defense of my country, my chief opponent being a tough little Scotch boy with square knees and nasty things to say about George Washington. Summers were spent in Peitaiho, a seaside resort north of Peking, where a person in need of transportation stepped out of his door to call a donkey, the way one would call a taxi in New York. Communism and war moved to Hankow during our last years there. A shell fell in our yard on one occasion, a riot broke out in our living room on another, and my mother and I were repeatedly forced to evacuate to Shanghai for a few weeks. In 1928, when I was ready for high school, we moved back to the United States — just in time for the Depression!"

The family settled in Hartford, Connecticut, where Ms. Fritz attended high school. She later earned her degree at Wheaton College and did graduate work in education at Columbia University.

From the time she was a small child living in China, she knew she wanted to become a writer. One day at the age of five, she announced to her father, "I know what I'm going to be when I grow up. I'm going to be a poet." Her father answered, "Well, that's fine, but you'll have to do something more than that. You'll never make a living writing poetry."

Taking her father's advice, she immediately wrote a story titled "Sue and Margery." It was about twins — Americans — with a bathtub that was white and shaped for lying down!

Her first book for children, *Fish Head* (Coward),* was revised in 1972. She had always written, however. After her marriage in 1941, the Fritzs traveled to the West Coast where they lived, according to the author, "five years of a pillar-and-post existence in the army." During this time Ms. Fritz held a variety of jobs doing research, book reviewing, and editing. When her own children were born, she became interested in children's books.

"During one year, when I ran the children's depart-

---

*All titles, unless otherwise noted, were published by Coward-McCann.

ment of our local library, I found that I not only wanted to read children's stories, I wanted to write them, too. But to be honest, most children's books, like most other books, are only a writer's way of traveling his individual river and, with luck, finding some of the sources," she explained.

"*Fish Head* started at our dinner table with the story an oceanographer friend told of an experiment at sea off Bermuda when a cat stowed away on his research vessel. This was the germ of an idea that appealed to me, probably because I was house-bound with young children at that moment and would have liked nothing better than to have escaped to sea!"

Although she continued to write books for younger readers, her earlier inclinations to write stories about America remained dominant for some time. Now, however, she is best known for her writings in the area of historical fiction: *The Cabin Faced West* (1958), a story of pioneer life in western Pennsylvania; *Brady* (1960), a story of a boy who discovered his father was an agent for the Underground Railroad; *I, Adam* (1963), a vivid recreation of life in New England during the 1850s; and *Early Thunder* (1969), a book Henry Steele Commager called one that "faithfully mirrors the life of revolutionary Salem . . . a spirited story . . . authentic history."**

**An excellent letter from Ms. Fritz to her editor about the development of *Early Thunder* is available free by writing to Coward-McCann, Inc., 200 Madison Avenue, New York, N. Y. 10016.

"These four historical stories were the most satisfying to write," she remarked, "and although it's hard for me to pick among them, I suspect *The Cabin Faced West* is emotionally closest to my own experience. After I had written it, I realized the story, although presumably about my great-great-grandmother, a lonely little girl in pioneer Pennsylvania, was really about me as a lonely girl in an equally foreign environment."

The Cabin Faced West was her first historical book. "With it I discovered the joys of research. It was like exploring, only you could sit down. And you were always on the edge of a surprise. Digging into American history also seemed to satisfy a need that I had, having grown up in China, of finding my roots, of trying to come to terms with just what it has meant historically to be an American.

"I am not one of those people who can mine for ideas. I simply stumble across them or do without. Once I have an idea, however, I worry it, lie awake with it, walk the floor with it, and make countless false starts before I can successfully launch it. I work an eight-hour day—not from discipline but because I can't put the story down. I work slowly, writing in pencil and typing it up at the end of each day's work; however, it is often not more than one or two typed pages. Rewrite? Of course I do. By the law of averages one would think there would be a certain percentage of sentences that would turn out right the first time. None of mine seem to, though. My children have been my most severe critics and have often been the ones who gave my books their titles."

Ms. Fritz's life is a full one. "Every day begins with coffee and the *New York Times*. The good days include several pages of manuscript that seem, at least at the moment, to be right. The best days have friends in them or family—a visit from our son or daughter, perhaps with talk around a fire if it's winter, a walk on the beach or a swim in a pool if it's summer. The red-letter days have perhaps most often been on trips —on an island in Maine, on horseback in the Tetons, in Delphi, Greece, or on a hillside in Wales. Such a description of life, however, overlooks the hours— the hundreds of hours—that accumulate in supermarkets, P.T.A. meetings, and other necessary but unexhilarating activities. It also overlooks a whole area of national and international concerns with which one struggles and for which one suffers every day. I join groups, write letters, make phone calls, and have on occasion demonstrated; in short, my life, like that of other Americans, is caught up in the special agonies of the times."

She likes going to beaches, new countries, art galleries, second-hand bookstores, garage sales, back roads, the theatre—places where she "always feels that she is on the edge of some lovely surprise. I don't even mind answering the telephone; who knows what may be waiting?"

At the time of this interview, Ms. Fritz had just "recovered from a four-year project"—a long adult nonfiction book about several Massachusetts families before and after the American Revolution, *Cast for a Revolution: Some American Friends and Enemies — 1728–1814* (Houghton, 1972).

"I hope," she concluded, "my next project will be some writing about present day mainland China. My husband and I have applied for visas; there's no way to know if or when they will be granted, but we wait and hope."

Also by Ms. Fritz

And Then What Happened, Paul Revere?
(Coward-McCann, 1973).

* Jean Craighead George

Jean Craighead George has described herself as having "the build of Cousin Bessie," but this doesn't do her justice — not at all. She is a handsome woman, chic and sparkling, with a face that seems to belong more in front of stage-footlights than on book jackets. She lives in Chappaqua, New York, in an old chalet-like house "of uncertain architecture." Woods surround the house "as well as a nice settlement of people who have children. The children," she continued, "bring me snails, beetles, robins, poems, essays, and little brothers and sisters. In winter here I can see the birds at my feeder and an occasional deer. It's a beautiful part of the world and close to the excitement of writers and editors in New York City."

Ms. George was born on July 2, 1919, in Washington, D. C. "I grew up in the wild edges and riversides of Washington, spending summers at the old family home at Craighead, Pennsylvania. My father, an entomologist, and my twin brothers, now wildlife ecologists, took me with them on hunting and camping trips, to the tops of cliffs to look for falcons, down the white water rivers to fish and swim, and over the forest floors in search of mice, birds, wildflowers, trees, fish, salamanders, and mammals. So absorbing and carefree were these excursions that my childhood in retrospect seems like one leaping, laughing adventure into the mysteries and joys of the earth.

"Our home was always full of pets—falcons, raccoons, owls, opossums, and dozens of sleeping insects that would metamorphose into the most miraculous things—thousands of praying mantis, a trembling luna moth, or a strange beetle that could snap his thorax and abdomen while lying on his back, flip into the air, and come down on all six feet. Hounds and kids ran in and out of the animals as other children run in and out of furniture. It was a rollicking childhood."

With this kind of early background, it seems natural that Ms. George's works are mainly about science and the world of nature. The late 1960s and the decade of the 1970s may well be The Age of Ecology, but this author was very concerned with the subject long before it became the popular thing to write about. Her first book for children, *Vulpes, the Red Fox* (Dutton), co-authored with her former husband, John L. George, was published in 1948. They also collaborated on *Vision, the Mink* (Dutton, 1949), *Masked Prowler, the Story of a Raccoon* (Dutton, 1950), and *Meph, the Pet Skunk* (Dutton, 1952), books dealing with the animals' struggle for survival. Besides co-authoring these titles, Ms. George provided illustrations for them.

Her own first book, *The Hole in the Tree* (Dutton, 1957), is a story for younger readers and traces the history of a hole in an apple tree from its beginnings as a tiny opening in one limb until it is large enough to attract a raccoon. The writer skillfully weaves natural science into an exciting, suspenseful tale. "When I sat down to write *The Hole in the Tree*," she recalled, "I realized that I was putting down the mysteries and details of animal life that had so excited me as a child. I could see no reason to try to work and struggle to get across to adults the things that children breathe in so easily."

She began writing while in the third grade. "I hoped I would become a writer and illustrator one day. Consequently I took many English and writing courses. Fortunately I had several remarkable teachers who overlooked my bad spelling and punctuation for the feelings and ideas. At Pennsylvania State College I had the opportunity to study under the Pulitzer Prize-winning poet, Theodore Roethke."

Ms. George holds both a bachelor of arts degree in English and a master of science degree from Pennsylvania State University. After graduating she worked for the International News Service and the *Washington Post*. "Here I learned the discipline of writing. From then on it was learning in the field from skilled newsmen and seeing myself in print.

"My ideas usually come in single words, like *seasons, migration,* or *living-off-the-land* (I consider that one word). Then I hassle the idea until personalities evolve to lead the story. Having gotten that far, I begin to write fast and furiously until I have a book, technically known as an outline. I put this away and, now familiar with the characters, events, and place, rewrite. I try this draft out on an editor or occasionally on children, but children are so nice they like anything you'll read or ask them about. Consequently I usually bounce ideas off adults who have good feelings about their own childhood. Then I rewrite and rewrite and rewrite. My record is eight completely different drafts!

"Once in print, a manuscript becomes less a part of me, and I am able to be more critical. I think some of my books would have been better if I could have rewritten them after they came out. Fortunately for me, this is impossible. If it were possible, I'd still be on *Vulpes, the Red Fox!*"

It is a lucky thing that she isn't still writing *Vulpes.* In the late 1960s and early 1970s, Ms. George completed a series of books, "The Thirteen Moons" published by T. Y. Crowell. She conceived the series to describe a significant moment in the life cycle of thirteen animals living in specific regions of the United States. The life of each animal throughout the rest of the year is also described, as are the flora and fauna in its environment. The series enables young readers to see a full picture of nature's activity in one geographic area. The books are geared to children in grades four and up. Animals included in the series are the owl, the bear, the salamander, the chickadee, the fox pup, the monarch butterfly, the mountain lion, the wild pig, the deer, the alligator, the gray wolf, the winter bird, and the mole. Each book presents scientifically precise data expressed in the poetic language that is characteristic of Ms. George's writing style.

The author said of this series: "It took about three years to write and prior to that several years of travel, for this is a series that includes the major life zones of North America from the desert to the mountain tops. Several times during the writing of these books, I got stuck and had to rewrite several of them many times before I felt I had conveyed the feeling of the changes of life as the earth and the moon swing around the sun. This series describes true ecology—the relation of plants and animals to their environment and the specific influences of the weather and the changing light.

"One of the most difficult problems in writing the

books was keeping the main character doing what he should be doing in that particular moon of the year. Elaborate life histories kept creeping into the manuscripts, for the lives of each animal were intriguing, and I wanted to go on and on."

Her personal favorite in the series is *The Moon of the Fox* (1968). "This was a joy to write. It centers on the learning time of one of North America's cleverest animals. Foxes learn by sniff, try, poke, and experiment—exactly the way children learn best. I learned in that kind of classroom and hope other children will get a good grin out of the moon of puppy curiosity and go out in the yard and poke around."

One of her most popular titles is *My Side of the Mountain* (Dutton, 1959), a first person account by an adolescent city boy who decides to try living off the land in the Catskill Mountains in an area once owned by his ancestors. The book has been translated into several foreign languages, including Dutch, Africaans, German, and Swedish; it was also made into a major motion picture by Paramount Studios in 1969.

Another popular title is *Coyote in Manhattan* (T. Y. Crowell, 1968). This is an absorbing tale of Tako, a young lively coyote who is discovered in a cage on the deck of a freighter in New York's East River by Tenny, a teen-age girl. The story deals with Tako's survival in the concrete canyons of New York, thousands of miles from the desert, the natural home of the coyote. I asked Ms. George how this unusual tale developed, and she replied: "My mammalogy friends told me several years ago about the arrival of the coyote in the East. Fascinated, I began to study how he got here, and in the course of this found that he was earning a living at night in many towns and cities of New England and New York by catching mice and rabbits at garbage dumps and pigeons in their roost. To have one come into New York City, which is entirely possible (red foxes are here), began to intrigue me. For a year or more I thought about how this might happen, and one day read that a coyote had arrived in Maine as a pet who got loose and took up residence in that state. A perfect way to get him into New York City was via a little girl who needed to do something daring to prove herself to her friends. The coyote also gave me a chance to talk about the incredible wildlife in New York City, something that has always interested me because of its richness and variety.''

1973 brought Ms. George the Newbery Medal for *Julie of the Wolves* (Harper, 1972). I asked her how she felt. ''Of all the awards I've ever won, the Newbery is the most important. I'm very proud to have won it; it's better than getting the Pulitzer Prize!'' she exclaimed.

Julie of the Wolves is a finely crafted novel evolving around a young Eskimo girl who becomes lost on the North Slope of Alaska's tundra while on her way, to visit her pen pal, Amy, in San Francisco. In the process of fighting for survival, she is aided by a pack of Arctic wolves whose friendship she wins. Her rich Eskimo heritage is an integral component of this novel that leaves the reader and the young heroine pondering the question—is contemporary life really civilized?

The book developed by a curious mishap. Ms. George had read two interesting articles on wolves in *Scientific American.* "These were fascinating studies of the leadership and dominance of wolves," she told me. "I asked *Reader's Digest* (where she works as a free-lance writer) to send me to Alaska to do a story for the magazine on the habitats of Arctic wolves."

She and her son, Luke, visited the Arctic Research Laboratory at Barrow for two weeks to study the wolves and the Alaskan tundra. There she talked with scientists, ecologists, and physicists, gathering information. Next she went to Mount McKinley National Park to observe a wolf pack there.

Returning to New York she wrote an article for *Reader's Digest.* It was never published! Then she began the novel, which stemmed from two inspirations: one, a little girl she had seen walking toward the vast and lonesome tundra; the other, a magnificent alpha wolf who was the leader of the pack in Mount McKinley National Park.

A high school student suggested that she make the heroine of the book an Eskimo girl, and she did. "Each incident in the book" she told me, "is based on scientific studies." *Julie of the Wolves* will be made into a major motion picture.

The author's profession is *writing.* "And raising three special kids, also dogs, cats, owls, iguanas, alligators, house sparrows, robins, crows, sea gulls, raccoons, mink—all the beautifully adapted and multi-sensitive animals that I write about and live on this unique planet with us," she added.

She still continues to illustrate and paint. "But more to sharpen my senses and make me see more than meets the eye than to become a professional artist. I live with and draw every character (animal) I write about, except bears and mountain lions. I do this more to become a better writer than a better artist.

"I am one of those fortunate people whose work is enjoying, and I can stitch everything into writing for children. Hiking, camping, boating, and keeping the pets, from one-celled animals to children, are all a part of my work. I travel a great deal for I find it essential to wander about the various parts of the globe that I write about."

Ms. George's three children are Twig, who attends Bennington College, Craig, who is at Utah State University, and Luke, a teen-ager who is still at home. "The children are more than offsprings. We all have a whale of a time together, be it cooking or shooting the Snake River in Wyoming in rubber boats."

I asked the author how she would describe herself: "This is a challenge!" she exclaimed. "I have my father's eyes, my mother's hair, and the build of Cousin Bessie. My driver's license says I am 'Bl-eyed, Bl-haired, 140 pounds, and white.' Actually if the license told the truth it would read '?-eyed, ?-haired, 143 pounds (I still cheat), and sort of an unbleached raffia color.' I look best in red, strange yellows, and off-greens. I look pretty good when I'm walking, horrible when I'm filling out income tax forms, and beautiful when I'm lighting the fire each morning and night. I also love modern dance, skiing, canoeing, hiking, and camping out. At these times, in particular, I think I look respectively like a bird, a leaf, a whirling beetle, a fox, and a dormouse."

Also by Ms. George

Gull Number 737 (T. Y. Crowell, 1964).

Hold Zero! (T. Y. Crowell, 1966).

Who Really Killed Cock Robin? (Dutton, 1971).

All Upon a Stone (T. Y. Crowell, 1971).

*Shirley Glubok
* * Alfred Tamarin

I was quite excited when Shirley Glubok (Glue-bach) and her husband, Alfred Tamarin, invited me to their New York East Side apartment. This team is responsible for the beautifully written, designed, and produced "Art of . . ." series. When I was a teacher, I used

this series over and over again with my students for these books open the door to the world of art and history to readers of all ages. Leafing through such titles as *The Art of Japan* (Macmillan, 1970), *The Art of India* (Macmillan, 1969), or *The Art of Colonial America* (Macmillan, 1970), is almost as good as going to the best museum, for they impart tremendous understanding and appreciation of the art world.

But I must confess a degree of disappointment when I visited the couple. I had expected their apartment walls to be jam-packed with treasures and oddities —paintings and pieces that I could drool over. But there are only a few artifacts in their modest apartment. Ms. Glubok explained why: "I work at the Metropolitan Museum of Art giving gallery walks and talks to children twice a month. Alfred and I also travel widely in our work to see, write about, and photograph the best art in the world. We don't collect a lot because we live with great art all the time. So why settle for second-bests?"

Ms. Glubok writes the texts for their books; Mr. Tamarin provides many of the photographs. Ms. Glubok was born and grew up in St. Louis, Missouri. "As a child I went often to museums with my parents. I grew up around the corner from a Y.M.H.A. with its many facilities where I spent after-school and summer hours. Nearby Forest Park offered the museum historical society. Also there were many opportunities for sports and the outdoors," she told me.

After graduating as an art and archeology major

from Washington University, Ms. Glubok taught kindergarten and second grade for about eight years. During her teaching years in St. Louis, she discovered that none of her pupils had visited the St. Louis Art Museum. But then, her principal had never visited it either! She was horrified at this and planned a field trip to the museum. That's when she found out that there were no books for children about the many treasures found in museums. She had a catalog of the museum's collection at home, brought it to school, and set it on the library table in the back of her classroom. When the children had free time, they would go to the table to read and browse. "I had never taken children to a museum before," she recalled. "I thought they would be interested in the Indian art most of all, so that's what I told the museum people we'd want to see.

"When the class arrived at the museum, a guide met them and said, 'Let's see, you wanted to see Indian art, didn't you?

" 'Oh, no,' the children replied, 'we want to see a knight and a mummy and Jesus on the cross.' That's what they had liked in the catalog!"

Thus began Ms. Glubok's long love affair with museums, children, art, and books. Her first book, *The Art of Ancient Egypt* (Atheneum), was published in 1962. This opened the door to a new career.

In each book she writes she continues her marriage between children and art. For each she recruits one or more "junior literary advisors" who read over her manuscript and help select the works of art to be photographed. And she listens to them! These advisors are given acknowledgement on the copyright pages of her books. She can share hundreds of anecdotes about the contributions of her junior co-helpers; this is one of the reasons she is so popular on the library-speaking circuit. Here are just a few examples.

On *The Art of Ancient Mexico* (Harper, 1968):
Ms. Glubok was afraid the human sacrifices described in the book would be too much for young readers, but the advisors disproved her theory. "The children were fascinated. What they objected to were the little pottery dogs modeled after the *real* dogs the Aztecs raised for food: 'Human sacrifice is O.K., but eating dogs is *different,*' the children insisted."

On *The Art of Africa* (Harper, 1965):
Her junior advisor insisted she use photographs of two masks which she had discarded. "They turned out to be the most popular pictures in the book!"

On *The Art of India* (Macmillan, 1969):
The boy advisor selected scenes of violence and rejected a picture of two lovers in the woods. Ms. Glubok discovered—by a lucky accident—that girls loved that picture and so she retained it. Since then she has had *both* a girl and boy advise her about each book.

Ms. Glubok not only respects the judgement of young girls and boys, she enjoys being with them. "Some of my best friends are seven-year-olds," she stated.

In addition to the junior advisors, she also has one

or more experts in the field she is covering look over manuscripts for accuracy and authenticity.

"To do these books I comb museum collections and private sources, examining both the materials on display and objects in storage. My objective is to find appealing material for young eyes and minds. These are narrowed down to the ones with the most interesting information. I rework material dozens of times."

In 1968, Ms. Glubok married Alfred Tamarin—a permanent advisor—and photographer. Together they have produced over thirty books.

Mr. Tamarin was born and grew up in Hudson, New York, an area rich in early Dutch, English, and Indian history. His first book, *The Revolt in Judea: The Road to Masada* (Four Winds Press), was published in 1968. He has also done advertising and public relations work for the Theatre Guild, United Artists, and In-flight Motion Pictures.

The couple travel a great deal in their work, "We have made marvelous friends all over the world. We cherish these friendships and work incessantly to keep them. They include university people, museum curators and directors, newspaper and television people, book publishers and sellers, and the like. After traveling extensively in Europe and Central and South America, we have discovered the United States and are now writing about its history and people," commented Mr. Tamarin.

Ms. Glubok has "discovered" *The Art of the North American Indian* (Harper, 1964) and *The Art of the*

Eskimo (Harper, 1964) as well as colonial and federalist America. Mr. Tamarin has edited *Benjamin Franklin: An Autobiographical Portrait* (Macmillan, 1969) and *Fire Fighting in America* (Macmillan, 1971) and is currently at work on other titles dealing with American people and life.

Taking the photographs for his wife's books is not always an easy task for Mr. Tamarin. For example, the full-color photograph on the cover of *Knights in Armor* (Macmillan, 1969) took a week to shoot because it was almost impossible to make a knight in the Metropolitan Museum of Art look as though he were riding out of a castle. Photographs for the books are taken in museums around the world, including the British Museum in London, the Archeological Museum in Mexico City, the Museum of the American Indian in New York City, and hundreds of others.

"I carry more cameras on my trips than clothes!" he exclaimed.

And Ms. Glubok added, "Yes, and the one difficulty I have traveling with him is that I have to help carry all of them."

When not at work the couple enjoy tennis, skating, and swimming; Mr. Tamarin is an A. A. U. backstroke swimming champion. The cheerful couple love their life and work together—and most of their time is spent working.

I enjoyed my winter afternoon with the Tamarins and even forgive them for not having a few mummies or knights or a real Grandma Moses painting in their apartment for me to admire.

Also by Ms. Glubok

(All published by Macmillan)

Discovering Tut-Ankh-Amen's Tomb (1968).

Discovering the Royal Tombs at Ur (1969).

Home and Child Life in Colonial Days (1969).

The Art of the Spanish in the United States and Puerto Rico (1972).

The Art of China (1973).

Also by Mr. Tamarin

(Both published by Macmillan)

The Autobiography of Benvenuto Cellini (1969).

Japan and the United States: The Early Encounters, 1791–1860 (1970).

✳ ✳ ✳ ✳ **Lorenz Graham**

Lorenz Graham on Lorenz Graham:

"Height: 64 inches
Weight: 150 pounds
Age: 71 of which I try not to boast. Kids are frightened by it!
Miscellany: I am a dark brown color. Although the top of my head is bald, there is white to gray hair left

on the sides. My health is remarkably good; my energy abundant. I believe I am cheerful and generally optimistic. So far as I know, I have no enemies. I have firm opinions and actively oppose people and ideas I believe are detrimental to human welfare."

Mr. Graham and his wife, Ruth, live in a one-story house in the college town of Claremont, California, where he teaches a course on Black writers at a nearby state college.

He was born on January 27, 1902, in New Orleans, Louisiana. His father was a minister of the African Methodist Episcopal (A.M.E.) Church and was transferred often to different churches. Thus the author's childhood years were spent all over the United States from Michigan to the state of Washington. "I started school in Chicago and finished high school in Seattle," he reminisced. "Family life was somewhat austere, but I never felt deprived. Among the things we had were books, thrift, and hope!"

While in his junior year at the University of California at Los Angeles, he gave up his studies to teach in a Liberian mission. In Africa he discovered how stereotyped his ideas about the "Dark Continent" had been. "My teaching experience in Africa made me know that African people were very much like people everywhere, that they had the needs and wishes other people did, and that they were individually diversified. There were no books that described Africans as people or as personalities and individuals. Writers had presented stereotypes. I wanted to change that."

Mr. Graham decided then that he would become a writer. His first two books, *How God Fix Jonah* (Reynal and Hitchcock, 1946) and *Tales of Momolu* (Reynal and Hitchcock, 1947), were about Africans. "I set these stories in Africa because I enjoyed the sounds of the speech and the storytellers' figurative language and natural rhythm. The stories are set down in the idiom of the African who has newly come to use English," he explained.

Mr. Graham's sister, Shirley Graham, the honored biographical historian and wife of the late W.E.B. Du Bois, whose works were being published in the 1940s, told a publisher about her brother's African tales. Thus the two books were published.

While in Africa, Mr. Graham met Ruth, a fellow teacher, and married her. When they returned to the United States, he completed his education in 1936 at Virginia Union University. Since that time he has worked with young people as a teacher, social worker, and probation officer. These experiences convinced him that writing about people could promote understanding. "I recognized the need for a clearer image of Black people in America as well as in Africa," he commented.

Perhaps his best known works are a trilogy for mature readers dealing with a Black American family. In the first novel, *South Town* (Follett, 1958), the Williams family is introduced—Mr. and Ms. Williams, David, and his younger sister, Betty Jane. The book deals with the injustices in a small southern community after World War II and the Korean War. In *North Town* (T. Y. Crowell, 1965), David and his family leave South Town because of violence, bigotry, hatred, nightmarish intimidations by night riders, beatings, unjust imprisonment, daily humiliation and condescension, and the eventual killing of a White. The family feels its only salvation lies in moving North. The story evolves around sixteen-year-old David and his adjustments to life in a northern industrial city. *Whose Town?* (T. Y. Crowell, 1969) carries on the family's odyssey—its search for better opportunities for work and education. But in this third novel issues are more tense and pressing; it describes the Black community's growing impatience and anger over continued racial injustice and its urgent debate about whether to work for equality by militant or nonviolent actions.

The growing cleavage between the Blacks and Whites precipitates many ugly situations, including David's arrest after a fight with several White boys and later the cold-blooded murder of a friend by a White man. Confronted with the harsh reality of injustice, David wonders, "Whose town is this, whose country? It doesn't just belong to White people. I live here too."

I asked Mr. Graham if the adventures of David Williams and his family were based on a real family. He answered: "Very real. Veritably real. The scenes are an honest composite out of my own life. Many of the situations I wrote about I have experienced within my own family. The background characters are people I have known. David and the immediate members of his family are not real in blood and sinew, but they are very real to me."

South Town has received a number of awards, including the Charles W. Follett Award in 1958 and the Child Study Association of America Children's Book Award in the same year.

"Getting ideas for stories presents no problems to me." he said. "Developing the idea takes much time. My most difficult task is eliminating and selecting."

Recently the author turned his pen to nonfiction and wrote *John Brown's Raid* (Scholastic Book Services, 1972), a biography in the "Firebird Book" series. "Here, said Mr. Graham, "is where research was of paramount importance. To do this book I went to Harper's Ferry and drove and walked around the countryside; I talked at length with people who had inherited knowledge of 'Captain Smith,' as Brown called himself."

When working, he stays in his own studio quite apart from the house. His next major project is to be another book in the "Town" series.

Leisure time is spent gardening, "care of which is shared with my wife." The Grahams also enjoy company. "We love having guests, young and old, domestic and foreign, new acquaintances, and/or family." The Grahams have four adult children, all with several children of their own. "One daughter died following the birth of her first child; this grandchild is very dear to us," said Mr. Graham.

Favorite possessions include artifacts from travels around the world "and most recently and most precious a copy of *Leslie's Illustrated Newspaper,* dated December 10, 1859, which describes with line drawings the execution of John Brown." Another favorite is his wife to whom he's been married since 1929. The author boasts most proudly, "She is deeply involved in good work—church and civic groups. And she has one book of her own published, *The Happy Sound* (Follett, 1970) and another now under consideration by a publisher."

Recently Mr. Graham has prepared a series of picture books for younger readers—Bible stories which first appeared in *How God Fix Jonah.* Titles include: *Every Man Heart Lay Down* (1970), *A Road Down in the Sea* (1971), *God Wash the World and Start Again* (1971), *David He No Fear* (1971) and *Hongry Catch the Foolish Boy* (1972; all published by T. Y. Crowell).

As a final question, I asked Mr. Graham if he felt that the 1960s and early 1970s had produced more realistic books depicting Africa and its people. "Yes," he replied, "but I do feel that the promotion has been inadequate. I believe publishers, distributors, and educators fail to realize the relation between the problems today—here and now—and the concepts, the false concepts, of Africa and its people. Since I first started to write, I have heard over and over, 'You may be right, but we don't think the public will accept your picture of life among *those* people.' *Those people* meaning Black people from both the United States and Africa."

But since his first book was published in 1946, times have changed. And Mr. Graham's characters, whether they live in America or Africa, have opened up a world that has always been there, one which too few have ever really seen before.

Another book by Mr. Graham

I, Momolu (T. Y. Crowell, 1968).

✳ ✳ Virginia Hamilton
✳

Audree Distad

Virginia Hamilton describes herself as being "chronically overweight, foul-tempered and given to alternate fits of depression and elation. In sum," she continued, *"I am a textbook neurotic who never sleeps. I love life, freedom, lazing around, and daydreaming. I read all the time—everything from Bulfinch to seed catalogs."*

Despite her self-analysis, she is the kind of person one loves to be around. And it's hard for me to think of her being either foul-tempered or one who might laze around! I know her as being bubbly and bouncy, with a never-stand-still way about her that makes one quickly perceive her sparkling, contagious enthusiasm for life.

Ms. Hamilton grew up in Yellow Springs, an Ohio village that had been a station on the Underground Railroad. The rural community, about sixty miles north of the Ohio River, is the home of Antioch College. The population of the village includes descendants of abolitionists and fugitive slaves.

Recalling her childhood she said: "I was born in a miserable corner of southern Ohio and dutifully raised there, where it is said that God, Himself, has seen the place only twice: once, when he created it and the time he came back to apologize for what he had done. Actually, Yellow Springs, where I grew up, is quite a pretty place. My mother's Perry family came to the town before Emancipation. The progenitor was, of course, a runaway slave. He settled down on the rich land. He married, prospered, and the family grew into the large, extended Perry clan. I grew up with the warmth of loving aunts and uncles, all reluctant farmers but great storytellers. I remember the tales best of all. My own father, who was an outlander from Illinois, Iowa, and points West, was the finest of the storytellers besides being an exceptional mandolinist. Mother, too, could take a slice of fiction floating around the family and polish it into a saga."

Ms. Hamilton was the fifth child born to Etta B. and Kenneth J. Hamilton. Her parents were "dollar-poor" in the 1930s when she was born. She described their situation: "Franklin Roosevelt's New Deal hadn't touched our household nor much of the Miami Valley where our village lay. But my parents turned acres of rich soil into a working farm with enough extra produce to sell by the bushel to the local grocer.

"By the time I was seven, I knew that life must be freedom; there was no better life than those acres and the surrounding farmlands. Being the 'baby' and bright, mind you, and odd and sensitive, I was left alone to discover whatever there was to find. No wonder, then, that I started to write things down at an early age. I'm a writer, I think, nearly by birth. There was no other way, really, that I could go," she said in a serious tone.

As she approached college age, she was drawn to the Antioch community of books and writing, parties and dances. But at the close of these gatherings, when the students returned to their dormitories, she would return to her family's home, a mile out on the Dayton Pike.

After attending Antioch College and Ohio State University, Ms. Hamilton moved to New York City where she married Arnold Adoff.*

Her first book for children, *Zeely*** (1966), received wide critical acclaim. The book tells a haunting story of eleven-year-old, Elizabeth "Geeder" Perry, and her brother, John "Toeboy" Perry, who spend a summer on their Uncle Ross's farm. One day Geeder finds a

---

*An interview with Arnold Adoff appears on pp. 1-9.
**All titles have been published by Macmillan.

photograph of a Watusi queen in an old magazine. The portrait reminds Geeder of Zeely, the grown daughter of Mr. Nat Tayber who rents a small part of Uncle Ross's land. Geeder decides that Zeely must also be a queen and becomes swept up in her fantasies until Zeeley tells her the truth, and they both realize that it is realistic to be one's own self.

The publication of *Zeely* came about via an old college chum who was working at Macmillan. The woman had remembered a short story Ms. Hamilton had written in college. "I had mostly forgotten it; but she reminded me about it and thought that if I tried making a book out of it, it would be a great story for children. Well, that's what I did! I took those eighteen moth-eaten pages and worked them over. It took a long time, but *Zeely* came from that. It was a happy accident—the kind of luck that hits you if you hang around New York long enough. I never really decided to write for children. It happened about the time I was thinking about giving up being a writer, since I was having trouble breaking into the adult writing field. I thought I might become an athletic instructor, or a singer—anything was better than the part-time book-keeping, cost-accounting work I had been doing."

Her second book, *The House of Dies Drear* (1967), dramatizes the history of the Underground Railroad in Ohio viewed from the present-day. It is a taut mystery, one which youngsters gulp down quickly and find hard to forget. Ms. Hamilton remarked: "*The House of Dies Drear* is my favorite book, I think, because it is so full of all the things I love: excitement, mystery, Black history, and the strong, Black family. In it I tried to pay back all those wonderful relatives who gave me so much in the past. And I tried to show the importance of the Black church to my being; also the land and the good and bad of small town, rural life."

Her third book, *The Time-Ago Tales of Jahdu* (1969), is a modern fable. The tales are told by Mama Luka, an old lady who cares for Lee Edward after school while his mother is at work. The story is set in New York's Harlem. Ms. Hamilton's second Jahdu book, *Time-Ago Lost: More Tales of Jahdu* was published in 1973. She commented: "Little Jahdu's out on the road again. Looky there, little brother! Here he is!"

The Planet of Junior Brown (1971), her fourth book, was selected as a Newbery Honor Book in 1972. As in all her works this novel is a fine example of literary craftsmanship. The tale centers around Junior Brown, a two hundred sixty-two-pound musical prodigy with a neurotic, over-protective mother; Buddy Clark, a loner who has no family whatsoever; and Mr. Pool, once a teacher but now a janitor — the custodian of the high school broom closet.

I asked Ms. Hamilton if any of her characters are based on real people she knows or knew. "Oh," she responded, "I'd say that Uncle Ross in *Zeely* is somewhat similar to my Uncle Lee who was a collector of antiques and stray cats. Geeder and Toeboy talk and act and sleep outside in much the same way my brother and I did. I don't really base any of my characters on real people. I do take the atmosphere of known people, their emotions, and give them to my characters. Zeely, of course, is completely imagined as a character. I never knew anyone like her. But then, a writer deals in possibilities. My childhood was immensely free, rural, and at times, lonely. There could have been a Zeely; it would have been fun if there had been. When I grew up, I simply rewrote the past and put Zeely into it. I think I'd have to say my characters are for the most part based on me. If you'll notice, every lead character is something of a loner, imaginative, and contemplative from Zeely up through Thomas Small in *The House of Dies Drear* to Junior Brown. My characters are the way I see the artist, the *human,* isolated, out of time, in order to reveal himself more clearly. I am tremendously interested in the human as oracle and as spirit isolated. I tried to speak of that in *The Planet of Junior Brown* with the use of planets and the lonliness of mankind in the immensity of space and time. That is why Junior Brown futilely sees himself as the center of a wheel or spiral, trying desperately to find a place for his mental isolation.

"I hope children and adults will accept my characters, all of them, in the manner they were given — with love and warmth for all that is uniquely human. A child — anyone — must know me through my books.

I reveal myself only reluctantly, if at all. Not that I'm trying to hide exactly, but more that I feel there is not really much to know. What I am is simply very personal and is revealed somewhat through what I write."

Like many of her characters, Ms. Hamilton is a loner; "an introvert, with no companions other than my immediate family. I do not like to talk, although I am called upon to do that more and more. Why is it writers are thought to be speakers as well? Writers never tell the truth; that is, they tell more than one truth, depending on what they had for breakfast or what they dreamed about the night before. I am fond of telling lies, about my age, creations, the past, and my husband!"

She then told me about her work habits: "When I get an idea, I keep it to myself until I find out whether I have a good story working. When I know that, well, then, I'll read parts to my husband. A story idea simply comes to me, and I accept the wonder of that sort of thing without probing to find out where it comes from. Usually, though, I get a title in my head, like *Dies Drear* or *Junior Brown,* and then start thinking about it. I'm not really aware of the thinking, for it is lightning swift. I get bits and pieces of conversation, flashes of atmosphere, a location. It's all a jumble at first, until I begin to write it and sort it out. I rewrite very little; when I'm ready to write it out, it comes along pretty clean."

Ms. Hamilton and her family recently returned to Yellow Springs after living in New York City for several years. The Adoffs have two children—a daughter, Leigh, "who is a high-spirited nine-year-old," and Jaime, a son, "who is a highly-motivated five!"

"My children take up a good deal of my time, of course, and I don't mind that one bit. They are so active and creative; they want to know everything and so I have to know everything in order to tell them. We have a good time. Life with two writers in the house is very hectic, very difficult, and often very amusing. My husband is basically a poet, although he is an anthologist too. As everyone knows, poets talk all the time as does Arnold. He not only talks forever but he works forever as well. He has a tremendous capacity for getting things done and can juggle work on three books at once. Plus he chops down trees and generally spends a good deal of time being a gentleman farmer. Having been born in the Bronx, he took to the land like an alligator out of water. Arnold is like a whirlwind. He keeps everything stirred up and noisy. He's never boring because he's always thinking up some outrageous new thing to do. We both work in the mornings and usually late at night. We get very little sleep. Who needs it anyway? The long last sleep is long enough."

The Adoffs live at the end of a dead-end gravel road in the middle of a two-acre field. The land was once part of the farm on which Ms. Hamilton grew up. Their house has high peaks made out of redwood, one deck, and two patios. "Everything is sliding glass so that the outdoors comes right in whenever it has a mind to, exclaimed Ms. Hamilton. "My favorite possessions are mine eyes to see the wondrous farmland surrounding us. We don't live in a neighborhood as such. My mother still lives in the old homestead just down the field and through the roses and trees." Her brother and his family still live on Grandpa Perry's farm, the original Perry settlement, near her mother's house. "It is very quiet back in the field. The nights are still and cautious with the past and stars.

"We raise a lot of flowers and lot of hell in town," Ms. Hamilton chuckled. "I'm on the local Human Relations Committee and the Committee on Equal Education. I belong to the local writers group. We are all women, and the group has been in existence for at least fifty years. There are many professional writers in town. Yellow Springs draws artists, ecologists, socialists, and other rabble-rousers like moths to a light! You can perhaps blame Antioch for that and maybe the crystaline quality of the atmosphere.

"I don't feel like an adult as such. I feel maybe twelve sometimes. I feel like I'd like to slow things down a bit. We work and play so hard out here that the seasons do not merely turn—they streak away."

Also by Ms. Hamilton

W. E. B. Du Bois (T. Y. Crowell, 1972).

✳ **Esther Hautzig**

Myles J. Adler

Esther Hautzig is no stranger to the world of children's books. She has worked in the publishing field since 1951.

"Let's Cook Without Cooking (T. Y. Crowell, 1955), was my first book," she stated. "It developed on a hot and crowded bus in 1954 when I was returning home from a non-air-conditioned office to an equally non-air-conditioned apartment. I prayed for inspiration to come up with an interesting dinner that did not require cooking. That led me to collect and experiment with likely recipes and that, in turn, led to the book. It was published under my maiden name, Esther Rudomin, since no one knew me by that name at Thomas Y. Crowell where I was working promoting children's books. It was easier to work with my own title this way.

"I did not have a day of reckoning when I decided to write for children. All I did was to write a cookbook in which all the recipes did not need a stove; this turned out to be an especially good idea for a children's cookbook, so that is what it became."

In 1961 Ms. Hautzig published another practical how-to-book, *Let's Make Presents: 100 Gifts for Less Than $1.00* (T. Y. Crowell), a very useful book of suggestions and instructions for making gifts for women, men, and children. One section gives instructions for making "Good Things to Eat"—things that require only a little use of the stove.

"This book was the result of a lifelong habit, fostered by my arts-and-crafts loving mother, of making gifts rather than buying them—long before the arts and crafts boom of today. I simply wrote down a list of all the things I had been making since goodness knows when and proposed the idea to my editor at Crowell. She accepted the idea."

A third title, *Redecorating Your Room for Practically Nothing* (T. Y. Crowell, 1967), came about much the same way. But in 1968 Esther Hautzig temporarily turned away from craft books. This was the year that *The Endless Steppe: Growing Up in Siberia* (T. Y. Crowell) appeared.

Ms. Hautzig told me about the book's development: "After I finished *Let's Make Presents,* I started working on *The Endless Steppe,* which actually had been in the making for some seven or eight years. Whenever the *Steppe* got too much for me, I'd make new curtains, or cover a headboard, or embroider some pillows or what-not for our apartment—a wonderful antidote to writing. Anyway I had said to my editor at Crowell that what I ought to be doing instead of writing the Siberia book was prepare a book on redoing a room on very little money," she laughed. "Well, the joke turned into reality and in between Siberia I did *Redecorating Your Room for Practically Nothing.*"

Although we are all grateful that Ms. Hautzig cooked, made gifts, and redecorated, if she had continued concentrating on such home crafts, she might never have given the world her poignant, autobiographical account of her young years in Siberia. Using beautiful prose she tells in *The Endless Steppe* the true and harrowing story of the five years she and her family spent in forced labor in Siberia. The text begins in June 1941, when the Russians declared ten-year-old Esther, her parents, and one of her grandparents of being "capitalists" and sent them from Vilna, in the northeastern corner of Poland, to Siberia where they were housed with twenty-two other people in a single schoolroom and put to work in a gypsum mine.

The remainder of the book relates Esther's hardships, joys, her schooling, her emotions, and finally her "exile" from Siberia at the war's end.

The volume has received many awards including the 1971 Lewis Carroll Shelf Award as a book "worthy enough to sit on the shelf with *Alice in Wonderland,*" a 1969 Honor Book in the National Book Awards, and a 1968 Honor Book in the Book World Spring Book Festival. It has also been translated into many foreign languages and has appeared in many editions of *Reader's Digest.*

But the book was not an easy one for the author to sell. It was submitted by her agent to adult trade book editors at first. They all wrote uniformly enthusiastic letters about the manuscript, but they were also afraid that Americans would not be interested in reading about what happened in Siberia in the 1940s. However, the editor of one Boston publishing house who liked the book enormously showed it to his children's book editor. She was anxious to publish it as a book for young people and wrote to Ms. Hautzig's agent to that effect. But since Ms. Hautzig worked at T. Y. Crowell at that time and since it had published her previous books, she felt obligated to submit *The Endless Steppe* there first, and it was accepted. The book, begun in 1959, was finally published nine years later.

Ms. Hautzig credits the late Adlai E. Stevenson for prompting the writing of *The Endless Steppe*. In 1959 Mr. Stevenson went to Russia and wrote a series of articles on his trip for the *New York Times*. One article was about Rubtsovsk.

"I wrote a three-page, single-spaced, typed letter to him about my own experiences in Rubtsovsk, and he answered me," she recalled.

Mr. Stevenson's reply read in part: "It was very good of you to write me, and I think you should write about life on the frontier of the Soviet Union during those trying war days. It would be a more useful contribution to our understanding than my pieces—and better literature."

Ms. Hautzig recounted for me more about her experiences after leaving Siberia. "I returned to Poland, a year of untold grief and misery for me. I was scared of crowds, noise—scared of my own shadow. I refused to venture out into the street for a long time. Perhaps I expected to be in some sort of heaven after the Siberian years. Instead I was thrust into a war-torn, largely bombed-out city where everyone still alive seemed, to my frightened eyes, to be in a desperate hurry to make up for lost time.''

In 1947, at the age of sixteen, she left Poland for Sweden and finally sailed alone to the United States. On the boat to America she met Walter Hautzig, a concert pianist who was returning from his first tour of Europe. He later became her husband. Luckily they both spoke German so they were able to communicate. Upon arriving in New York City, she lived in Brooklyn with her aunt and uncle, whose children, her cousins, spoke to her *very* loudly and *very* slowly in the hope that in this manner she would learn to understand the English language! After spending two years at Hunter College in New York City, she married and left school.

"I still regret not finishing college," she told me, "and may go back to get a degree in education, since teaching appeals to me."

Instead she ventured into the publishing world. For two years she was a secretary at G. P. Putnam's and then she did publicity for The Children's Book Council. In 1954 she became head of children's book promotion at Thomas Y. Crowell, working for the juvenile editor there, Elizabeth M. Riley.

Currently Ms. Hautzig is a housewife, although she regularly keeps her hand in the publishing world by both writing and doing free-lance assignments for publishers. She and her husband live in an apartment on New York's Upper West Side.

"We are very fortunate in that we have an apartment in an old house where Rachmaninoff once lived and where no one bothers my husband about his practicing. Walter is a concert pianist as well as professor of piano at Peabody Conservatory in Baltimore, Maryland. He commutes! Our neighborhood is full of all sorts of marvelous and not so marvelous people. In upper New York State, we have a house near the Massachusetts border. It is set on twenty-four acres of land, which encompasses everything from cleared fields to thickly wooded acres. We prize our land, trees, and pond above all our physical possessions.

"I like best of all to be around the house with my family and, sometimes, close friends. I like to bake, embroider, do needlepoint—not from kits but of my own design. I also love to knit all sorts of things. I love the ballet and figure skating and go to performances regularly as well as watch them on television. Ballet, to me, combines all the beauty of music, movement, and staging. Of course, music for the piano is also a favorite; I prefer the classical and romantic composers to modern ones."

Ms. Hautzig said of her work habits: "They are highly erratic. When I have a deadline, I find it best to go to bed around 10:00 or 11:00 p.m. and set my alarm clock for 1:00 or 1:30 a.m. I then get up and work until 4:00 or 5:00 a.m. and then it's back to sleep.

This avoids telephone interruptions, or urges to run the vacuum cleaner, scrub the bathroom, or visit a neighbor. Without a deadline, I work whenever I find a quiet or reasonably unhectic minute in my daily life. The first draft of *The Endless Steppe* was written in a nearby hotel room. I checked in to avoid being disturbed by normal household noises. I never had any formal writing training but sometimes wish I did.

"I don't have a favorite book since all of my books are fairly diverse. I like and dislike them all equally and impartially. Moreover, the three picture books were pure joy from beginning to end."

The three picture books include *In the Park: An Excursion in Four Languages* (Macmillan, 1968), illustrated by the Caldecott Award-winning artist, Ezra Jack Keats, *At Home: A Visit in Four Languages* (Macmillan, 1968), illustrated by Aliki, and *In School: Learning in Four Languages* (Macmillan, 1969), illustrated by twice-Caldecott Award-winning artist, Nonny Hogrogian. Each book includes English, French, Spanish, and Russian texts. Ms. Hautzig also speaks Jewish, Polish, and German. "*In The Park* was growing in me for over ten years. I have first drafts of this picture book text dating back to 1958," she said.

The author is five-feet five-inches tall, has brown hair, and hazel eyes that "turn green" when she is angry. "I am incapable of making-up my pale skin to look rosy and healthy. If I remember, I put on lipstick, but otherwise I look rather dowdy and highly unfashionable. I've worn my hair in a bun since I was seventeen.

"I get angry very quickly and forget what I've been mad about even quicker. I tend to be anxious over unimportant things and reasonably calm in a real crisis. I like personal contact and am forever hugging and kissing my kids and family."

The children include Deborah, seventeen, and David, eight. "Deborah is very interested in children's books and hopes to go into this field. David says, in occasional desperation, 'Let's read a book by someone we *don't* know!' And on occasion we do that."

As our bagel-and-lox luncheon session ended, Ms. Hautzig explored a possible sequel to *The Endless Steppe* by telling me of frequent letters she receives from children. "From letters it seems children want to know what happened to me after the book's end. One day perhaps I will do a sequel but right now I prefer to stick to other kinds of writing, including more arts and crafts books. Actually in replying to their letters I almost feel I am writing a sequel to *The Endless Steppe*. What I ought to do, I guess, is to make carbon copies of all my letters and someday use them as a basis for the sequel."

Also by Ms. Hautzig

Let's Make More Presents (Macmillan, 1973).

Cool Cooking (Lothrop, Lee and Shepard, 1973).

Carolyn Haywood

Lotte Meitner-Graf

Carolyn Haywood suffers from one of the problems common to all popular writer-illustrators. She receives bundles and trundles of letters from girls and boys across the country, many of whom request an autographed copy of one of her books. Although she would like to fill children's requests, she cannot mail copies of her books to them as gifts because she has to purchase them from her publisher.

Most children and many adults do not realize that authors have to buy their own books; because they have written them, it doesn't mean they can have as many as they want for nothing. The usual number of free copies they receive is a low five! Any author filling requests for free autographed books would quickly go bankrupt.

One of the reasons Ms. Haywood is so popular with children is that her books span a wide range of age and interest levels. Her first book, *B Is for Betsy* (Harcourt), was published in 1939. Here Betsy is depicted as the kind of child one might find anywhere in any first-grade classroom. She is a real girl with real adventures. Betsy's life is continued in a series of books. In *Betsy and Billy* (Harcourt, 1941) Betsy is in the second grade; *Back to School with Betsy* (Harcourt, 1943) and *Betsy and the Boys* (Harcourt, 1945) continue her growing up through the third and fourth grades. Betsy and her friends are also subjects of additional titles such as *Betsy's Winterhouse* (Morrow, 1958) and *Betsy and Mr. Kilpatrick* (Morrow, 1967).

In addition to this series, Ms. Haywood has created another popular series evolving around the character Eddie Wilson. *Little Eddie* (Morrow, 1947), the first in this series, depicts Eddie as a seven-year-old who is a collector of all sorts of curious things. Although his family calls it junk, it is valuable property to Eddie. Throughout the series Eddie continues adding to his collection, which grows to include stray cats, a parrot, a pail of pay dirt, and a saddle. Like Betsy, Eddie grows older throughout the series.

Ms. Haywood's books are perfect for reading aloud because each chapter is a complete story. Some readers in grades two and three can read the books themselves.

Ms. Haywood was born in Philadelphia, Pennsylvania, on January 3, 1898, and grew up in Germantown, a nearby suburb. Her mother was a third grade teacher in Philadelphia's public schools. "There were only two children in my family," she told me, "myself and a younger brother. In later years, he became a silversmith; he died in 1958. As a young girl I spent most of my spare time drawing and painting with the ambition of becoming an artist. after graduating from the Philadelphia High School for Girls and the Philadelphia Normal School, I taught for a year. At the end of the year I was granted a scholarship to study art at the Pennsylvania Academy of Fine Arts. I studied there for three years; it was here that I won a Cresson European Scholarship."

She began her career as a portrait painter specializing in children. She is still much involved in this area of art.

In the 1930s she decided to try her hand at writing and illustrating children's books. She planned a picture book with little text, but Elizabeth Hammond, a former editor in the juvenile department at Harcourt, suggested she write about American children and the things that interest them. *B Is for Betsy* evolved from this suggestion, and her children's writing career was launched.

Besides the above-mentioned series, Ms. Haywood created many other books including *Robert Rows the River* (Morrow, 1965), *Taffy and Melissa and Molasses* (Morrow, 1969), and *A Christmas Fantasy* (Morrow, 1972).

I asked her where she gets her many ideas for plots and characterizations. "I derive experiences from various sources," she answered. "I just listen to everything people tell me, and in that way ideas come to me. Many of my own experiences while a child have found their way into my books. I travel fairly widely and make notes and sketches. Travel has given me background material for a number of books, especially

Robert Rows the River, which is set in England, and *Eddie and Gardenia* (Morrow, 1951), which is in Texas, to name just two."

She rewrites her manuscripts "a bit," but usually the majority remains as written in her first draft. "Of all the delightful features about make-believe children, the most convenient one is that their author can control not only their growing up but their growing down. The world of books is indeed an *Alice in Wonderland* world where there are bottles marked 'Drink me' and cakes marked 'Eat me' with the inevitable Alice results."

One of the questions children most often ask her is, "Are the children in your books real?" I asked this question, too; she told me: "The children in my books are not real children, but I do use children to pose for the illustrations," she explained. "There have been many little Eddies, but only one by that name—Eddie Wilson. He posed for the illustrations in *Eddie and the Fire Engine* (Morrow, 1949). The character is actually a composite of typical little boys."

Master Wilson and Ms. Haywood spent three riotous days together while he posed for the illustrations. Ever since then Eddie Wilson has never quite been make believe.

She uses boys and girls in her neighborhood as models for the art in her books. They find it great fun to come to her studio, listen to her read the latest manuscript, and then take the part of the characters in the stories. Often their pets participate as well.

She receives many letters from girls and boys who write, "I have read all your books in the library. Why have you stopped writing?"

"I'd like children to know," she told me "that because they have read all my books that doesn't mean I've stopped writing!"

Currently the author lives in a house with an attached studio wing in Chestnut Hill, Pennsylvania, a suburb of Philadelphia. "I find life full of interesting and unexpected challenges and solutions. What with my work, I find there is never a dull moment."

She enjoys people, reading, and travel and does illuminated manuscripts as a hobby. She is five-feet two-inches tall, has grey eyes, and brown hair flecked with a bit of grey. In 1969 she was made a Distinguished Daughter of Pennsylvania.

Carolyn Haywood's books have sold well over twenty million copies and have been read by over twenty million readers. All of the "Betsy" books have been translated into three Scandinavian languages; other titles have been translated into French. The universality of her writing is certainly due to the "me-too" syndrome voiced by her readers.

Also by Ms. Haywood

Eddie the Dog Holder (Morrow, 1966).
Ever-Ready Eddie (Morrow, 1968).
Merry Christmas from Betsy (Morrow, 1970).
Away Went the Balloons (Morrow, 1973).

*Irene Hunt

"I believe I am one of those people who remember what it is like to be a child—the bewilderments and uncertainties as well as the joys. I have an excellent rapport with adolescents because I sincerely like most of them and sympathize with their problems," declared Irene Hunt.

Ms. Hunt knows children and knows them well. She has been actively involved with girls and boys from kindergarten youngsters to college students throughout her career. She began teaching in the Illinois public schools in 1930. After a four-year post at the University of South Dakota, she returned to Illinois and again taught there until the late 1960s.

Ms. Hunt was born on May 18, 1907, in Pontiac, Illinois, but was "transplanted" at the age of six weeks to Newton in southern Illinois. "My early childhood years were happy until my father died; I was seven then. After his death, I was a very lonely child, living with grandparents until I was twelve. I lived on the farm mentioned in *Across Five Aprils* (1964).* I had a

---

* All titles have been published by Follett.

kindly, storytelling grandfather whose stories greatly influenced my writing. I spent much time making up stories of my own as a child, although I did not write them, and I often told stories to other children.

"During the early sixties while teaching social studies to junior high school students, I felt that teaching history through literature was a happier, more effective process. My grandfather's poignant old stories had floated through my mind for years. Suddenly I realized how they might be put to use. My books were generated by the needs of my students."

Thus, *Across Five Aprils*, the sole 1965 Newbery Honor Book, was born. A Civil War story, it spans the five Aprils of 1861–1865 and relates how a frontier family endured this turbulent era. Fascinated by the troubles of the border states at the time of the American Civil War, Ms. Hunt saw a chance to help children see the many faceted problems of that day. "I hoped also to make children realize the need for critical thinking about social and political problems."

Across Five Aprils is her personal favorite among her books because the emotional impact of it was strongest.

Her second novel for children, *Up a Road Slowly* (1966), was suggested by a memory that has haunted her adult life. "I was one of a thoughtless group of children who once rejected a retarded child. Writing about Aggie was therapeutic for me—equal to a session in a psychiatrist's office. Other aspects of *Up a Road*

Slowly were either autobiographical or experiences that had happened to others. I had long felt the need to tell girls that no matter what our age, the problems of growing up are universal."

This book received the 1967 Newbery Award. It chronicles ten years in a young girl's life. Julie suffers the loss of her mother and goes to live with a spinster aunt, and the reader grows along with Julie from the age of seven through the age of seventeen. Ms. Hunt was nominated for the 1974 Hans Christian Andersen Award, which is given to an author for the entire body of his or her work.

I asked Ms. Hunt if she had any formal writing training. "Not much," she replied. "One year while at the University of Illinois, I took a course in short story writing. The letter Uncle Haskell wrote to Julie (in *Up a Road Slowly*) concerning her writing contains almost exactly the same comments made by my professor about my writing."

Now retired, Ms. Hunt lives in St. Petersburg, Florida, where she gardens, travels, and does some "etcetera!" She likes to read, cook, play the organ, and has a wide selection of recordings; she enjoys golf and loves animals, especially Beau, a clownish pug puppy who is her constant companion.

I asked Ms. Hunt if she occasionally misses the classroom. "Yes!" she responded. "I've been close to children and their problems. I believe I know many of them very well. I have read much in children's literature, largely because of teaching, and have come to realize the role that good literature plays in self-understanding, in compassion, and in literary discrimination. I do miss the classroom at times. That's why I try to have children in my house and near me as much as possible."

But even though she is friends with children in the neighborhood, many still wonder if it's true that she's a real live author. But it is true. She is real, alive, and an author.

Also by Ms. Hunt

(Both published by Follett)
Trail of Apple Blossoms (1968).
No Promises in the Wind (1970).

* * Harold Keith *

Harold Keith's recollections of his life as a child might well be the basis for a Hollywood feature film: "I was born Harold Verne Keith on April 8, 1903, in Lambert, which was Oklahoma Territory. We lived in Watonga, Oklahoma, a small-ish county seat town that had a population of 1,500. My father owned the ice house and ice cream plant. As a young man he had been the horse wrangler, the cowboy and cook of a small northwestern Oklahoma ranch, the Bar-Z. He also taught in a dugout school on the ranch. Once when a heavy snow marooned them (there was no busing then), a friend who had a small farm two miles away, drove over in his wagon and moved the whole student body, consisting of twelve pupils, to his home where dad taught for a week in the ranch house until the roads were opened.

"Dad was a sportsman. He always took my younger brother, younger sister, and me out on the North Canadian River. In spring and summer we camped, trotlined for channel catfish, and swam. In fall and winter we'd still go out and camp and fish with bank lines. We did lots of ice skating, too. Dad bought my brother and me each a shotgun and taught us how to hunt duck and quail.

"In those distant days at Watonga there was no radio, television, or paved roads. The big event was the arrival each evening of the railroad's three-coach passenger train and seeing the sporty-dressed traveling drummers descend from it and climb aboard the horse-drawn hotel bus. Billy Masters drove it, and he often let me ride with him. I can still smell the hot bread baking in the town bakery and hear the ringing of the blacksmith's anvil three blocks away.

"In spite of the town's isolation, its inhabitants knew how to have fun. Town baseball was the annual summer craze. Enthusiasm even carried over into October. I recall that during the 1919 World Series between Chicago and Cincinnati, Hooper's corner drugstore was jammed with people watching my high school pal chalk up the score by innings. It was my job to run back and forth to the Rock Island railroad station where the agent obligingly bootlegged this sketchy information off the depot wire. It was like a message on the bush telegraph. Nothing was available on who was pitching or who drove in the runs. Just the bare score by innings scribbled on a small ash-framed blackboard. Yet the town hung as breathlessly on this paltry bit of news as modern fans do seeing the entire game on color television.

"Across the street from our home was the Blaine County Court House. The town library was in its basement. Winifred Schofield, a tall, sweet girl, was the librarian who helped us find books. My favorites then were the various series of the time written for boys —the "Dick Prescott" series, "The Motor Boys," the "G. A. Henty" series, and the like.

"Gradually my father introduced me to some of the books that had interested him. As a young man Dad had sold the novels of Opie Read on the Santa Fe passenger trains while working as a news butch. Later I found out about Mark Twain, Arthur Conan Doyle, Zane Grey, and Jack London. The stories that grabbed me hardest then were Doyle's *The Hound of the Baskervilles*, Twain's *Tom Sawyer*, and London's *The Sea Wolf*.

"My mother, who is still living in Oklahoma City at the age of ninety and still jumping around like a high school girl, was also a schoolteacher. She played the guitar and taught us how to sing. She went to college at Northwestern Normal of Alva. As a girl she had devoured *The Youth's Companion* and introduced us to it. She had a great sense of humor. Oklahoma then had just been taken from the Indians, and the country had very little culture."

After graduating from Lambert High School in 1921, Mr. Keith attended Northwestern State Teachers' College in Alva. Following in his parents' footsteps, he taught school—seventh grade—for one year and served as a coach to high school girls' and boys' basketball teams. In 1929 he graduated from the University of Oklahoma in Norman with a B.A. degree in history; in 1938 he received an M.A. degree in history from the same university.

His early interest in sports has lasted throughout his life. Sportsminded children should enjoy his record as an athlete:

- 1921—Received track letters in mile and 880 at Lambert High School.
- 1925—At Northwestern won Oklahoma Collegiate Conference two-mile race.
- 1927—Placed second in Missouri Valley Conference five-mile cross-country run.
- 1928—As a long distance runner at Oklahoma won Penn Relays 3,000 meter steeplechase, captured the Missouri Valley Conference indoor mile and two-

mile championships, the Kansas City Athletic Club mile championship, and anchored Oklahoma's victorious distance medley relay team that won at Texas, Rice, and Kansas Relays.

- 1945—At the age of forty-two, won the Oklahoma AAU three and one-quarter mile cross-country run.

On July 1, 1930, Mr. Keith left his job as a reporter on the Hutchinson, Kansas, newspaper and began a career as sports publicist for the University of Oklahoma—a position he held until his retirement in 1969.

I asked him why he decided to write for children. "Probably because I began doing it early in life," he replied. "At fourteen I began writing fiction for a weekly magazine, *Lone Scout.* Boys from all over the nation wrote the entire magazine and also did the artwork. The Lone Scout organization paralleled the Boy Scouts but was designed for farm and small town kids. We weren't paid for our work. However, we did compete for medals—bronze, silver, and gold— and finally the Gold Quill. Later I wrote short stories about sports for *The American Boy;* my stuff was probably the reason the magazine folded in the late 1930s! But I enjoyed it; the magazine's standards were high, and we got paid!

"My first book was *Boys' Life of Will Rogers* (1936).* When Rogers, an Oklahoman, died in 1935 in an Alaskan plane crash, the Crowell company

---

*Unless otherwise noted all titles were published by T. Y. Crowell.

sought an author to write a biography of him. They wanted an Oklahoman preferably. Bob Crowell, then assisting his father with the publishing company, wrote to his friend, Franklin Reck, editor of *The American Boy.* I was the only Oklahoma writer Reck knew; he suggested me.

"I researched the book that summer and wrote it at night during Oklahoma's football season. My copy wasn't very good; part of the book had to be re-written."

The author's second book, *Sports and Games,* was published in 1940. It was a Junior Literary Guild selection; the fifth revised edition appeared in 1969.

Rifles for Waitie, his sixth book, won him a place in the history of children's literature—it received the 1958 Newbery Medal. The book tells the story of Jeff Bussey, who joined the Union army in 1861. His mission was to discover how the infamous Stand Waitie and his Confederate Cherokee rebels were receiving repeating rifles from northern manufacturers. I was curious to know how the book came about, since it seemed a far cry from the author's sports interest.

Mr. Keith explained: "As a history student at the university back in the 1920s, I became interested in the Cherokee Indians living in eastern Oklahoma and how superior their culture, wealth, and education was to that of the Whites living around them.

"Researching *Boys' Life of Will Rogers* brought me in contact with Clem Rogers, Will's father, who was a

Cherokee politician and had been a captain in General Stand Waitie's Cherokee cavalry during the Civil War. I thought him a more interesting man than Will Rogers. So for my master's thesis in history I chose the subject 'Clem Rogers and His Influence on Oklahoma History', and again I drove to eastern Oklahoma to do research. This time I talked mostly to old people, some of whom had lived in Oklahoma during the Civil War as children. They'd say, 'Sure, I'll tell you about Clem Rogers in the Civil War but first let me tell you about my own daddy's part in it.'

"From all this I felt *Rifles for Waitie* developing. During the summers of 1939 and 1940, I obtained a list from the state capitol of all the rebel Civil War veterans still living in Oklahoma and called on them; there were about twenty. I interviewed each, writing down their personal memories; the facts filled three notebooks. I have always enjoyed interviewing old people. You get a great deal more color and personality and characterization. You can ask them questions. While advancing Oklahoma football, I haunted the various state historical societies, scanning letters and diaries of Union Civil War soldiers. I let all this information lie dormant until after I'd taken a few courses in the University of Oklahoma's professional writing school. *Rifles for Waitie* was my first book thereafter.

"Winning the Newbery Award changed my life in that I've become a prolific writer of letters. I've received hundreds of letters from youngsters about this book, and I've answered every one. I still receive them, and I still answer them."

Following *Rifles for Waitie,* Mr. Keith wrote *Komantica* (1965) a novel about Comanche Indians. "I drew the inspiration for this story from devouring all the printed information I could find on these fascinating people as well as personally visiting several Comanches still living in Oklahoma. One of them was Topay, the seventh and last living wife of War Chief Quanah Parker. Although Indian captive stories are out of fashion today, I enjoyed doing this book and I think it still has some strengths."

Commenting on his work habits, Mr. Keith said: "About 8:00 or 8:30 a.m. I usually arrive at my faculty study, a small area on the fourth floor of the University building where most of the historical collections are located. It's a very private, quiet place to work; telephones are not allowed. It's lonely up there. I miss the sports writers, coaches, and athletes like the dickens, but I am averaging two books per year up there. Now that I have retired, I plan to research and write full time; most of it for young people.

"I write until about 12:00–12:30 p.m. and then go to the stadium and run four miles around the football practice fields. Sometimes I run hard. I usually run with faculty, coaches, and townspeople. After the run I go home, take a nap, then return to the library, and work several more hours, usually revising what I did in the morning. I develop ideas for books from research. When I find a field I like, I research it heavily, apply a plot formula, and out comes a book. I revise six or seven times. Sometimes I check the manuscript with children.

"When I'm at work on a book, I become very enthusiastic about it and think it's going to be the best book I ever wrote. The writing is great fun. No matter how tired I am, I dislike stopping. I can't wait to resume the following morning."

Mr. Keith acknowledged that he learned a great deal from the courses he took at the University's professional writing school. "The school is a small one, but very sound. I lived within three blocks of it but didn't enroll for two decades. I had published four or five books and didn't think I needed it. When I did enroll, I discovered in the first five minutes of the first class that I didn't know anything about writing. And I still don't know much. The school operates on the theory that genius is made as well as born. Foster Harris, the dean, says that he thinks he could teach a monkey how to write if somebody would first teach it how to type. Before I took the course, I was taught the rudiments by Elizabeth Riley, my editor at T. Y. Crowell. The letters she wrote explained writing so superbly and simply that I sold four books. Although she stood only about four-feet eight-inches and weighed only eighty-seven pounds, I called her 'Coach'; she was my coach by U. S. mail."

Mr. Keith and his wife, Virginia, live in Hall Park, Oklahoma. "In 1965 we built a new home exactly as we'd always wanted it, a seven-room, one-story brick house, five miles from the University. Virginia is an artist who paints in watercolors and oils. Her studio is the northwest room; I sometimes work in my room on the extreme southeast of the house. That way we don't bother each other when we're working. Walking is her hobby. Despite my running, when I walk with her, she's hard to keep up with.

"My favorite possession is a plaque I received when I retired. It says 'Most Good-for-Nothing Graduate of L.H.S.' and was given to me by my old Lambert High School class at our forty-seventh reunion. We still meet every three years."

The Keiths have two children. Johnny took over his father's job as sports publicist after his retirement; Kathleen (Kitty) is married to a doctor and lives in Houston, Texas. Life's pleasures include visiting with his four grandchildren, singing in a barbershop quartet and, of course, sports activities of all kinds.

"Having lived in Norman for the past forty-three years, we feel we know nearly everybody in town. We've always had a dog. Now she is Betsy, a sheltie."

At the time of this interview Mr. Keith had just completed *The Blue Jay Boarders* (1972). "I like to mix up the fields for my books," he told me. "I think it would be very boring to write novels about the same subject matter. That's why I've jumped around from biography to blue jays."

His next project to look out for will be a mystery story for youngsters.

Also by Mr. Keith

Shotgun Shaw (T. Y. Crowell, 1949).

A Pair of Captains (T. Y. Crowell, 1951).

Go, Red, Go! (Thomas Nelson, 1972).

* Elaine L. Konigsburg

What happened to Elaine L. Konigsburg (Kō-nigs-berg) in the year 1968 is a writer's dream come true; it also made history in the field of children's literature. Her first book for children, *Jennifer, Hecate, Macbeth, William McKinley, and Me, Elizabeth* (1967),* was cited by the American Library Association as a Newbery Honor Book. (It was recently the basis of a N.B.C. television special entitled "Jennifer and Me.") But her second book, published in the same year, *From the Mixed-up Files of Mrs. Basil E. Frankweiler* won the 1968 Newbery Medal and received the William Allen White Award chosen by an annual vote of Kansas schoolchildren in grades four through seven.

Both of the above titles, as with most of her future writings, are sparked from real-life situations. *Jennifer, Hecate, Macbeth, William McKinley, and Me, Elizabeth* developed from an experience her daughter, Laurie, had when the family moved from Port Chester, New York, a suburb of New York City. Laurie, being somewhat independent and shy, had a difficult time making new friends at school and in her new environ-

---

*All titles have been published by Atheneum.

ment. After several weeks, Laurie asked her mother's permission to go to a friend's house to play; the new good friend was a tall, Black girl. This friend became the basis for the development of the fictional character, Jennifer. The plot tells of a lonely girl's adventures with Jennifer, a child who pretends she is a witch and can do tricks. The witch's game in the story came from Laurie's own imagination.

From the Mixed-up Files of Mrs. Basil E. Frankweiler grew in part from a family picnic in Yellowstone National Park. This seems far from the book's plot—two children running away from their suburban Connecticut home to live for days in New York's Metropolitan Museum of Art. But Mrs. Konigsburg's comments on the idea cleared things up: "I purchased bread, cold cuts, chocolate milk, and paper cups from the commissary and found a clearing where we could eat. There were no picnic tables, so my small group ate squatting slightly above the ground, and groaned about ants and flies and how could they keep the milk from tipping over. I realized that if my children ever left home, they would not revert to barbarism. They would carry with them all the fussiness and tidiness of suburban life, and they would hold onto these habits dearly. Where then would they go? They would probably consider nothing less than the Metropolitan Museum of Art. How they love it! And so do I! It contains those wonderful beds and all that elegance, and maybe they could find some way to live with caution and still satisfy their need for adventure."

All sorts of research was necessary to do the book, mainly research about the museum itself. When did they clean the place? What kind of security was there at night? Where could two children hide in the morning and at night when the museum staff was around but the Museum itself was closed?

The Museum naturally was reluctant to divulge such information, so the author spent hours, days, and weeks snooping to her heart's content. There were many trips to the Museum, but just how many? Ms. Konigsburg doesn't really know. "I never remember numbers," she told me, "I never keep track of anything, so I don't know how many actual trips I made. I loved them all, and there were many."

In the few years since the book was published it has been translated into seven foreign languages, making Claudia Kincaid and her nine-year-old brother, Jamie, international figures. At the time of this interview shooting had just begun on a film version of the book, which will star Ingrid Bergman in the title role. A *New York Times* report of August 1, 1972, stated:

The Metropolitan granted the request for use of its premises, for the first time "because of the integral role of the Museum in the film, the warmth and charm of the story, and the educational aspects of the film." The Metropolitan has never before given over its premises to a commercial film.

Among the distinctions of the movie will be that it is the first with a mixed nude bathing scene to receive the Hollywood Motion Picture Code G rating. Claudia and Jamie take a bath together in none other than the Museum's magnificent cafeteria pool. Again, to quote the *New York Times,* "(it) should be just about the prettiest thing that ever happened there."

New York and its environs are familiar places to the author. She was born in New York City, grew up in small towns in Pennsylvania, and graduated from Farrell High School in Farrell, Pennsylvania. After high school she worked for a year as a bookkeeper for a wholesale meat plant. She then attended Carnegie Institute of Technology in Pittsburgh, from which she earned a bachelor of science degree in chemistry in 1952. During her college years she worked at a number of jobs ranging from manager of a dormitory laundry and dry cleaning concession to waitress. During this time she married David Konigsburg, a fellow student.

After Mr. Konigsburg received his doctorate degree, they moved to Jacksonville, Florida, where Ms. Konigsburg taught chemistry in a private girls' school and took up painting and drawing. She has illustrated most of her own books. Three children came along, Paul, Laurie, and Ross. In 1963 the family moved to Port Chester, New York. This is when Ms. Konigsburg started writing and also furthered her art study by taking classes at the Art Students' League in New York City.

"I wanted to write books that reflected the kind of growing up my own three children were experienceing in middle class suburbia because I have always regretted that when I was a child there weren't any books that told what it was like to grow up in a small mill town, even though book jackets would promise that I would meet children in a typical small town.

"And my own children are all visible in my books. They pose for me. Laurie was Claudia; Ross was Jamie, and the studious-looking boy with the glasses sitting on the bus was Paul. Paul also posed as Benjamin Dickinson Carr in *(George)* (1970).

"All three of my children are bright and are excellent students. They all have a natural bent toward math and science. The children are my first editors. I read them what I have written and watch their reactions. I watch more than I listen, and I revise accordingly. I know that a book is truly organic when it changes as I write."

In the midst of her third book, *About the B'Nai Bagels* (1969), the family moved back to Jacksonville. Their house is on a quiet street set on a lot with many trees including beautiful magnolias and moss-draped oaks.

"There are so many trees here," she commented, "that we can't get grass to grow in the backyard and only on the hottest days will the bed linens dry on the line!"

Although the author loves to write and paint, she has "absolutely no musical or athletic skills; I never got past twosies in jacks! Writing and drawing are probably elaborate compensation mechanisms," she told me. She also enjoys gardening and long walks, and loves miniatures—tiny things like salesmen's samples. She laughed about a salesman's sample of a coffin into which her youngest son laid a marionette skeleton to rest.

The things she hates most in the world? "Liver and phonies!"

Currently her one occupation besides writing and illustrating is walking Jason, the family's "ill-mannered, ill-trained dog." But who knows? Maybe liver and phonies and an independent dog will be the subjects for still another Konigsburg adventure.

Also by Ms. Konigsburg

Altogether, One at a Time (Antheneum, 1971).

✳ ✳ Nancy Larrick
✳ Alexander L. Crosby

Frank Fosbenner

A *few years ago I spent a most* memorable evening with Nancy Larrick and her husband, Alexander L. Crosby. I had driven with a friend from New York in a torrent of rain to have dinner at their house near Quakertown, Pennsylvania. Only a mile from our goal, we pulled off a narrow pavement to check a map. The night was pitch dark; we could not see that we were on a soft shoulder until our two right wheels sank axle-deep into the mud. We were hopelessly mired.

I plodded through the mud to a nearby house to phone the Crosbys. Mr. Crosby arrived in a few minutes.

"Leave the car here—nobody could steal it," he said. "Let's go eat now."

A few hours later we returned with a flashlight, a jack, a shovel, and several short and heavy planks. Mr. Crosby dug out enough mud to get the planks under the wheels, which had been raised by the jack. The car was started and, by the grace of God, it crawled back onto the pavement.

In 1972, when I compiled a mini anthology of poetry, *When I Am All Alone,* for Scholastic's Individualized Reading Program, I borrowed a perfect word from e. e. cummings and dedicated the book:

> For Nancy Larrick and Alexander L. Crosby
> who are *mudluscious.*

The Crosbys don't write books together. Each is unique in his writing.

Arnold Arnold, writer of the syndicated column "Parents and Children," once commented on Nancy Larrick:

Miss Larrick (is) among the few who have a feeling for children and poetry. (She knows) what kind of poetry stimulates an interest in language for young children. (She) has combed the literature for ideas, sounds, and rhymes that are imaginative and childlike. (She ex-

cludes in her anthologies) the tired old standbys . . .
that have drawn generations of children away from
poetry.

As of this writing, Dr. Larrik has compiled eight
anthologies of poetry for children and young people.
The first was *You Come Too* (Holt, 1959), a selection
of poetry by Robert Frost for young readers. "I read
everything Frost had written at that date," she recalled,
"then selected the poems I thought young people
would enjoy, grouped them into sections or chapters
for which I chose titles from the poems themselves,
and then submitted the plan to Robert Frost's publisher. We were all very pleased that the poet liked the
whole combination."

Her second anthology, *Piper, Pipe That Song Again*
(Random House, 1965), includes the work of many
poets. All the poems were chosen with the help of
more than one hundred second- and third-graders,
"good readers and not so good," who met with Dr.
Larrick twice a week for several months. They gave
their reactions to hundreds of poems and their reasons for liking some and rejecting others. "The
common reason for rejecting a poem," she remembered, "was that 'It's too sweet,' which I have come
to think is the most damning comment today's child
can make."

To select the title, Ms. Larrick listed five possibilities on a large poster and asked children and teachers
for their opinions. The teachers' choice was *The Easy-
to-Read Poetry Book,* but almost every child preferred

Piper, Pipe That Song Again. "That title makes me feel good," explained a third-grader.

A second anthology on which she had the help of youngsters is *On City Streets* (M. Evans, 1968), a collection of poems about the city. "As I gathered children's responses to poetry, I found them rejecting poems about haystacks and pumpkin vines and favoring poems about their world, which is largely urban or suburban. Even rural children are so urbanized by television that they are more intrigued by traffic lights than a herd of cows." So she assembled as many poems about the city as possible and took them to inner-city and small-city schools to get student responses. "These are the poems they preferred over all others," she stated, "because as the children put it, 'These poems are real.'"

The youngsters with whom she worked showed her many poems they had written about the city, and she began collecting city poems by city children. Out of this collection came *I Heard a Scream in the Streets* (M. Evans, 1970), selections from more than five thousand poems gathered from city schools, storefront schools, and ghetto workshops. The words of these young poets are contemporary and stark, speaking harshly about poverty, brutality, and crises of city life today. This is poetry of protest.

Dr. Larrick was born and grew up in Winchester, Virginia. "I was an only child," she told me, "but in a small southern town, especially at that time, even an only child had a wide circle of friends and became a part of many families. We lived near a splendid public library, which meant my friends and I were all constant library patrons, slowed down only by the rule that each could borrow just two books at a time and no returns the same day. My parents were readers, too, and I was constantly a part of adult discussions about politics, economic issues, and social problems that were of particular concern to my father, a country lawyer."

At fifteen, Dr. Larrick graduated from high school and entered Goucher College in Baltimore, Maryland. Upon graduating, she returned to Winchester and began teaching in her hometown school.

"Soon after I began teaching, I took a course in modern American poetry. I had always loved poetry and at college had explored the poetry of the past, but I had little acquaintance with such modern poets as Robert Frost, Carl Sandburg, e. e. cummings, and Edgar Lee Masters, Now I began bringing the poetry of these moderns into my classes, and I found the children just as enthusiastic as I was. Seventh and eighth graders soon began collecting favorite poems and compiling their own poetry booklets from the work of contemporary poets. We read and read, but we did not make any attempt to analyze a poem line by line, a practice that has killed the love of poetry in the past. It was the melody and the feeling that got us."

From the classroom, Dr. Larrick went on to earn both her master's degree and doctorate. She has been an editor of children's magazines and books and has taught in the Graduate School of Education at New

York University, Indiana University, and the Bank Street College of Education in New York City. She has served as president of the International Reading Association and was editor of the I.R.A. journal, the *Reading Teacher.* Currently she is Adjunct Professor in the School of Education at Lehigh University and Director of the Poetry Workshop. Most of her students are in-service elementary school teachers.

"I try to get my students doing the same kinds of things their children might be doing—writing poetry, singing and dancing and dramatizing poetry, and making films and filmstrips that grow out of poetry. Then they go back to their classes and try the same things with their students.

" 'But the kids write better poetry than we do!' someone always wails. And often that's true!" she exclaimed.

Interest in the Poetry Workshop led to a one-day Poetry Festival at Lehigh University in the spring of 1969 at which more than one thousand teachers spent the day with poets, anthologists, critics, and student commentators in an effort to learn how to capitalize on the youthful surge to poetry. *Somebody Turned on a Tap in These Kids* (Delacorte, 1970), edited by Dr. Larrick, is a report of this extraordinary day. Chapters of the book were written by seven of the speakers, a group of inner-city youngsters, and Dr. Larrick.

I asked the author to tell me just what poetry is. "I like to think of poetry," she answered, "as a means of helping both adults and children understand themselves better; not as 'a heritage' which sounds like a heavy document from the past. A poem should sing out to the reader or listener and help him identify with the poet and begin to wonder whether he feels as the poet feels.

"I hope adults will never try to feed poetry into children. That suggests that adults will make choices and spoon the poems into the gaping mouths of helpless children sitting down to a rich bill of fare where there will be all kinds of poetry to sample and choose from and where adults and children as partners can share and enjoy what appeals to them."

Dr. Larrick is handsome and statuesque; a woman whose love for children and their literature is contagious.

She shared with me this anecdote of a visit she paid to a second grade: "One little girl seemed especially interested in what I was saying. When I asked if there were any questions, she raised her hand and said, 'Yes, aren't you awfully tall for your age?' I had to admit I had *always* been tall for my age!"

She is tall in two ways—tall physically but even taller as an educator. Her forward-looking comments on children's literature and on education in general have reached a vast audience through books and numerous magazine articles that have stirred lively debate and have been widely quoted.

Her best known book, *A Parent's Guide to Children's Reading* (Doubleday, third edition, 1969), was initiated by the National Book Committee and sponsored by nineteen organizations in a nationwide effort to encourage children to read more widely. The volume has sold close to a million copies in its various editions. It is written with the warmth and in the simple direct style that mark all of her work. It is must reading for parents and for all teachers of children as well.

Alexander L. Crosby, Dr. Larrick's husband, was born in a farmhouse in Catonsville, Maryland, on June 10, 1906. His father cared about farming, reading, politics, and nature; his mother had taught in private schools and always wished for more money than she ever had. The family moved to National City, California, when Mr. Crosby was nine. The trip by the Southern Pacific Railroad got the lad interested in trains, a lifelong romance.

His closest friend in childhood was his sister, Elizabeth, who was two years younger. "Elizabeth and I went for walks in the sagebrush hills that began less than half a mile from our house. We saw roadrunners and mourning doves. We discovered a colony of trapdoor spiders and occasionally met a tarantula. When there were fights with other children, Elizabeth and I always stuck together—sometimes without any allies," he recalled.

Mr. Crosby returned to the East after graduating from the University of California and got a job on S.I. Newhouse's *Staten Island Advance.* "In 1934 I tried to organize a chapter of the Newspaper Guild there; the publisher fired me. I held several jobs afterward, including two years on the WPA Federal Writers' Project as an editor of the *New Jersey Guide*. In 1958 I was fortunate enough to marry Nancy, then editor of children's books at Random House. The first product of our marriage was a children's book called *Rockets into Space* (Random House, 1959; retitled *The World of Rockets* in 1965). I was never really interested in rockets, but the book brought in enough money to pay off my last debts."

Most of Mr. Crosby's early books deal with science and geography. Several were sparked by the Crosbys' move from New York's Greenwich Village to Quakertown, Pennsylvania, in 1960, where they had found an old stone house and barn, thirty-three acres of fields and woods, and a pond. "I then began to write about things that were more important to me than rockets—beavers, ponds, rivers, and American history.

This new locale figured in *The Junior Science Book of Pond Life* (Garrard, 1964) and *The Junior Science Book of Canada Geese* (Garrard, 1966). Regarding this latter title Mr. Crosby remarked, "In the early fall as many as three hundred Canada geese come to our pond for cracked corn. That's a lot of geese and a lot of cracked corn!"

One of his recent titles, *One Day for Peace* (Little, Brown, 1971), is a novel for teen-agers and tells the story of a junior high school girl who organizes a parade against the war in Vietnam. "I wrote this book," he said, "because I believe that our killing hundreds of thousands of Vietnamese and wrecking their land is the most terrible thing the United States has ever done. My hope was that more and more young people would be encouraged to demand a stop to the killing."

Mr. Crosby's first book of fiction, *Go Find Hanka!* (Golden Gate, 1970), was based on the story of a small boy who was lost in the tall grass of the Illinois prairie more than a century ago. The original account, anonymously written, was published in 1869 in a book of articles and anecdotes about the Rocky Mountains and the West.

"I try to choose subjects I know a little about and care a great deal about," he declared. "My heart influences me more than my head—which is why I'm through with rockets."

Mr. Crosby has two sons from a former marriage and three granddaughters.

The old stone house in which the couple live is comfortable, friendly, and mirrors their interests. The walls are adorned with two Audubon prints from the Elephant Folio, old religious paintings from Peru, and modern abstract oils. Animal sculpture by George Papashvily is inside the house and in their gardens.

Among Dr. Larrick's favorite possessions are the rare children's books she has collected here and in England, many dating from the eighteenth and early nineteenth centuries. Some are tiny chapbooks colored by hand, some are first editions illustrated by Kate Greenaway and Randolph Caldecott, some are modern books autographed by friends.

Mr. Crosby enjoys planting trees, especially the small white pines he has saved from destruction along the edges of highways. All year long he feeds birds, rabbits, squirrels, muskrats, and other animals that enjoy cracked corn. He is a collector of United States stamps and coins and particularly cherishes those that show railroads.

Both the Crosbys like to travel, "especially when we get off the tourist tracks," said Dr. Larrick. Expeditions have included a float trip on the upper Missouri River following the route of Lewis and Clark, a horseback trip in the Pecos Wilderness of New Mexico, a backpack trip through the Lost Canyon of Cantil in Baja, California, and a railroad trip from Lima over the Andes to Juancayo. They are also fond of people, especially those who are doing things and raising questions. They have guests almost every weekend they are at home.

Anthologies edited by Dr. Larrick

Poetry for Holidays (Garrard, 1966).

Piping Down the Valleys Wild (Delacorte, 1968).

Green Is Like a Meadow of Grass (Garrard, 1968).

The Wheels of the Bus Go Round and Round
(Golden Gate, 1972).

Also by Mr. Crosby

The Colorado: Mover of the Mountains
(Garrard, 1961).

Steamboat up the Colorado (Little, Brown, 1965).

The Rio Grande: Life for the Desert
(Garrard, 1966).

The Rimac: River of Peru (Garrard, 1966).

Old Greenwood (Talisman, 1967).

* * Jean Lee Latham
*

Jean Lee Latham (Lā-thum) is a five-feet two-inches, white-haired, seventy-year-old bundle of energy. She's quick, witty, gregarious, loves to travel, speak, and write, and cooks all sorts of things she doesn't eat. "People have always described me as 'tiny'. Then when my basso profundo voice comes out, they jump!" she declared. "It's *very* difficult for me to prove to Western Union that I am *Ms.* Latham when a telegram is to be delivered on the telephone. When it comes to doing something new, I ain't got no shame about flubbing it, so I have more fun than most people."

The author was born on April 19, 1902, in Buckhannon, West Virginia, where she spent "a lot of happy years at the three R's—readin', ritin', and runnin' around! For years I lived just across from a lovely bit of unpruned forest. We had swings, trapezes, log houses, and tree houses. The only things I did indoors, sometimes, were to read, write poetry, and tell stories to my younger brothers and their pals. So I'm doing what comes naturally when I write for children — especially for boys."

Ms. Latham began writing plays while she was in high school and continued writing through her college years at West Virginia Wesleyan College. After college she filled a variety of teaching roles. In 1930 she became the editor-in-chief of the Dramatic Publishing Company in Chicago, Illinois, a job she held for six years.

Leaving this, she turned to free-lance writing until the United States' entrance into World War II. During the war years she was in charge of training Signal Corps inspectors for the United States War Department and later received the War Department Silver Wreath for her work.

Her first book for children, *The Story of Eli Whitney* (Aladdin, 1953, 1962), was issued about eighteen years after her first adult book, *Do's and Don'ts of Drama: 555 Pointers for Beginning Actors and Directors* (Dramatic Publishing Company, 1935). "A scientific man showed me a model of the first cotton gin and said, 'I wonder what would have happened if Whitney had been a lawyer as he started out to be?' Since I'm a dramatist at heart, I look for suspense in a man's life. If there's not enough suspense, the man's just not my cup of tea. Some small quirk like the scientific man's statement rouses my interest. That's enough to start me tally ho on a subject's trail.''

Medals for Morse (Aladdin, 1954) about Samuel Morse, was her second biography for children; her third, *Carry On, Mr. Bowditch* (Houghton Mifflin, 1955), was a biography of Nathaniel Bowditch, a self-taught man who became one of the leading mathematicians in the United States. The book was awarded the Newbery Medal in 1956. The inspiration for it came after she had read one paragraph in Bowditch's book on navigation, *The American Practical Navigator,* a work that superseded the previous standard work on navigation by an Englishman and one that is still used by sailors the world over.

I asked Ms. Latham how she came to write about a man who lived from 1773–1838. She answered me with a series of *thats:* "That the undersized son of a drunkard had to stop school when he was ten. That when he was twelve, he was given six weeks of training in bookkeeping and then was apprenticed to a ship chandlery and could not leave the premises by night or day without permission until he was twenty-one years old. That by the time he was thirty, he had conceived of a new method of nautical calculations and had written the book that is still the sailor's Bible. That he could read Latin, French, and other languages. That he was the outstanding mathematician in the United States and was awarded a master's degree from Harvard: Well, there just *had* to be a story there, no?

There was, and I wanted to tell it—even though I knew absolutely nothing about anything I'd have to know to do it!

"I started with titles from the children's room at the library—books about having fun with stars, mathematics made easy, and the like. After some earnest study there, I worked up to Sea Scout manuals and on and on and on."

Discussing the Newbery Award, she reminisced: "Before the news came of my winning the Newbery, I had written *Trail Blazer of the Seas* (Houghton Mifflin, 1956), a book about Matthew Fontaine Maury, and was deep in *This Dear-Bought Land* (Harper, 1957), a story of the early settlement of Jamestown. This was early in 1956. The three hundred fiftieth anniversary of Jamestown was to be celebrated in April 1957. I read the letter telling me that I had won the award, looked up Newbery Award in the encyclopedia, called my sister to borrow some winter clothes for a trek to New York City for the announcement, then returned home and got back to work. April 1957 was breathing down my neck!"

Between 1957 and 1973, Ms. Latham has written scores of books, plays, retellings of famous stories, and biographies and histories dealing with the American scene.

"For my biographies I read, research, and travel. I research with a tape recorder and may collect half a million words before I start writing. I make an historical chronology in squared-off blocks on shelf paper, about two yards long or so, and number the squares. I can start writing scenes around any historical incident, file them in order, and go on to another. And I certainly do rewrite! I may spend a month doing twenty different versions of an opening chapter."

She often tests out her material on children: "I find a keen, but non-studious boy, have him read the manuscript and tell me 'what can come out.' That's my acid test!"

Her interest in Americana stems from her birthplace, West Virginia, "A completely hybrid state," as she describes it. "Easterners think we're pretty rough; Westerners think we're effete Easterners; the North thinks of us as Johnny Rebs, and the South thinks of us as damn Yankees. I'd never been out of West Virginia until after my first college degree. Since then I've been in most of the states. My knowledge of history and geography was very, very minus until I started digging into the backgrounds of some of my characters."

Currently Ms. Latham lives in Coral Gables, Florida. Prior to this she lived in a trailer for twelve years. "Not to travel with but to live in during the World War II housing shortage. Since I am an 'unthing' person, I adapted to it easily. I had two doors. If something new came in the front door, something old had to go out through the back door. I wrote my first books in the trailer but finally realized I was discarding too much research material that I needed to keep. Since then I've lived in an apartment.

"I'm very busy when I'm at home writing. I have a great many friends, but I may not see them for two months at a time. If my phone rings before evening, it's a dire emergency or a wrong number. When I come up for air, I'm as gregarious as a curb stone sitter. A clerk in a big department store in Chicago said to me once, 'You must be from a small town.' You look at a clerk as though she were a human being. I think the small town background is still much a part of me.

"When I go off treking alone, sometimes someone will say, 'Way out *there?* Have you got any friends?' Sure, I tell them. One I've seen, and a lot I haven't met yet. Once in Nova Scotia I was with a friend who had kith and kin all over the place. We were in a new home for lunch or dinner, or both, everyday. One evening she started laughing and said, 'I've timed you; the time from the minute you enter a strange house till you are in the kitchen. Fifteen minutes is the longest time yet.'

"Again, that's the small town in me."

Whenever she can, she speaks to groups of youngsters about writing. "I hit all the assemblies I can cram in when traveling. On my first visit to Hawaii I spoke forty times in thirty days; the next time ninety in six weeks. It restores my bubbles! The remark I often receive in letters from boys is to this effect: 'I sure was disappointed when I saw you. But as soon as you started talking, it was all right. You're like us.'

"No wonder I have such a good time. Children are such fun to talk to. If I did all the talking I'd like to do,

I'd not get any writing done. I seldom go to market without some youngster grinning at me and saying, 'Hi! I'm from _____' (whatever school it is). Once a very shy little girl said, 'Is it all right to speak to you when we see you?' Since then I always close my talks saying, 'I'm going to ask you to do something for me. After I talk to the boys and girls I write for, I feel acquainted. I don't have time to memorize all your faces, but you've gotten a pretty good look at me. Think you'll know me when you see me? If you do, just say 'Hi' and tell me where you're from, and I'll know where we got to be friends.'

"Sometimes a very small youngster sings out, 'HI!' and the name of his school, and then to shocked parents says, 'She *said* we could!'

"Some of my best friends are adults, but I honestly like children better! If an adult doesn't like something in a book of mine, I tell him, 'That's all right, dear. I didn't write it for *you!*' "

Also by Ms. Latham

Sam Houston: Hero of Texas (Garrard, 1965).

George W. Goethals: Panama Canal Engineer (Garrard, 1965).

Anchors Aweigh: The Story of David Glasgow Farragut (Harper, 1968).

Far Voyager: The Story of James Cook (Harper, 1970).

✳
✳ **Madeleine L'Engle**
✳ ✳

Bradford Bachrach

A Circle of Quiet (1972)* is Madeleine L'Engle's autobio-graphical account of her life as wife, mother, grandmother, teacher, speaker, concerned citizen, practicing Christian, and author of nearly twenty books for both children and adults. Her widely acclaimed science fiction novel, *A Wrinkle in Time* (1962), won her the 1963 Newbery Medal.

Ms. L'Engle and I planned to meet for lunch in the winter of 1972. I knew I'd recognize her easily for she wrote me: "My friends describe me as a giraffe, and it's only too true. I'm tall, long, thinnish, and apt to trip over my own feet. Look for a giraffe with mouse-brown hair and blue-grey eyes."

Instead of my searching for a giraffe, however, we decided to meet at my office at Scholastic. She appeared somewhat as she described herself; she is a tall, longish, thinnish lady—but not really as tall as a giraffe. She failed to tell me that she is plainly pretty with an unforgettable sparkle in her blue-grey eyes. After a

---

*Unless otherwise noted, all titles were published by Farrar, Straus.

brief period of warm conversation, we went to a small, West Side French restaurant. Over lunch we talked endlessly, sharing anecdotes, discussing everything from the drug culture to the Broadway show *Oh Calcutta!,* and, of course, chatting at length about Madeleine L'Engle.

"I'm one of those rare creatures, a native of Manhattan," she told me. She was born shortly after World War I, an only child, on November 29, 1918. Her mother was a pianist; her father, a foreign correspondent and writer, was gassed during the war. "I saw him dying for eighteen years; the gas just went on eating. Both of my parents were fairly old so I led a rather isolated, lonely city life until I was twelve years old, with lots of time to write, draw, and play the piano.

"I always wanted to write even though I wasn't encouraged to do so at home, for father was a writer. I was well into adolescence when I really started to do something about my writing."

During this period of her life she attended a "perfectly ghastly school" that placed great emphasis on prowess in the gymnasium. "My being lame didn't help me much in this institution. My homeroom teacher went along with the kids in labeling me the lame, unpopular girl in the school and also decided I wasn't very bright. The last year there I entered a poetry contest and won. This homeroom teacher of mine declared Madeleine wasn't bright enough to write, that I couldn't have written a poem, and that I must have copied it. My mother had to go to school with a mountain of poems, stories, and novels I had written to prove that the contest was rightfully won!''

At the age of twelve, her parents were forced to move to France because the New York fumes were too much for her father's lungs. "I was put in an English boarding school where I was the only American —speak of culture shock! I was very close to my parents, although I saw less of them than most children today. I had an English nanny, who still, at age ninety-one, telephones me regularly to see if I've polished the silver or washed all the curtains for Christmas. I admired my parents and felt a terrific sense of responsibility to them. I grew up in a manner that was already obsolete when I was a child and certainly no longer exists. It's a world my children have glimpsed only because my mother, their grandmother, died last summer at the age of ninety.''

After graduating from Smith College, she submitted several of her writings to magazines, and her articles were published sporadically. She also returned to New York City to work in the theatre, thinking of it as an excellent school for aspiring authors. While touring with Eva Le Gallienne and Joseph Schildkraut in *Uncle Harry,* she wrote her first book, *The Small Rain* (Vanguard, 1945), an adult book. She met her future husband, Hugh Franklin, when they both appeared in *The Cherry Orchard* with Ms. Le Gallienne. They were married during the run of *The Joyous Season* starring Ethel Barrymore. When she became Ms. Franklin, the author gave up the theatre in favor of the typewriter. Her husband temporarily retired too. The couple settled in Connecticut in an old farmhouse they bought for $6,300 and began to raise a family—and a business.

"Hugh bought a general store—a completely dead store in the center of town. He had mortgaged us to the hilt to buy it. He had no experience in this sort of thing. He comes from a family of lawyers, and being an actor was strange enough! Yet we ran that store for many years. He built it up from nothing to a flourishing business. It reached the point where the only thing to do would be to buy more stores.

"One night when we were sitting in front of the fire having a drink, I asked him, 'Hugh, are you still happy with the store?' 'No,' he replied. I said, 'Sell it.' And why not? The only thing I was selling was the stuff from the store and not my writing! But a lot of what I learned in our store was of immense value to a writer. Our customers included gypsies, carnival men, farmers, factory workers, artists, and philosophers. *Meet the Austins* (Vanguard, 1960), came directly out of our lives at that time; it could easily have been called *Meet the Franklins.*"

Next she wrote *A Wrinkle in Time,* but the manuscript was rejected by a number of publishers. Finally, her agent returned it at her request. Rather than becoming hysterical, as she sometimes did over her writing failures, she took this calmly.

"*Wrinkle* was turned down for about the twentieth time just before Christmas. I was sitting on the bed wrapping presents and thought, 'Madeleine, you've really grown up. You're being terribly brave about all this.' I didn't realize until some time later, however, that I had sent a necktie to a three-year-old girl and some perfume to a bachelor friend!

"My mother was at our house for the holidays, and I had a small party for her. At the party one of my friends said, 'You must meet John Farrar from Farrar, Straus.

"At this point in time I was down on publishers, but my friend insisted. I set up an appointment to see him. He had read my first book, *The Small Rain*, liked it, and asked if I had any other manuscripts. I gave him *Wrinkle* and told him, 'Here's a book nobody likes.' He read it and two weeks later I signed the contract. The editors told me not to be disappointed if it doesn't do well and that they were publishing it because they loved it. The book (published in 1962), did very well as it turned out. It is still doing very well, and because of it my life certainly changed in all kinds of ways.

"It's very pleasant to be a small success after a long period of failure. One of the best things is the people I've met and who have taught me so much. And I've learned a great deal from the letters children and grown-ups write me and from writing or talking with them."

The author and I did not talk at length about her science fiction work *A Wrinkle in Time,* for so much has already been written about this book dealing with such subjects as tesseracting (traveling in time), extrasensory perception, and inhabited planets in outer space. Being curious about Charles Wallace, the brilliant five-year-old boy in the book, I asked if he was based on a real person in her life. "Charles Wallace is Charles Wallace!" she answered. Then she paused for a brief moment and added, "Well, he's the next son I never had!"

Ms. L'Engle has just completed *A Wind in the Door* (1973), which "is by no means a sequel to *Wrinkle,* though it is definitely a companion piece. Despite the fact that it is about Meg and Charles Wallace and Calvin, it is completely different. In *Wrinkle* the children went into galactic space; in *A Wind,* they go into the incredibly minute world of mitochondria—those strange little creatures that live in our cells, are genetically independent of us, and with whom we have a symbiotic relationship. I've had to learn a lot more about cellular biology than I ever expected to know, but I don't think it shows in the story, which is a story first and foremost. Nevertheless, the background had to be scientifically accurate, so that the strange happenings have a basis in scientific possibility. I hope it's an exciting story—that's the main thing."

After ten years in Connecticut, Mr. Franklin returned to Broadway, and they moved into an apartment near Columbia University, after taking a ten-week camping trip to the Pacific Coast. One result of the trip was *The Moon by Night,* a mystery-suspense-science fiction story for older readers about the Austin family's adventures on a trip across the United States. The book was published in 1963—the year of her Newbery.

I asked Ms. L'Engle why she so wanted to write for children. She replied: "I didn't! I don't! I write for the child in everybody, that part of us that is aware and open and courageous. It's also that part of us that isn't afraid to explore the mythical depths, that vast part of ourselves we know little about, and which we often fear because we can't manipulate or control it. That's where art is born."

In 1965 *The Arm of the Starfish* appeared. Ms. L'Engle told me of its development: "This book came about as a result of a trip to Portugal my husband and I made when I needed to do on-the-spot research for *The Love Letters* (1966), an adult novel about an actual seventeenth century Portuguese nun. Our plane, like Adam's in *Starfish*, couldn't land at Lisbon because of the fog and went on to Madrid; we were taken to the same hotel Adam was, spent the day at the Prado, ate the same food, were finally flown to Lisbon in the same Caravelle. We both stayed at the Ritz in Lisbon, where Adam first met Joshua, and at the Avenida Palace where Dr. O'Keefe took Adam. Canon Tallis is one of two characters in all my books where I can see a resemblance to an actual human being. Some young readers understand right away that Dr. and Ms. O'Keefe are Calvin and Meg from *Wrinkle*—but nobody needs to know this to enjoy *Starfish*. This island is a mixture of the south coast of

Portugal and the beach in north Florida where my grandmother had a cottage. It is essential for me to see, feel, smell, taste, and hear all the places where my imaginary characters move. I may change the size of a house or the curve of a beach, but I have to know the locale before my characters can come to life for me. Then they take on complete lives of their own; they are as real to me as my family and friends, and sometimes surprise me completely. For instance, when Adam woke up in the Ritz in Lisbon, it was as much of a surprise to me as it was to him to find Joshua Archer sitting in his room; Joshua changed the story entirely and caused me to do a great deal of rewriting.

"I hope that *Starfish* is first and foremost an exciting story of international intrigue, but I was concerned at that time about how one cares about the fall of the sparrow.

"When Hugh first read my manuscript, he said, 'It's good, but you left strings untied here and there. The plot isn't tight enough; the book isn't nearly good enough.' I became really furious with him because I knew he meant I had to rewrite the whole book. But I did rewrite it changing the last third completely.

"An invaluable thing Hugh does that saves both my agent and my publishers a great deal of time is to go over a manuscript with me word for word, cutting. I usually scream, 'You want me to cut the whole thing; you don't want anything left!' But it all ends up tighter and tidier because of his vigilance. I always over intellectualize, and he takes it right out. And he's right.

Speculation doesn't belong in a novel; it belongs in an essay. The world lost a good editor when Hugh became a great actor."

Since 1965 the author has done many other books for children including *The Journey with Jonah* (1967), a dramatized version of the Old Testament's Jonah and the whale, *The Young Unicorns* (1968), a novel for older readers, and *Dance in the Desert* (1969), a beautifully designed picture book illustrated by Symeon Shimin.

Commenting on her diverse writing, Ms. L'Engle said: "My story ideas are somewhat like a big, old fashioned French stove, with several pots on the back keeping warm. As ideas come along, I drop them into the appropriate pot, and when one book is finished, I pull forward onto the fire whichever pot seems most ready to be written into a book. I get my ideas from everywhere, everybody, and everything. I rework in that I rewrite and rewrite and rewrite, and each book gets more revisions than the previous one. I don't try ideas on anyone, but I do like to read bits and pieces of manuscript to people—either children or grown-ups, whoever is available. But not too much; an idea that is talked about too much seldom becomes developed in writing."

Currently the Franklins live in New York City. Mr. Franklin is at present playing in the TV soap opera "All My Children" and in off-Broadway shows. "During the academic year we live on Manhattan's Upper West Side in a neighborhood that is a melting pot—

White, Black, Wasp, Jewish, Oriental, Puerto Rican, rich, poor. We live in a big, old fashioned apartment with huge rooms and high ceilings. In the summer we live in a large, two hundred-plus-year-old farmhouse in the foothills of the Berkshires, on top of a windy hill. My favorite possession is my magnificent piano, which was given to me and has been played by both Rachmaninov and Paderewski. I enjoy getting everything inside me quiet and into perspective by an hour of playing Bach fugues.

"I enjoy dinner and an evening of conversation with friends, sitting over a drink with my husband, and traveling with him anywhere, anytime; we love freighters. I've been married for twenty-seven years, and for an actor and a writer that's a bit of a miracle. My family have also been tolerant, patient, and encouraging about my writing, and it is well understood that if I don't write everyday, my temper is apt to get short. They know, even when I dump a hundred pages into the wastepaper basket, that I love to write."

The Franklins have three children and two grandchildren. Their son is a junior in college; their two daughters are married. "I know I'm prejudiced, but I think they're all marvelous!" she asserted.

As mentioned earlier, the inner L'Engle is well-exposed in *A Circle of Quiet*. Her last words in the book best describe her philosophy of life: "The shadows are deepening all around us," she writes. "Now is the time when we must begin to see our world and ourselves in a different way."

Also by Ms. L'Engle

For younger readers

The Twenty-Four Days Before Christmas
(Farrar, Straus, 1964).

*
* **Milton Meltzer**
*

I had met Milton Meltzer several times at various publishers' gatherings, but the first time I had the chance to really talk with him was up in the air when we flew together to Dallas, Texas, in 1971 for an annual American Library Association Convention. High above the clouds we chatted. Mostly we talked about the late Black poet, Langston Hughes, who was a close friend of Mr. Meltzer and my own private poet laureate.

It's difficult to describe this five-feet nine-inches, one hundred forty-five pound bundle of scholarship, so I asked him to describe himself. "Besides having grey hair, green eyes and a rusty voice," he replied, "I have a rapidly aging body that can't do what I want it to do at times. I also have an explosive laugh that astonishes people in dark theatres and movies, an inability to slow down and take it easy, a rapid walk that's like a run—and eyeglasses, of course. I can't find my pillow at night without them! I talk too fast too."

Mr. Meltzer's work in the area of nonfiction writing for older children has been widely acclaimed. He began writing for boys and girls via one of his daughters. His first juvenile, *The Light in the Dark: The Life of Samuel Gridley Howe* (T. Y. Crowell, 1964), is a biographical account of the abolitionist. "I'd run across this fascinating social rebel while working on a book about abolition. I talked about him so much at the dinner table my daughter Amy said, 'Stop talking about Sam Howe and start writing. Write it for me!' I did and I was hooked."

Mr. Meltzer has a profound interest in social reform and its effect upon all Americans, as his writings well document. Following the biography of Howe he wrote a second biography about the abolitionist Lydia Maria Child, which is entitled *Tongue of Flame* (T. Y. Crowell, 1965). "I fell in love with her while writing about her," he exclaimed.

Other popular titles dealing with America's past include *Bread and Roses: The Struggle of American Labor, 1865–1915* (Knopf, 1967), *Thaddeus Stevens and the Fight for Negro Rights* (T. Y. Crowell, 1967), and his highly praised three-volume series "In Their Own Words: A History of the American Negro (volume I, *1619–1865;* volume II, *1865–1916;* volume III, *1916–1966;* T. Y. Crowell, 1964, 1965, 1967).

In this stirring and important series, the author compiled a unique history of the role of Blacks in America's past through contemporary letters, newspaper articles, book excerpts, journals, and speeches. Each volume is illustrated with photographs and prints, and each includes an excellent calendar of Negro history and reading lists.

More recently Mr. Meltzer has served with Dorothy Sterling as a consulting editor to Scholastic Book Services' "Firebird Books," a series designed to help young readers understand some of the less publicized events of American history, especially those dealing with the experiences of minority Americans. His own book, *To Change the World: A Picture History of Reconstruction* (Scholastic, 1971), is part of this program.

Mr. Meltzer was born in Worcester, Massachusetts, and grew up there. "My parents were immigrants from Austria-Hungary. Father was a window cleaner, mother a factory worker. I was the middle of three sons. My parents were self-taught in English, intensely interested in education, and delighted when I early became a slave to the printed word, devouring library shelves from one end to the other. I saw less of my father because of his terrible, hard physical labor and long hours. We all went to work early to help the family. I worked as milkman, newsboy, warehouse worker, and shoe clerk among other things. But I had lots of fun at outdoor sports—swimming, skating, coasting, tennis. I attended good local schools, and I enjoyed going to them." He attended Classical High School and later Columbia University.

He began writing nonfiction because of his interest and "absorption in history." He worked for years as a journalist and editor for newspapers, magazines, radio, and television and was the producer of a three-part film series, "Free and Equal: The History of the American Negro."

"I never really thought of trying fiction until two years ago when I couldn't find enough documentation to do a biography I wanted to write. Defeated from fact, I wrote it as fiction. I had a wildly exciting, frustrating, disappointing, and loving time doing this one," he recalled. The book is *Underground Man* (Bradbury Press, 1972), a novel set in the 1800s and dealing with Josh Bowen, a slave-stealer working underground in Ohio and Kentucky.

I asked Mr. Meltzer why he had chosen to write *Langston Hughes: A Biography* (T. Y. Crowell, 1968). He replied: "I met Langston in 1955 when we began collaborating on two big history books *(A Pictorial History of the Negro in America,* Crown, 1956, 1963 and *Black Magic: A Pictorial History of the Negro in American Entertainment,* Prentice-Hall, 1967). It was then that I came to know and love him. I felt I wanted to express my feelings to others. He consented and let me try it, but he died shortly before the book was finished. The book is in no sense an official biography. Langston saw some of it in early draft but did not try to set any limits on what to include or how it should be written. After his death my research continued and extended considerably, but with one important limitation. Access to the Hughes papers in the James Weldon Johnson Collection of the Yale University Library, which I had referred to earlier, was cut off by the literary executors of his estate." The book was nominated for the National Book Award.

The author and his wife live in a New York City apartment on the West Side. The apartment has a broad view of the Hudson River and the city. Books are his favorite possessions, and he has "thousands and thousands of them—all over every room." He enjoys tennis "winter, summer and forever, though I'm only a mediocre player. I used to travel a lot abroad but have had enough of that. Now I like staying in one place, the country, and preferably mountains. People? I love some, like a lot of others, am still ridiculously shy with too many. They probably think me standoffish."

The Meltzers have two grown children, Jane and Amy.

As a final question I asked if there is anything else he felt his readers would enjoy knowing about him. "Yes. A lot," he said, "but nothing I'll give away!"

Also by Mr. Meltzer

Time of Trial, Time of Hope: The Negro in America, 1919–1941 (co-authored with August Meir, Doubleday, 1966).

The Right to Remain Silent (Harcourt, 1972).

Hunted Like a Wolf: The Story of the Seminole War. (Farrar, Straus, 1972).

✳ ✳Jean Merrill
✳

Ronni Solbert

"If I had to single out a favorite book of mine for no reason whatsoever, perhaps it would be *The Black Sheep* (Pantheon, 1969), for a black sheep has always been a favorite character of mine," stated Jean Merrill.

"I first encountered the expression as a child and ever since have felt an instant admiration for anyone who might be called a black sheep. It seemed to me that one could not earn the general disapproval of one's group without possessing an unusual degree of conviction, courage, or creativity—or some combination of them—each of which impress me as enviable qualities.

"How many times as a child I must have heard my mother say, as perhaps all mothers say from time to time with a mixture of exasperation and pride, 'Why do you always have to be different?' But I should count my blessings. Perhaps not all mothers acknowledge pride in their children's differences. The truth is that we all want to be different, which is only to say that we are different and crave the freedom to be ourselves. I think one of the things children unconsciously seek in the books they read is the strength to discover and be themselves."

The word *different* is wholly applicable to Ms. Merrill. If you stack up the more than twenty books that she has created, you'll find just about everything—picture books, poetry, fantasies, and tales for every aged reader, young and old.

Ms. Merrill was born on January 27, 1923, in Rochester, New York. "I was the oldest of three girls. During the years I was growing up, my father was the manager of an apple and dairy farm on the shores of Lake Ontario in upstate New York. Living six miles from the nearest village and such diversions as team sports and movies, most our entertainments were self-made. My mother often read aloud to us in the evenings over bowls of popcorn and apples. My sisters and I put on plays I wrote for our aunts, uncles, and cousins who came for Sunday family dinners. But most of our lives were spent out-of-doors, inventing and building things and exploring the countryside.

"For three years I went to a one-room country school where our teacher would often join us at lunch hour playing kick-the-can or killy-I-over, forgetting to ring the schoolbell for the afternoon session. In good weather my sister, Marge, and I walked the two miles to school, and the walk home was enlivened by such projects as filling our lunchboxes with frogs from a creek we passed and trying to sell them at the farmhouses along the way. I remembered reading somewhere that frogs' legs were considered a delicacy in some parts of the world and persuaded Marge we could make a fortune on frogs' legs. Alas, no one else on the Lake Road had read about them and weren't persuaded by my recommendation.

"The physical freedom of those years in which I had the whole countryside to explore and opportunities to invent, build, daydream, and discover may have had a great deal to do with my eventual choice of writing as a congenial profession."

Ms. Merrill attended Allegheny College, where she received her B.A. degree, and Wellesley College, where she earned an M.A. degree.

"College efforts in creative writing affirmed for me the possibilities of writing as a profession. However, I was not at all certain on completing my college education, that I would be able to make a living as a writer. Fortunately the Wellesley placement office encouraged me to apply for a position as a feature editor and writer with Scholastic Magazines in New York City.

"During the several years I wrote for the various Scholastic publications, my assignments were varied from writing reviews to interviews and an occasional story and play. This experience gave me sufficient confidence as a writer to hazard the uncertainties of free-lance writing, which has been my way of life ever since, except for a year when I returned to Scholastic to edit *Literary Cavalcade* and another year when I worked as an editor on the "Bank Street Readers," one of the first series of readers to be urban-oriented."

Ms. Merrill's first book, *Henry, the Hand-Painted Mouse* (Coward, 1951), appeared shortly before she completed graduate work at the University of Madras, where she was a Fulbright Scholar studying Indian folk stories, an interest that led to her several adaptations of stories from the Far East, such as *Shan's Lucky Knife* (Scott, 1960) and *High, Wide and Handsome* (Scott, 1964).

Ms. Merrill reminisced about her first book: "Looking back on this story, I see it essentially as a celebration of the creative impulse and its potential for enlivening lives, a theme that seems to reoccur in different contexts in many of my books for children."

"Ronni (Ronni Solbert, the illustrator of this book) shared my interest in children's books," she continued. "Discovering that we had liked many of the same books as children, I suggested that we collaborate. We have since collaborated on many others. I have never ceased to delight in her great range as an illustrator. Ronni's ability to capture a variety of moods from comic to poetic to dramatic to satiric is unusual; people often find it hard to believe that the bold childlike drawing of *Red Riding* (Pantheon, 1968) or *The Elephant Who Liked to Smash Small Cars* (Pantheon, 1967) can be the work of the same illustrator who did the elegant pictures for *The Superlative Horse* (Scott, 1961) or the droll, witty drawings for *The Black Sheep*."

One of Ms. Merrill's most popular titles is *The Pushcart War* (Scott, 1964), which received the Lewis Carroll Shelf Award in 1965 as a book "worthy enough to sit on the shelf with *Alice in Wonderland*." The story was recently bought by a major Hollywood studio to be produced as a musical film.

Ms. Merrill told me about the development of this

modern classic; her story about the background of the book is as delightful as the book itself.

"*The Pushcart War,* like most of my books, derived from a feeling and an image rather than from an idea — although I suppose it impresses many readers as an ideological book, one in which the author had a message. I perhaps had, but I did not 'think up' the book to convey a message. I remember reading with astonishment a comment in a *School Library Journal* review that said:

> . . . this is a satire on almost every conceivable aspect of modern urban life: the city politician, the union, children, secret weapons, war and mechanization, and ever so much more.

And I marvelled to myself, 'Is *that* what I've done?'

"Actually the book originated in a persistent fantasy that I'd had for four or five years. The fantasy stemmed from a feeling of rage I experienced whenever I observed an enormous truck bearing down upon, or otherwise taking advantage of, some poor little Volkswagon or pedestrian. I had not always felt hostile to trucks. On the farm where I grew up, I was on intimate terms with three trucks — the milk truck, the pickup truck, and the big truck. I recall them having distinct personalities. They were all friendly trucks with friendly drivers, and any day when time dragged slowly, one could always hitch a ride on the back, top, hood, side, tailgate, or running board of one of the three.

"After I finished college, however, and had been

working in New York City for a number of years, it seemed to me that the trucks I began encountering were of a different breed from the friendly, obliging trucks of my childhood. They were bigger for one thing, often half-a-block long—and the bigger they were, the more belligerent their drivers seemed, as if the size of the trucks entitled the drivers to coerce everyone else on the streets.

"My reaction to their tyrannical behavior was to take refuge in a fantasy of suitable revenge. The one that gave me the most satisfaction was imagining myself equipped with an inconspicuous weapon, a kind of miniature blow-gun that propelled a tiny dart sufficiently lethal to penetrate a truck tire. Gargantuan as the trucks might be, I had found their Achilles wheel!

"The vision was so satisfactory that I found myself returning to it everytime I witnessed a particularly aggressive act by a truck. Walking down Fifth Avenue, I found myself mentally getting out my glorified peashooter every few blocks and taking aim. And with the hordes of people hurrying along the Avenue and the confusion of traffic in the streets, no one ever saw the eccentric, middle-aged lady, braced against a lamppost, taking aim at an offending truck. And the lady would watch with pleasure as the truck driver limped to the curb with no idea what had incapacitated him.

"This fantasy got to be a kind of obsession, occurring with increasing frequency since the provocations in

New York streets were everywhere. Walter Mitty had nothing on the lady with the peashooter. During the years I indulged in this fantasy, I must have shot down thousands of trucks.

"And then one day, as I was about to take aim, I stopped dead in my tracks to ask myself whether I was completely sane. Children, we know, enjoy such fantasies of revenge. But an adult? One sophisticated enough to distinguish between real and imaginary remedies? At this point, I heard my rational self reply to my peashooting self, 'Of course you're sane. What you feel about the trucks is what everybody feels about bullies.'

"Having made this simple observation, it occurred to me instantly that any situation that provoked such strong emotion in me, and one that I additionally identified as an emotion many people share, was probably very good material for a story. I seemed to sense the whole central idea of the book at once, —the truck as the epitome of The Aggressor, its ugly, metal grillwork bearing down on a defenseless populace like a tank. The image was so compelling that I abandoned my errand of the moment and went directly home and jotted down two or three paragraphs amplifying this idea.

"Thinking of the Big vs. the Little, I thought of the pushcarts indigenous to my part of the city. If trucks were the biggest things on wheels, the pushcarts were the smallest. Beside the massive steel forms of the trucks, the wooden pushcarts looked frail and human in scale, since a cart is about the length of a man's body and as wide as his reach.

"I then proceeded to sketch out characters who might represent the leadership of the two factions, and then just began to write, letting the story dictate its own form, which turned out to be a genre I'd never thought of attempting. It never occurred to me to write a 'funny' book, never having thought of humor as one of my gifts. I had also thought comedy one of the most difficult types of writing. The fact that book took on the character it did may have been an unconscious realization that often the best way of cutting a bully down to size is to make him look ludicrous.

"But despite the variety of satiric elements that found their way into the story—all the items that *Journal* review recorded are there, though I never consciously set out to include them—I think it should be obvious from the foregoing that the tale is essentially an elaboration of my personal David and Goliath fantasy, the original simple image from which it springs being comparable to the metaphor on which a poet can hang a whole poem.

"Curiously, from the day I started the book, I never had the peashooter fantasy again!"

In 1969 Ms. Merrill and Ms. Solbert collaborated on a collection of haiku poetry by Issa, *A Few Flies and I* (Pantheon). The volume was sparked by much of the same concern that prompted *The Pushcart War:* "Dismay at the violence and brutality so omnipresent in our world today," she noted. "If *Pushcart* tackled the problem head-on by dramatizing the misuses of power, Issa's poetry, I hoped, might affirm that there are other ways of 'being' in the world.

"I had always enjoyed haiku for its immediacy and concentrated purity. Since acquiring my farmhouse in Vermont, where I spend some part of each day in the fields or woods, I have felt even more acutely the rightness of the way the great haiku poets looked at the world. Their feeling of reverence for life and the sense of kinship with the whole natural world is illuminated in their writings.

"A friend once asked anxiously, when I had been staying one fall at my country house, four miles from the village without a car and for some six weeks without company, 'But didn't you get lonely?' And I laughed, 'Lonely? With all those creatures out there — birds, mice, chipmunks, deer, and trees and grasses — I talk to them all.' I realized this sounded eccentric, even psychotic, and perhaps it is by our civilized standards. But when I have been in the country by myself for a time, I find I do talk to crickets and frogs as easily and unselfconsciously as Issa and Basho did.

"In making a selection of haiku that I felt would be especially meaningful to young readers, I decided to introduce them to the work of Issa, as he is my personal favorite among the four great Japanese poets — Issa, Basho, Buson, Shiki — who perfected the haiku form.

"Children instinctively understand haiku; its simplicity and directness are close to a child's own immediate and unintellectualized manner of perception."

Ms. Merrill now lives full-time in Vermont. "I feel most at home in the Vermont farmhouse on a dirt road. Six months of the year I live without electricity, phone, mail delivery, or central heating in what I think of as nineteenth century grandeur. The farmhouse is surrounded by three hundred acres of woods and meadows in which I spend any time I am not working.

"During the six months of the year when mud or deep snow make the road to the farmhouse impassable, I return to the twentieth century. Until recently my winter home was in New York, but now I have a winter base in the town of Randolph, two valleys east of my summer place. I move there in late November when the chores of survival such as lighting kerosene lamps, stoking the parlor stove, and restocking the woodpile begin to consume too many hours of my working day.

"I don't feel too much attachment to possessions and consider them an unnecessary clutter in one's life. Part of me aspires to the simplicity of a Zen Buddhist's cell, a small, white room, furnished with nothing but a sleeping mat and one perfect drawing on the wall. My rambling farmhouse, however, does tend to be a cheerful clutter of treasures from children and friends and piles of books and newspapers I haven't finished reading. The sort of possessions I do feel some affection for are my snowshoes, a lightweight mountain pack, a pocketknife I take on mushroom walks, and paintings, drawings, or objects friends have made for me."

I asked Ms. Merrill where her many diverse ideas spring from. "My story ideas are more apt to come from an emotion or an image that suggests the feeling of a certain kind of experience. Sometimes the emotional tone is the first perception, and I consciously look for an image that expresses that emotion. Sometimes an image comes out of the blue; if it is funny or strong or memorable, I sense that it is expressive of a significant feeling.

"I can't ever remember saying to myself, 'I think I'll write a book about . . .'. Subject matter, plot, and characters are usually secondary considerations.

"Although I once wrote a book in two hours and only changed two words, I usually rewrite a story many times, sentence by sentence, until I feel it has been told in the fewest and most vivid words possible. I suppose, like a child who wants to do it himself, I don't want an editor revising my work, and the only way to avoid this is to be sure the manuscript is not a rough draft but as careful, exact, and right as I can make it."

She never tries ideas out on children. "If you are a skillful reader," she asserted, "or the kids you are reading to are fond of you, you could read them the Manhattan telephone book and they'd think it was great. But there's a child in *every* writer who is still very much alive and kicking. It is that child-reaction I rely on a lot."

Also by Ms. Merrill

The Tree House of Jimmy Domino (Walck, 1955).

The Travels of Marco (Knopf, 1955).

A Song for Gar (Whittlesey House, 1955).

The Very Nice Things (Harper, 1959).

Emily Emerson's Moon (Little, Brown, 1960).

Please Don't Eat My Cabin (Whitman, 1971).

∗ Emily Cheney Neville

James A. Rackwitz

In 1963 Emily Cheney Neville's first book, It's Like This, Cat* was published. It deals with the pleasures, problems, and adventures of Dave Mitchell, a fourteen-year-old, and his pet, Cat, living and growing up in the Gramercy Park neighborhood of New York City.

Soon after publication, the book received the 1964 Newbery Award. No one was more surprised than Ms. Neville. The manuscript was not the first one she had submitted to Harper & Row.

"I started writing picture book fantasies for my

---

*All titles mentioned have been published by Harper & Row.

youngest child about 1963. I didn't begin writing until the youngest was triumphantly installed in kindergarten and I had the house to myself for a few hours each day. Although none of my early efforts were accepted, Ursula Nordstrom, Harper's juvenile editor, asked me in to talk with her and urged me to continue writing. She also suggested that I try my hand at writing stories for older boys. An adult short story, "Cat and I," had just been published as a one-page piece in the *Sunday Mirror. It's Like This, Cat* grew out of this," she told me.

I asked Ms. Neville to discuss the development of *It's Like This, Cat* further. "I happened to start writing an argument between a boy and his father," she continued, "writing from the boy's viewpoint. This made me feel very free — like wearing a mask and costume — and I could just have fun and say whatever I wanted to. It's also much easier, though more limiting, to organize a book told in the first person. The book progressed with several hitches; when I seemed to run out of steam, I thought of another place for Dave to go, another character such as Mary's mother, or a new friend, Ben. At the time I signed the contract with Harper, the book ended with the chapter where Kate gets the money, but then I added on to tidy up and concluded the events with Mary and with Dave's father and Tom."

Ms. Neville is slender and blue-eyed, with light brown hair that she cuts herself. Her favorite attire are jerseys, shorts or jeans, and sneakers. "The end of this long, sharp-pointed nose of mine gets very red in winter," she said. "One day a strange child on the street looked at me and asked, 'Are you a witch?' Well, I'm not, unless by witch you mean anyone who does some peculiar things—then I am! I have no hobbies. I like to have each day filled with a combination of sedentary and active things. I'm not a good conversationalist in ordinary social occasions, but I do enjoy talking and arguing with my family and a few friends. I have found that I rather like some public speaking and teaching work; winning the Newbery got me into all that. I'm restless by nature and probably walk more than any other sport. It's so much the simplest, since no scheduling or equipment are needed. I drive the car a good deal, and I also like swimming in cold water brooks. I like all animals, though I still have a foolish fear of snakes. I also have a moderate, rather slapdash liking for cooking and sewing."

Currently Ms. Neville lives in the Adirondacks, but she maintains a sparsely furnished apartment in "an old, decaying part of St. Louis, Missouri."

"I inherited a big Victorian summer house in the Adirondacks and have made it somewhat livable in winter. I like it sometimes, though there is a constant battle over who owns whom—me or the house. Ideally I think I would like to get rid of all my possessions but actually, even furnishing an apartment from Goodwill, I've acquired a few new ones that I want to keep. I enjoy the people-ness of cities, but the sidewalks kill my feet. When this happens, it's back to the Adirondacks."

The author was born on December 28, 1919, in Manchester, Connecticut. "I was born at home!" she declared. "I was the youngest of seven; my father was one of twelve. I grew up surrounded by cousins and never played with or went to school with anyone but cousins until I was eleven. The families set up a little school on the place for their children. My father and uncles ran a silk mill. We never had a radio, therefore my constant indoor occupation was reading—anything. There were plenty of books at home, and we also went to the library. I read stories about dogs and knights-in-armor most often. My cousins and I had a fairly rich and independent outdoor life—bicycling, building, tunneling, keeping pets, and gardening. I disliked almost all food and tried to live on sugar lumps; consequently, I had many colds and many trips to the dentist. My real ambition was to be either a boy or a dog."

Her father, Howell Cheney, was a distinguished industrialist and a pioneer in the field of industrial education. One of America's finest vocational institutions, The Howell Cheney High School in Manchester, Connecticut, was named in his honor.

Ms. Neville attended Oxford School and Bryn Mawr College, where she received a Bachelor of Arts degree in 1940. After graduating, she worked in various positions on two New York daily newspapers, the *New York Daily News* and the *New York Daily Mirror*. In 1948 she married Glenn Neville, a newspaperman with the Hearst Corporation, and began to raise a family.

The couple had five children. Mr. Neville died in 1965.

Following the success of her Newbery Award title, Ms. Neville wrote several other books for pre- and adolescent readers. *Berries Goodman* (1965) relates the adjustments that must be made when a family leaves an urban environment and encounters life in the suburbs; it also presents a realistic view of anti-Semitism. *Traveler from a Small Kingdom* (1968) is a fictionalized autobiography. *Fogarty* (1969) tells of a young man who decides to become a dedicated loafer.

One of her most popular novels is *The Seventeenth Street Gang* (1966). I asked Ms. Neville to tell me about its origin. "The germ of this book came from one of those picture book stories I wrote. The Minnow, the main character in the novel was then a three-year-old, super-talented, bossy, little girl. It never was convincing in the short picture-book form, so I grew her up to ten and off she went. It is a happy book. I enjoyed writing it. *Flot* (a word used by Minnow to describe stuffy, bossy adults who talk down to children) is a word my children got from a sample tube or something, and we all used it during one Christmas vacation.

"When I was living in New York, a little boy I knew actually did fall through a manhole and was swept out into the East River; his father had to save him. We lived on a block on 17th Street, which is just as I described it. The characters are all entirely made up though."

She then described her work habits: "I start with a conversation or scene, work out from it in all directions and from both ways in time. I add characters as they seem needed. I have no real plan, certainly no outline at the start; I do have to rewrite a great deal, at least three times all the way through, and some parts need more rewriting than that. All my books start from a contemporary scene, someplace I am or know well. I never try a manuscript out on children or seldom anyone."

Concluding our interview, I asked if there was anything else she felt a child or adult reader would like to know about her. She replied: "Adult life is worrisome, but it has its moments. I dislike rules, almost all of them really, but I am forced to admit there is no way people can live with people without some of these artificial systems."

*
* Barbara Rinkoff
*

Herbert Rinkoff

*Barbara Rinkoff is a pert, out-*doorsy-looking type, a person who loves to laugh a lot. She was born in New York City and grew up in rural New Jersey. When she reached school age, her family moved back to New York, where she remained during her school years.

Ms. Rinkoff is an only child. "Recalling my early years brings back memories of tramping through woods, picking blueberries, wading in brooks, and climbing trees. I enjoyed hiking with my father to collect chestnuts to roast in our fireplace and picking grapes in the fall. I often sat on our porch and listened to my parents and their friends hotly debate politics and philosophy. I read all the time and loved all kinds of books, not only what was on the pages but the feel and smell of them as well. I looked forward to gifts of books from my mother and my aunt for birthdays, Christmas, and when I was sick in bed. I pretended a lot. I wrote stories, poetry—even made my own greeting cards. Mother was a social worker, so I was exposed from a very early age to people's problems—mental, physical, and financial. This made me aware of conditions outside my experience. I liked to put myself in other fellows' shoes to find what motivated reactions," she told me.

Ms. Rinkoff studied at New York University where she took graduate courses in social work. Having a deep commitment to urban and social problems, she was a medical caseworker for four years on New York's Lower East Side and in Harlem, working with children with behavioral problems at home and in school and with children in trouble with the law. She also served on the Curriculum Council of the Bedford-Stuyvesant School District in Brooklyn for six years.

Many of her novels for middle-grade readers stem from her social work experiences. One such title is

Member of the Gang (Crown, 1968). "Although the characters are not real persons," Ms. Rinkoff said, "they are based on children I have met through the years. Their problems and homelife are drawn from life. At the time I wrote the book, 'color' was the central problem in stories with Black characters. I wanted my readers to be so involved in the characters that they would not stop to consider their color.

"The book does not obviously deal with race relations. Yet, by absorbing the White reader in an action story about Black children, he, by being able to identify with the characters, can realize that people are people regardless of race. He can learn something about life in a slum area and realize that people living there have aspirations and desires similiar to his own. The main character, Woodie, is a boy with a problem. He just happens to be a Black boy. But Woodie could be White, Yellow or Red. His is the story of *any* boy placed in such circumstances.

"Woodie is striving for recognition, as all people do. If he cannot attain it one way, he tries another. His decision about choosing a way of life for himself is one that boys and girls of every color must face.

"I hoped the reader would identify with and have empathy for Woodie, Sonny, and the other characters and care about what happened to them. I wanted to reach the prejudiced child, involving him so that he would look upon the characters as kids like himself rather than as Blacks first. Letters from readers tell me that this has really happened."

Other books that have been somewhat influenced by Ms. Rinkoff's social work background include *Name: Johnny Pierce* (Seabury, 1969), *Headed for Trouble* (Knopf, 1970), *I Need Some Time* (Seabury, 1970), and *A Guy Can Be Wrong* (Crown, 1970). All of her books do not, however, deal with social issues. Her first book, *A Map Is a Picture* (T. Y. Crowell, 1965) is a simple introduction to map reading. It was written for her daughter, June, when she was in the second grade.

"June wanted to know more about map reading," she recalled. "I found nothing available in print for this level, so I wrote a book introducing and explaining different types of maps."

After her first book was published, Ms. Rinkoff decided to try her hand at writing fiction. Her first efforts, *The Remarkable Ramsey* (Morrow, 1965) and *The Dragon's Handbook* (Nelson, 1966), are humorous novels. As her social work background came to the fore, she turned to writing more serious fiction. Occasionally she still creates a humorous novel such as *Harry's Homemade Robot* (Crown, 1967).

Ms. Rinkoff said of her writing and work habits: "My ideas come from personal experiences. Once I have a nucleus of an idea, I decide on the point I want to make and a tentative ending, for I need to know where I'm headed. Without this framework a story can ramble like a poorly told joke whose punch line is dissipated before the teller gets to the point. Knowing where I'm going helps me to set my timing and story pace. Next comes the naming of characters. Once this is done, they come alive for me. Then the real fun begins. It's like being an actress and talking all the parts. I see the chapters as scenes to move the story to its climax. I make a general outline—a sentence or two—indicating what the high point of the chapter is to be. My characters may vary this for me; sometimes a piece of action takes longer to develop, sometimes it's more complex than I had planned, so the chapter has to be divided to avoid an anticlimax.

"I don't write each day, nor do I have special hours set aside for writing. I seem most inspired to work in the afternoons. Before I write, I mull. I can see the scene acting out in my head while doing housework or driving. When I feel the urgency to get it down on paper, I write. This is done in pencil on a legal-sized yellow pad, usually curled up on the chaise in my bedroom. I don't usually do much reworking of material, except perhaps to expand a scene or clarify a point. Writing is not traumatic for me. I love the creation of a story. I am totally involved. You could move the house from under me!

"All my work is read first by my daughter, June, now a senior in high school. My son, Richard, regularly read my manuscripts, too, before he went off to college. Both are extremely critical and do not hesitate to tell me where I went wrong. I can tell by how avidly they read a manuscript whether or not it passes the test." (The Rinkoffs' third child, Robert, is a doctoral candidate at Purdue.)

"Often I try stories out on children in our local elementary school. I have the librarian read, while I sit unobserved watching reactions. Afterwards I come forward and discuss the story—what the children liked or didn't like about it, where interest flagged, and what parts were particularly appealing."

Ms. Rinkoff enjoys children. For two years she taught creative writing to fifth and sixth graders in Mount Kisco, New York.

Her husband, Dr. Herbert Rinkoff, is a dentist. When she has time, she occasionally helps out as nurse in his office. The family lives in Mount Kisco, a suburban village near New York City. Their colonial ranch house sits at the end of a dead-end street. The area is woodsy and very quiet. Between books Ms. Rinkoff enjoys traveling to interesting areas in a trailer, talking to people who live there, and imagining their way of life. She also enjoys savoring the sound of waves dashing on beaches and collecting shells, particularly at Cape Cod. She also collects wood carvings, foreign dolls, and "I'm a rock hound too," she declared.

Also by Ms. Rinkoff

Elbert, the Mind Reader (Lothrop, 1967).

The Pretzel Hero: A Story of Old Vienna (Parents, 1970).

Tricksters and Trappers (Abelard-Schuman, 1970).

Rutherford T. Finds 21B (Putnam, 1970).

The Case of the Stolen Code Book (Crown, 1971).

The Watchers (Knopf, 1972).

* Keith Robertson

Memories of my teaching years in the Fair Lawn, New Jersey, public schools, come to me many times. One recollection is of one boy, one of those mischievous, devilish sixth-graders. No matter what I was teaching—mathematics, science, social studies—any-thing—Richard would frequently interrupt both me and the rest of the class with a tee-hee, a giggle and sometimes a guffaw!

But I always knew what Richard was tittering about. In today's lingo he would be termed a Henry Reed freak! Richard had been a poor reader until he dis-covered Henry Reed. After that he would go to the library, take out a Henry Reed book, devour it, and go back to borrow another in the series. When he finished all he could lay his hands on, he would start the first one over again. I had a class of twenty-five students, but I considered Henry Reed the twenty-sixth.

Henry Reed was created by Keith Robertson. Henry is a young, resourceful, and thoroughly candid hero of several genuinely funny novels. Beginning with *Henry Reed, Inc.* (Viking, 1958), Henry gets himself into and out of a maze of situations from book to book. All the tales are written in diary form, and all are amusingly illustrated by Robert McCloskey, twice-winner of the Caldecott Medal.

One of the first things I wanted to find out from Mr. Robertson was just how Henry was born.

"Our farm was a popular place to play when my children were small," he replied. "All their friends came here as we had animals, a stream, and woods. I used to observe so many amusing antics that I began keeping rough notes. Henry was based to a degree on a fourth-grade woman schoolteacher whom I know. For some strange reason she acted as a catalyst, and strange things always happened when she was around. In the first Henry Reed book she sort of half appears as Henry's mother. I couldn't have an adult female teacher as the central character of my books, so I created Henry.

"I didn't know Robert McCloskey before he illustrated *Henry Reed, Inc.* Now we are good friends. An author always has a picture of his characters in his mind, and frequently the artist sees the same character much differently. This was not the case with Henry. He is exactly as I would have drawn him had I McCloskey's talents. I was delighted with the illustrations from the very first."

Henry Reed, Inc. remains the author's favorite book in the series. "It was my first attempt at a humorous book, and I enjoyed writing it more than any I had ever written; particularly since many of the incidents were based on the crazy things my children and their friends had done."

Prior to creating Henry Mr. Robertson had authored

fifteen juveniles, including two popular mysteries— *Three Stuffed Owls* (Viking, 1954) and *The Crow and the Castle* (Viking, 1957). I asked Mr. Robertson why he feels mysteries are so popular with children in the middle grades. "I think children have a regrettable tendency to associate any reading with school," he replied. "Therefore, books with social messages smack of school work. Mysteries are pure escape for them as well as for adults. They know they aren't being taught anything—that a mystery is pure entertainment."

The author was born on May 9, 1914, in Dows, Iowa. "My father always saw greener pastures in the distance, and our family moved a great deal. I lived in Wisconsin, Minnesota, Oklahoma, Missouri, and Kansas during my elementary school years. We returned to Iowa by the time I entered high school; I consider Iowa my childhood home. During much of my childhood, we lived on farms in small rural communities. Our family was close-knit and happy. I have two sisters who still live in Iowa and of whom I am very fond. We were rather poor, but at the time I had no realization of that fact; it never occurred to me that we lacked anything.

"I was very fond of the out-of-doors and spent a great deal of time hiking, fishing, and camping. It was so simple for me—I could step outside the door and be in the open country."

After graduating from high school he enlisted in the navy and two years later entered the United States

Naval Academy at Annapolis. He returned to civilian life and worked as a refrigeration engineer until 1941 when he rejoined the navy and served for five years on a destroyer in both the Atlantic and Pacific. After the war he joined the John C. Winston publishing firm in Philadelphia. "Writing for children came about as an accident," he told me. "Like most struggling authors, I had the problem of having to eat. The company for whom I worked published a number of excellent children's books. I became so interested in them that I decided to write one of my own. My first book, *Ticktock and Jim* (Winston, 1948), was about a horse. It remained in print for more than twenty years."

Shortly after the book's publication he left his job to devote more time to writing.

Mr. Robertson and his wife, Elisabeth, live in Hopewell, New Jersey, on a small farm at the edge of a small village. The area is rural and hilly. The thirty acres of woods on the farm is a home for deer, raccoons, opossum, and other wild animals, many of which can be seen from the kitchen window. "We usually have a number of animals around and had even more when our children were small. At one time or another we had sheep, goats, steers, horses, dogs, cats, rabbits, ducks, geese, chickens, a pet raccoon, and a pet crow. At the moment we are down to two horses, one of which was born last year, a dog, a cat, and a parrot."

The Robertsons have three children and one grandchild. Ms. Robertson has operated a rare book business for many years, specializing in books on horticulture, landscape gardening, and wine. Until very recently she also specialized in cook books. She conducts her business almost entirely by mail from a separate building on the farm. "Since she has literally thousands of books and I have quite a few also, our place is aptly named Booknoll Farm," Mr. Robertson chuckled.

Regarding his work habits he said: "Each new book is mulled over for a considerable period of time. Then I outline it rather completely, even though this outline may be changed greatly during the writing. I make a character sketch and physical description of each character that I know will appear. When I start writing, I usually work very rapidly and steadily until the book is finished. My typing is terrible. I misspell words, make errors of grammar, and other mistakes in this first draft because I prefer to work at high speed. Then, when it is finished, I have to go over the entire manuscript word for word, making extensive changes and corrections. Sometimes my revisions on a page exceed the original typing. For some time I have been dictating my books on tape. I find this works well if I can dictate without interruptions. It is particularly good for conversation. However, one tends to be too verbose, and the first version needs to be cut considerably. Incidentally, that first draft is the most fun."

Mr. Robertson stands five-feet ten-inches, weighs one hundred-sixty-five pounds, and has dark hair and dark eyes. Leisure time is spent hiking through the woods, riding, sailing, and reading. Although he's spent seven years at sea, he still loves the ocean.

Also by Mr. Robertson

(All published by Viking)

The Year of the Jeep (1968).

The Money Machine (1969).

In Search of a Sandhill Crane (1973).

✳ ✳ ✳ Charlemae Hill Rollins

"*Is Charlemae Hill Rollins here yet?*" asked Augusta Baker, a friend of mine who works with the Children's Service Division of the New York Public Library. The place was Chicago's old-world Palmer House Hotel. A large group was assembled waiting for the chairwoman of the 1972 Newbery-Caldecott Committee, to announce the 1972 book awards. I told Ms. Baker that I had never met Ms. Rollins, although we had corresponded when her book *Black Troubador: Langston Hughes* (Rand McNally, 1970) was published.

"Well, you'll just have to meet her," said Ms. Baker. After the announcements were over and the reception was in full swing, she introduced Ms. Rollins to me.

Ms. Rollins was born on June 20, 1897, in Yazoo City, a small farm community in Mississippi. "That was a long, long time ago!" she exclaimed. She grew up in Oklahoma when it was still Indian territory. Her grandmother was a slave, "a bad one—a runaway. Grandma told wonderful stories of her life as a slave. I've always loved books because of her. She gave us all the books that belonged to her master who was the father of her children, one of whom was my father. We enjoyed the books in his library, even though most of them were medical books. But I would read anything and everything!

"We were quite poor as far as money goes, but we were very rich in family life—parents, brothers, a sister, and lots of cousins, aunts, and uncles. My father was forced to leave Mississippi and he 'fled' to the Indian Territory which is now Oklahoma. My mother was one of the first Black teachers in this Indian Territory."

Ms. Rollins' love of books as a child continued throughout her life. For over thirty years she was children's librarian at the George C. Hall branch of the Chicago Public Library. Now retired, she continues to lecture about children's books and reading.

"I got hooked on books and children while working at the library," she remarked. "I was also hooked on writers and listened to all the authors who visited the library. I attended lots of lectures on writing by many famous authors. I just had to try to do a book of my own."

This determination led her to compile *Christmas Gif'* (Follett, 1963), a handsome, delightful anthology of Christmas poems, songs, and stories by or about Black people and featuring both traditional and contemporary works.

"Of all the books I've done, this one's my favorite," she said. "It's a part of my life, my heritage, my family, my philosophy. It's me!"

In the foreword to the volume Ms. Rollins further explains:

> Over the years, in my experience as a librarian, I have been asked by teachers and parents and children for Christmas stories and poems specifically related to Negroes. I have found such material in old magazines, in collections of the work of Negro writers, but never have I found one single book about the Negro and Christmas. I felt there was a place for such a book, and that is how *Christmas Gif'* began. It is a book for people of all ages, for families to read together, for everyone to enjoy . . . .

> It is my earnest hope that this book may help every reader to appreciate the Negro's contribution to the love and reverence, the joy and brotherhood, that is the universal spirit of Christmas.

The author's books of nonfiction for middle-grade readers have the same objective. "I try to give young people a feeling of belonging—love, warmth, truth, and yes, beauty, as well as an appreciation of the Black heritage.''

She continued to give this warmth and appreciation in titles such as *They Showed the Way: Forty American Negro Leaders* (T. Y. Crowell, 1964), *Famous Negro Poets* (Dodd, Mead, 1965), and *Famous Negro Entertainers* (Dodd, Mead, 1967)—all biographical accounts depicting the part that Blacks have played in the history of the United States.

Black Troubador: Langston Hughes developed from her life-long friendship with the Black poet. During the thirties when writers were not being published because of the Depression, Ms. Rollins met Langston Hughes. ''He visited our branch library many times,'' she recalled. ''Ours was one of the branches that sponsored a W.P.A. Writers Project. Langston spoke to our various groups and read and discussed his poetry. We all fell in love with him. He visited in my home often. He enjoyed southern cooking, which is one of my hobbies.''

Ms. Rollins also enjoys being with people young and old and reading books whenever she has a spare moment, particularly children's books. She has collected perhaps one of the best home libraries of literature concerning the Black experience and is always happy to lend a volume to anyone who wants to know something about Blacks.

She and her husband, Joseph, a retired government employee, live on the sixteenth floor of a Chicago highrise apartment overlooking Lake Michigan and

"Old John"—the John Hancock Building, one of Chicago's highest skyscrapers. "At night the view of the lake and the Loop skyscrapers is like fairyland. We can't afford this apartment, but we need it," she exclaimed.

The Rollins' one son, Joseph, Jr., lives in Cambridge, Massachusetts. *Black Troubador: Langston Hughes* is dedicated to Ms. Rollins' two Josephs.

The author's work and contributions to the field of librarianship have earned her many awards and honors, including the American Brotherhood Award of the National Conference of Christians and Jews, the Library Letter Award of the American Library Association, and the 1970 Constance Lindsey Skinner Award given by the Women's National Book Association.

✻ George Selden

Bruce Nicholson

There are many reasons why I treasure my worn copy of George Selden's *The Cricket in Times Square* (Farrar, Straus). The book was published in 1960 and given to me as a gift when I began my teaching career that year in Fair Lawn, New Jersey. I read the book aloud, several chapters each day, to my sixth-grade class. Before we finished the book, all of us were completely captivated by the characters: Mario Bellini and his parents who operate an unsuccessful newsstand in New York's Time Square subway station; Chester, the liverwurst-loving cricket who had been carried there in a picnic basket from his Connecticut home; Tucker, a mouse resembling a Damon Runyan character; and warm hearted Harry, the cat. After finishing the book, the class wrote the author personal letters, and several urged him to write a sequel as probably hundreds of other readers had. We sent the letters in care of the publishing house and more or less forgot about them. Several weeks later the following letter arrived:

Dear Mr. Hopkins and Members of the Sixth Grade:

I have just spent a delightful and flattering half-hour reading all your letters, and truly I don't know how to thank you! I enjoyed every one of them, and I know I should have taken the time to answer each one individually. But I have just finished the first draft of a novel I'm writing—for adults this time—and frankly, I am so exhausted that I hope this one note to all of you will be sufficient.

Your encouragement is heartwarming! I would like very much to write a sequel to *The Cricket . . .*—along the lines you suggest—and I think some day I will, if I can ever find the time!

Several of you asked whether or not I have had any other books published. Well, I have. *The Dog That*

Could Swim Under Water (out of print)* and *The Garden Under the Sea* (out of print). Both were released by Viking Press. The first is about a dog I owned when I was a child, and the second is about a fish, a crab, a lobster, and a starfish that live together at the bottom of Long Island Sound.

Thank you all again—and thank *you* especially, Mr. Hopkins, for your compliment of calling *The Cricket* a novel! Coming, as it did, just on the day that I finished the first version of my big one, the word struck me as a good omen. Which I hope it is!

Sincerely,

George Selden

Sometime during the decade of the 1960s, Mr. Selden found time to write that sequel; *Tucker's Countryside* (Farrar, Straus) appeared in 1969 and presented further adventures of the three animal heroes. *The Cricket in Times Square* has now become a modern classic in children's literature. Besides being cited as a 1961 Newbery Honor Book, it was chosen in 1963 for the Lewis Carroll Shelf Award as a book "worthy enough to sit on the shelf with *Alice in Wonderland*." In 1972 the book was turned into an excellent dramatized recording by Miller-Brody Productions, Inc. And if that's not enough, many critics have praised the book, putting it into the same category as

---

*This has now been revised by Harper, 1966, with the title *Oscar Lobster's Fair Exchange*.

E. B. White's *Charlotte's Web* (Harper, 1952). In April 1973, *The Cricket in Times Square* was televised by ABC-TV. Although the half-hour animated version was loosely based on the book, it brought the story into the homes and hearts of many youngsters. The telecast, produced and directed by Chuck Jones, who has done Dr. Seuss's *How the Grinch Stole Christmas* and *Horton Hears a Who,* is one that will undoubtedly appear season after season on television.

The day after the production was telecast, I phoned Mr. Selden to talk with him about the show. Mr. Selden commented, "I was so glad that Chester's adventures could be seen by so many viewers. Just think how many new friends Chester, Harry, and Tucker have made!"

Like Chester Cricket, George Selden was born in Connecticut—Hartford—and grew up there. "I didn't have a particularly artistic home, but I realized early that I wanted to be a writer. Both my brother and I had plenty of exposure to music, especially opera, through my mother. And it was my father, a doctor, who read a lot. I never had any idea that one day I'd write for children. I always liked children's literature, even as an adult. A friend suggested I try my hand at it as an experiment, and the experiment got published. The book was *The Dog That Could Swim Under Water;* a book I don't like now."

Cricket was born later, inspirated late one night when Mr. Selden heard a cricket chirp in the Times Square subway station. "The idea for the story formed instantly," he recalled. "And I am grateful for that late night."

Tucker's Countryside is his personal favorite. "Although I had hundreds of requests for a sequel, I put it off until I thought I had an equally good idea. Also the conservation theme is dear to me. I used my own childhood home and the meadow across the street as the book's setting. I think some of the passages in it are the best writing I've done for children."

"My stories have to first please me. I strongly believe in an outline. I usually work in the afternoon. When I start something, I work everyday on it. I search for new ideas, am gratified when I find one, am nervous at the thought of putting even one down in words, and feel happiness when I think I've succeeded."

Mr. Selden lives in New York's Greenwich Village. His apartment is small. "The furniture is too big for the size, but I like it. My favorite possession is a needlepoint a girl made me of one of the banners from J. R. R. Tolkien's fantasy, "The Lord of the Rings." As for pleasures in life there is music, particularly opera, and reading. And of course, people. Archeology is a hobby of mine."

Also by Mr. Selden

Oscar Lobster's Fair Exchange (Harper, 1966).

The Dunkard (Harper, 1968).

The Genie of Sutton Place (Farrar, Straus, 1973).

* *Louisa Shotwell
* *

Pach Bros.

The Grady family was packing up. "Beans all run out, said (Roosevelt's) father. "Nothing more to pick here. We'll pull out early in the morning. Head north."

Roosevelt's heart dropped. Here it was happening all over again. Not ever, probably, could he get to stay put in one school long enough so he'd really belong.

Thus ends the first chapter of Louisa Shotwell's *Roosevelt Grady* (World, 1963), a story about migrant workers.

Although Ms. Shotwell's family weren't migrant workers, they too moved around a lot during her childhood years. "The first eight years of my life, my father, mother, and I moved around almost as much as families do today whose employers keep transferring the fathers. I was born in Chicago and lived there my first two years; then three years were spent in Des Moines, Iowa, where we had a house with a garden and I had pets galore—a cocker spaniel, a rabbit, a burro, a goat, and a goldfinch from Ireland. Then we went back to Chicago for two years. I was six and seven then and went to private school. We lived in an apartment, and I could have no pets there. Then there was a brief year in Philadelphia, where I was very lonesome. We always spent our summers in the Finger Lake district of central New York in a village called Skaneateles, my father's boyhood home. When I was nine, we moved there for good, and I loved it. I was an only child, and in Skaneateles there were plenty of children to play with. I still spend summers there," she told me.

For the past twenty-five years, she has stayed in one place. Her apartment is located in Brooklyn Heights, a section of Brooklyn, New York, near the East River just across from lower Manhattan. Her windows look out on wharves and freighters, barges, tugs, and all sorts of river traffic. Governor's Island, the Statue of Liberty, and the Manhattan skyline are also dramatically in view. "I feel very much at home here. I love living in two places—city in winter, country in summer—and I enjoy the many different people of all ages, backgrounds, and interests," she declared.

After preparing her book *The Harvesters: Story of the Migrant People* (Doubleday, 1961; a nonfiction adult book), her agent prodded her to write a book for children.

"I wasn't a bit sure I could write so that any child would turn the page. My agent said, 'You've taught school, haven't you?'

" 'Of course,' I answered, 'but that doesn't prove I can write for children. Besides my teaching was in high school and college. But, well . . . all right, I'll try.'

"But, I thought to myself, if I'm going to write a story for children, it has to take place in a setting I'm familiar with. I had spent a number of years traveling around the country visiting migrant labor camps, talking with families, interviewing crew leaders, growers, and residents in communities where migrants came to work, and I'd written a good many articles besides *The Harvesters.* So I thought it had better be about a migrant child, probably a Mexican-American child if the story takes place in the Midwest or Far West, or a Black child if the story is to be located on the Eastern Seaboard where most of the migrant stream is made up of Black workers. In *The Harvesters* I had written some fictitious sketches of migrant families from different ethnic groups, and one of the Black children in the sketches was Roosevelt Grady. It was hardly more than a name but enough to set me going."

Thus, *Roosevelt Grady,* her first book for children, was born. One year after its publication, the book received the Lewis Carroll Shelf award as a book "worthy enough to sit on the shelf with *Alice in Wonderland."* The novel has also been translated into German, Danish, and English. Ms. Shotwell is not very happy about the English-English translation. "It is so very grammatical that some of the flavor disappears," she asserted. "They changed so many words—like *diapers* to *nappies.* Can you just imagine a woman like Ms. Clay hanging her *nappies* on the clothesline? Oh, no!"

Although Roosevelt Grady and his family are Black, the text never indicates color. The fact is revealed through the illustrations by Peter Burchard.

Many readers think Ms. Shotwell is Black. "The nicest compliment I ever received came to me one day when I met with a group of school librarians in Brooklyn. One of them, whose school is predominantly Black, told me this anecdote. Several of her nine-and ten-year-olds had been reading *Roosevelt Grady*. She told them she would be hearing me speak the next day and asked if they had any questions they'd like her to put to me. One boy asked, 'Is she White or Black? The librarian replied that she had never met me but had a recollection that someone had told her I was White. 'Well, if she's White,' said the boy, 'ask her how come she knows how to write so good about Black children.' "

Ms. Shotwell is wrapped up in her writing career. She knows her characters well long before they become words on a printed page. "No matter where I am, even in between books, I get lonesome for my characters. I can hardly explain this, but all the time I'm working on a story, the characters become more and more real to me, and sometimes I can hear them talking. This sounds peculiar, I know, but it's true. It's then I know it's time I get them down on paper.

"Ideas for my stories come from observation, experience, and memory. I'm a slow worker, and my working habits are deplorable. I seem to depend on my characters to take off and carry the story. They develop gradually, and I'm never completely sure where they are going.

"I have some children friends, both in the city and in the country, with whom I occasionally talk over ideas. But so far I have never read them any part of a book in advance."

Two other books by the author include *Adam Book-*

out (Viking, 1967), a perceptive story about a young boy who runs away after his parents' death, leaving his midwestern town where he lived with two aunts to stay in Brooklyn with an aunt and uncle, and *Magdalena* (Viking, 1971), a novel about a Puerto Rican girl in Brooklyn.

At the time I spoke with Ms. Shotwell she was preparing for a six-week trip on a freighter heading for the Mediterranean. "I'm very independent," she said, "and I'm a private sort of person. I don't especially like to talk about myself, though I'm an inveterate question-asker of other people. I dearly love to know about them—where they came from, their families—everything!"

＊ Isaac Bashevis Singer

Patt Meara

"*I was born in Radzymin, Poland, on July 14, 1904, and grew up in Warsaw. My father was an orthodox rabbi; my mother was the daughter of the Rabbi of Bilgoray. I studied in Chada, a religious school, and only studied one subject, religion,*" stated Isaac Bashevis Singer, (B∂-shā-vis).

His family included a younger brother, Mosha, and an older brother and sister, Israel Joshua and Hinde Esther.

It would seem pretentious to write further of Mr. Singer's childhood years. One can read about it in the author's own words in *A Day of Pleasure: Stories of a Boy Growing Up in Warsaw* (Farrar, Straus, 1969), a book that won the 1970 National Book Award for Children's Literature. In this volume he describes his early days in Poland from 1908–1918, depicting a bygone era of the hardships and wonderments experienced by a curious boy. *A Day of Pleasure* is truly a book for many age levels; it can be read and appreciated by upper-grade students as well as adult audiences.

Although he was a student at the Rabbinical Seminary in Warsaw, he chose not to become a rabbi. "Thank God, I did not finish," he declared. "I do not deserve to be a rabbi. In our Orthodox household every second word was 'forbidden.' In my later years, I'm practicing many of the things that were forbidden!"

Instead he went to work as a journalist for the Yiddish press in Poland after completion of his studies. In 1935 Mr. Singer came to the United States and since that time, has worked as a journalist and book reviewer for New York's *Jewish Daily Forward*.

"In 1935, when I came here, I got a job on the *Forward*. I said to my editor, 'What I want is a steady job.' He replied, 'A steady job? In a language that will die in ten years?' Yet, you see, Yiddish is still with us."

And indeed it is. Writers such as Sholom Aleichem,

Sholom Asch, and I. L. Peretz have done much to make the culture, customs, and idiomatic language of the Jewish people familiar the world over. Mr. Singer has done for children's literature what these writers have done for adult audiences. Of course, he, too, is well-known for close to a dozen adult titles including *In My Father's Court* (Farrar, Straus, 1966) and the recent *Enemies: A Love Story* (Farrar, Straus, 1972).

Although he originally wrote in Hebrew, he long ago adopted Yiddish as his medium of expression; he personally supervises the translation of his works into the English language.

His first book for children was *Zlateh the Goat and Other Stories* (Harper, 1966). I asked Mr. Singer why he turned to writing for children. "Because I felt I could do it," he answered. "I still believe there is no basic difference in writing for grown-ups or for children."

Zlateh the Goat is a collection of seven tales set in Chelm, a village of fools where the seven elders are the most foolish of all the inhabitants. The book's illustrations, done by the Caldecott Award-winning artist Maurice Sendak, beautifully capture the bittersweetness of Jewish folklore and perfectly depict what Mr. Singer's text is all about. In 1967 *Zlateh the Goat* was designated a Newbery Honor Book.

The same year *The Fearsome Inn* (Scribner, 1967) and *Mazel and Shlimazel or the Milk of a Lioness*

(Farrar, Straus, 1967), a handsome picture book illustrated by Margot Zemach, were published. This tale was inspired by his memory of a story his mother told when he was a boy. *The Fearsome Inn,* illustrated by twice-Caldecott Award–winning artist Nonny Hogrogian, was cited as a 1968 Newbery Honor Book. The tale is about three beautiful girls imprisoned in a remote inn as servants to a witch, Doboshova, and Lepitut, who was half-man, half-devil. How the girls outwit these demons is the basis of the story.

His fourth book for children, *When Shlemiel Went to Warsaw* (Farrar, Straus, 1968), also illustrated by Margot Zemach, was a 1969 Newbery Honor Book. Mr. Singer relates eight stories, some inspired by traditional Jewish tales, ranging from hilarious trickery in "Shrewd Todie and Lyzer the Miser" to the tender "Menaseh's Dreams."

As mentioned earlier, in 1970 the author received the National Book Award for his unforgettable *A Day of Pleasure.* The stories in this volume actually took place during the first fourteen years of his life. The last story, "Shosha," deals with a later time. The volume is illustrated with dramatic black and white photographs.

In a brief forward to the text, the author wrote: "I have a good deal more to tell about myself, my family, and the Poland of days gone by. I hope to continue these memoirs and reveal a world that is little known to you, but which is rich in comedy and tragedy, rich in its individuality, wisdom, foolishness, wildness, and goodness."

In 1972 his *The Wicked City* (Farrar, Straus) appeared. This is a retelling of the Biblical story about Abraham's wicked nephew Lot, Lot's wife and daughters, of the bargain Abraham tried to make with the Lord, and of "the raging fire that descended from the sky." This handsome volume is illustrated with red scratchboard drawings by Leonard Everett Fisher.

In preparing his books, Mr. Singer told me, "I write the stories, translate them, and edit them together with another translator. If they are bad, the critics let me know."

The author is not worried about the Yiddish language slowly disappearing. "I should worry? I put all my capital, you might say, in Yiddish. But I'm not at all worried. Declining it is. But you know that in our history there is a long way between declining and dying. Resurrection with us is not a miracle but a habit!"

In addition to his writing, he does a great deal of lecturing. "I also steal chickens," he jested. He lives with his wife in an apartment house on New York's Upper West Side. His favorite possessions are his books. In his spare time he enjoys "working and walking and visits with his son and three grandchildren." His son lives on an Israeli kibbutz.

Mr. Singer has only been on the children's literary scene for a short time, but his works have earned him much praise. In the *Horn Book* the late Ruth Hill

Viguers called Mr. Singer "one of the great creative writers of our time." The dust jacket for *Mazel and Shlimazel* . . . cites additional kudos. Consider the following tributes:

> He was born in 1904, but thousands of years of Jewish history are embodied in him, thousands of ghosts. — *Alfred Kazan*

> He is a Yiddish Hawthorne . . . It becomes obvious that Singer is more than a writer; he is a literature. — *Stanley Edgar Hyman*

> Above and beyond everything else he is a great performer, in ways that remind one of Twain, Dickens, Sholem Aleichem. — *Irving Howe*

But of all that has been said of Isaac Bashevis Singer, the *Chicago Tribune* possibly sums up his work best with the statement:

> (His) tales are no more for Jewish children than Andersen's fairy tales are for Danish children. They have the sweep, the direct voice-to-ear simplicity, the easy familiarity which make all folk literature universal.

Also by Mr. Singer

Magician of Lublin (Farrar, Straus, 1960).

Elijah, the Slave (Farrar, Straus, 1970).

Joseph and Koza (Farrar, Straus, 1970).

Alone in the Wild Forest (Farrar, Straus, 1971).

The Topsy Turvey Emperor of China (Harper, 1971).

Zilpha Keatley Snyder

"I was eight years old when I decided I was a writer, and in spite of many detours, I never entirely gave up the idea. I came back to writing after one such detour that included growing up, marriage, motherhood, and teaching. I almost automatically began to write for the children I'd been teaching in the upper elementary grades," Zilpha Keatley Snyder said to me.

For nine years Ms. Snyder taught in public schools in California, New York, Washington, and Alaska.

She was born on May 11, 1927, in Lemoore, California, but shortly thereafter her family moved to Ventura County where she grew up.

"I was the middle child in a family of three girls. We lived in the country during the Depression and World War II. Due to shortages of such things as gasoline and money, I didn't get around much or do many exciting things. In fact, my world might have been quite narrow and uninteresting if it had not been for two magical ingredients—animals and books. We always had a lot of both. There was a library nearby, which to me was an inexhaustible storehouse of adventure and excitement.

"I think I read almost a book a day during my childhood and loved every minute of it, so you can imagine that as soon as it occurred to me that books were written by ordinary human beings, I decided that was the kind of human being I'd like most to be."

She attended Whittier College in Whittier, California, where she met her husband, Larry, then a music student. After graduating she became a teacher, while Mr. Snyder continued his studies. Several years later she traveled around the country with her husband when he was serving in the United States Air Force. It was while the Snyders were in Alaska that their first child, Susan, was born; eventually they returned to California where their son Douglas was born. They have one other son, Ben. Between children, Ms. Snyder continued to teach. While Mr. Snyder attended the University of California at Berkeley, Ms. Snyder became a master teacher there, training student teachers and conducting demonstration lessons for educational classes.

When she began to write, she gave up her teaching career. Her first book, *Season of the Ponies,* was published in 1964.* Ms. Snyder's own comments on this book and her many succeeding novels are quite interesting:

"*Seasons of the Ponies* was based on a scene from a vivid dream I once had, and it combined two of my favorite childhood enthusiasms—horses and magic."

The Velvet Room (1965) came next. The story de-

---

*All titles mentioned have been published by Atheneum.

velops around Robin, a twelve-year-old girl in a large family of migrant workers. Robin, a dreamy, imaginative child finds a haven in the Velvet Room, the library of a deserted house. "I chose a setting of mystery and adventure" the author explained, "because children love it so. More than any of my other books, *The Velvet Room* was written for the child I once was. It is set in the time and place of my own childhood, and many readers who know this, are sure that it is autobiographical. Although it is full of old ghosts and memories, it is not at all a true story. Actually, many of the characters are lifted from an adult novel, unpublished, needless to say, that I wrote at the age of nineteen."

Black and Blue Magic (1966), a humorous fantasy with a modern setting was written for her son, Doug, because he "requested a funny story about a boy instead of more sad stories about girls."

The Egypt Game (1967) followed and was cited as a 1968 Newbery Honor Book. All six of the main characters are composites of boys and girls whom she taught at the Washington School in Berkeley, California. "My teaching experience was invaluable to me as a writer. I not only met many wonderful students whose ideas, attitudes or entire personalities have been inspirational to me; they also taught me to speak the language. Washington School was a well-integrated school in a well-integrated neighborhood. I always considered reading aloud to the class an important part of the school day, and there was a certain kind of book that I was never able to find. There were good books available that were about minority group children, but all I could find, for my grade level at least, dealt with racial problems—poverty, discrimination, and slavery. I began to look for a book that would encourage close and proud identification with a character who was of their own race and who would have exciting and wonderful adventures and face demanding problems. But the adventures and problems had to have as little as possible to do with race. I only wanted to give my minority children a happy and uncomplicated experience with a good book. And so, four years later, when I began to write *The Egypt Game,* I very soon knew for whom I was writing and for what purpose. Of course, I hope the story will have things to say to children of all races and in classrooms of all kinds. If it does, it will be because the children in *The Egypt Game* are *real* children, and their relationships are real in schools like Washington—and could be in other places. Someday there will be more integrated schools where the problems of childhood can be the problems of childhood and have nothing to do with race."

A haunted department store is the setting for *Eyes in the Fishbowl* (1968). "This story was the result of meeting a shoeshine boy in a very fancy department store and was also based on memories of my own reaction to seeing a big city department store for the first time."

In 1972 the American Library Association cited Ms. Snyder's *The Headless Cupid* (1971) as a Newbery

Honor Book. The story tells of a large family who have just moved to an old house in the country. The Snyders recently moved to an old farmhouse in Sonoma County in California, that was built in 1877 and is mysteriously similar to the one in the book. "The book, however, was finished before we found the house," insisted Ms. Snyder.

The following year *The Witches of Worm* (1972) was selected as a 1973 Newbery Honor Book. Its plot revolves around an ugly kitten named Worm who Jessica suspects is bewitched.

It is obvious that the author's story ideas develop from just about anything and everything: "Dreams, chance meetings, brief experiences, haunting memories, nagging curiosities, or even a fascinating place can suggest a good story setting. I rework my stories a great deal, dialogue the least, expository and descriptive passages more, and a first page perhaps as many as twenty times. My own children have been patient and indispensable guinea pigs as well as sources for ideas and inspirations. But all three are in high school now, and their present ages seem to make them function best as critics."

Her newest book is always her favorite. "It's like a new toy—because it isn't until later that you begin to see all the little faults and failures. However, I do have some special feelings about some of my books that don't change with time and the cooling off of creative fires. *The Velvet Room* is one of those."

She likes old things—a pair of antique candle-

sticks and an old clock are among her favorite possessions as well as items her readers have given her,
particularly pictures and models of scenes and characters from her books and many little souvenirs, including a blue rabbit's foot for good luck as a writer.

Ms. Snyder is also superstitious: "A long time ago I
accepted the fact that I'm probably incurably superstitious, gullible, and generally unsophisticated. I've
also known for some time that it's not too wise to
admit that I still believe in fairy godmothers and some
kinds of ghosts and all kinds of magical omens. I used
to keep it a secret, but I don't think I will anymore."

Also by Ms. Snyder
Today is Saturday (Atheneum, 1969).

✳ ✳ Virginia Sorensen
✳ ✳

Virginia Sorensen told me lots
of beautiful things about herself. "I was born in Provo,
Utah, the third in a family of
six children. When I was five,
my family moved to Manti, a
churchy little town settled by
Scandinavian Mormons. I'm
sure my brother is right when

he says we all felt obliged to be especially good and bright because our parents weren't active church people. But my mother wisely saw that we were baptized at the proper ages, so that we would really belong to the community. I have described my happy childhood in my book of adult stories, *Where Nothing Is Long Ago* (1963).* Out in Utah I was close to history as well as to nature and was familiar with Indians and animals and mountains, so all of these came into my early adult novels.

"My own two children were grown up before I became interested in extension library work and wrote my first book for children, *Curious Missie* (1953), about a small girl hungry for books in rural Alabama. After that I seemed to find children's stories wherever I lived. One was set in Utah, two in Pennsylvania, one in Denmark, and one in Alexandria, Virginia. The next seems to be emerging from my present home in Morocco.

"I don't seem to have any favorites among my books any more than I do among my children and grandchildren. But *Plain Girl* (1955) and *Miracles on Maple Hill* (1956) have been most successful, so I am grateful to them for many special blessings."

Plain Girl is the story of Esther, a young Amish girl and her growing understanding of her people, religion, and the conflicting values of her home and

---

*All titles mentioned have been published by Harcourt Brace Jovanovich.

school life. *Miracles on Maple Hill* earned the author the 1957 Newbery Medal. The novel tells of one year in the life of ten-year-old Marly and her family.

"The story behind the book is told in my Newbery acceptance speech, and I've told it to children a thousand times in great detail. So suffice it to say that I had lived in Alabama for several years and when I moved to Pennsylvania, I was charmed by the seasons, especially spring and the first manifestation of it there —the rising of the sap in the trees in February. That delight and Pennsylvania Dutch friends on a maple farm started the book going. The idea of rejuvenation happened later and made the eventual thread on which everything hangs," explained Ms. Sorensen. which everything hangs," explained Ms. Sorenson.

The changing seasons at Maple Hill are beautifully described in poetic prose. Here, for example, is Marly's first impression of a country morning:

> When Marly woke up the next morning, there was another miracle right outside her window. The sun was coming up, and it was clear and frosty out. And there were ten million little crystals shining on every single branch of every single tree, down to the littlest twig. The tree right next to the window was a wilderness of shining threads, as if every branch, every twig, was spun from ice. Among the threads hopped the cold little black figures of birds. Marly felt as if she could never in the world look at it long enough. (page 50).

The novel tells of the family moving to Maple Hill

after Marly's father returns from a war prison broken in health and spirit. They move to Maple Hill hoping for a cure for him.

I asked Ms. Sorensen if winning the Newbery Award had changed her life in any way. "Afterward one is more prosperous and independent, of course," she answered, "but the demands grow—the speaking and so on. I found writing the next book very difficult; it took me years. Mostly it was a matter of not being able to satisfy myself. But this feeling comes to most writers as they grow older, I'm sure. They all tell me writing becomes harder and harder."

Besides books for children, Ms. Sorensen has written adult novels and short stories that have appeared in *New Yorker, Story, Arizona Quarterly,* and *Rocky Mountain Quarterly.* "I am trying to get back into adult writing again after a long dry spell. I am working on a novel, one which I expect to work on for several years. I am also working on a book about Morocco for children which, I hope, will introduce the country to them intimately, historically, literarily, musically, every way, for it is a country I have come to love.

"As I like to tell children, a story is a bouquet of things—places, people, ideas, plot—and no matter which you start with, all the rest must come in and make it a whole indivisable work. The past few years I have had groups of children 'help' me with stories. I tell them the idea, the beginning of the story, and the main character, then they start to embroider. This is especially effective when a lot of children are sitting around in a school library. They send me a lot of writing afterward. In Tangier, at the American School where I now have my studio, I have a marvelous variety of children to work with, children of American diplomats, Moroccans, Italians, French, Spanish, and from deep in West Africa."

Ms. Sorensen travels extensively. In 1969 she married Alec Waugh, the English novelist. This was her second marriage. "Alec is one of the world's greatest travelers; his work has taken us all over the world. But I'm rather glad all this waited until I could enjoy it in full leisure and maturity. We live, when we are at home in Tangier, in an apartment that is the top floor of an immense French house. We have long balconies lined with flowers and a Moroccan room we fixed up for entertaining, which has turned out to be our favorite room even when we are alone. We have used Moroccan wool rugs and draperies everywhere — and my old Danish furniture seems made to go with them. My three loves, Denmark, Morocco, and the United States, seem somehow brought together in this new home, with, of course, a lot of English touches. We live a very modern life traveling in every direction from this central base on the Straits of Gibraltar. Tangier is on the Mediterranean but ten minutes over a mountain is the Atlantic Ocean. The Moroccan beaches end, as they say, in South Africa. The climate is semi-tropical and never hot; sometimes it's a bit too breezy. This was Alec's choice out of the whole world because, being writers, we could literally have lived anywhere. We belong to the American group in Tangier as well as the British, of course, so we have a busy social life; we go on the ferry to Gibraltar every time we need a good dose of the English language. We were married on the Rock four years ago. Alec has a study in our apartment, and I go almost every day to my studio in the American School. We both belong to P. E. N. (an international organization of poets and writers) and take pleasure in its annual conferences, which were lately in the Ivory Coast and Dublin and next in Istanbul."

I asked the author how life was in a home with two writers. She replied: "I think it's splendid for a couple to have two separate careers and pursue them; it makes for exciting arrivals and departures as well as filling the days. We both write mornings and meet for lunch, usually at the Tangier Yacht Club, a charming place on the shore where we like to bring our friends. I think the main thing is to respect each other's works and moods. If I'm in the middle of a scene, I simply send a message that I'm busy and Alec understands. And, of course, the same is true the other way around. Leaving a companion free is the main thing about any marriage, don't you think?"

Occasionally Ms. Sorensen does "a stint of teaching." Recently she taught creative writing at Central State University in Oklahoma. She also visits schools of all types wherever she goes. "Children always want to know where I've lived, so I make them look at maps and give them a long list, mostly, of course, in the United States. They want to know how much I earn, so I tell them about royalties and give them problems in arithmetic."

The only occupation she indulges in other than writing is doing things of "a housewifery nature."

"People seem surprised that I'm proud of my real age, which was sixty-one last February 17th (1973). It pleases me to have survived feeling better than I ever have before. I still ride my bicycle every chance I get, though I sometimes think I'm the only adult female in Morocco to be seen on one. I ride horseback a lot with my daughter Elizabeth and her three children in Tampa, Florida, and with my son Frederick in Alexandria, Virginia, but it's not unusual in the States, of course. None of my family goes gray, it seems, so I'm still dark-haired, and I wear my hair long so I can take care of it myself wherever I go.

"My son Frederick is my favorite poet and, next to Alec, my favorite traveling companion. He cycles and Alec doesn't, so you can see it's a different sort of traveling with him. Alec is a city man, and I grew up a country girl. It's a long way from Mormon Utah to life with a wine specialist in Tangier, Morocco!"

But can't you tell she loves it all?

Also by Ms. Sorensen

Lotte's Locket (Harcourt, 1964).

Around the Corner (Harcourt, 1971).

* * Elizabeth George Speare *

Elizabeth George Speare is one of the few people ever to receive the coveted John Newbery Medal twice. In 1959 she was awarded the Medal for The Witch of Blackbird Pond (1958) and again in 1962 for The Bronze Bow (1961).* The author was born in Melrose, Massachusetts, on November 21, 1908, and has lived her entire life in New England. "Though I love to travel, I can't imagine ever calling any other place on earth home. It is easy for me to feel right at home in colonial times, because in some ways the countryside and New Englanders themselves have not changed very much in three hundred years."

Although her immediate family was a small one consisting of her parents and one brother, she grew up surrounded by a large clan of aunts, uncles, and cousins. Some of her best memories are of family reunions — big Christmas dinners and summer picnics. "Whenever one branch of our family met, a favorite cousin just my own age and I, with barely a greeting to anyone else, used to rush into a corner clutching fat brown notebooks and breathlessly read out loud to each

*All titles mentioned have been published by Houghton Mifflin.

other the latest stories we had written. One summer day an aged uncle invaded our corner. To our dismay he asked permission to listen. He sat for some time very gravely and then got up and walked away shaking his head in bewilderment. But nothing ever discouraged us. Years later when we were in college, we still never visited each other without tucking into our suitcases, along with a new formal dress and the daring new lipstick, a few dog-eared manuscripts.

"Since I can't remember a time when I didn't intend to write, it is hard to explain why I took so long getting around to it in earnest. But the years seemed to go by very quickly. After I graduated from Boston University, I divided my time between teaching in a small private school in Boston and studying in graduate school, running three blocks back and forth between classes. At the end of two years I had acquired a master's degree and the illusion that I could teach. Then, still shy and naive, in the midst of the Depression, I ventured into a high school and offered my Shakespeare and Browning to a volcanic classroom crowded to bursting with boys who were only biding their time till the closed factories would reopen. I don't suppose any of them has ever remembered a word of what I tried to teach them, but I have never forgotten what they taught me. Surprisingly, in that first toughening year, I discovered that I really liked teaching."

In 1936 she married Alden Speare, an industrial engineer, and settled in Connecticut. Two children came along, and life was busy with the usual chores of rearing a family and keeping a house. Not until both children were in junior high school did Ms. Speare find time to begin writing. Her first success came with an article she wrote about skiing with children. "My husband was, and still is, an ardent skier, and by the time the children were five, they were schussing down the most terrifying hills with mother snowplowing behind!"

Other articles followed, and she occasionally "took a short flight into a story or a one-act play." Her first book for children, *Calico Captive,* was published in 1957. Based on real people and events, it tells of young Miriam Willard, who, with her sister, brother-in-law, their three children, and a neighbor, were captured by Indians and taken to Montreal to be sold as slaves. Ms. Speare recalled the development of this book: "One day I stumbled on a true story from New England history with a character who seemed to me an ideal heroine for a book. For a long time this girl haunted my imagination, and finally I began to write down her adventures, filling in the outlines of the actual events with new characters and scenes of my own creation. It was like living a double life, stepping every day from my busy world into another time and place and into a family that came to seem as familiar as my own. In the evenings, as breathlessly as I had once read those brown notebooks, I read the latest chapters to my patient daughter, Mary. Her encouragement kept me writing, and her fresh comments kept me

strictly down to earth. When *Calico Captive* finally
was published, it was dedicated to her."

Her second novel, *The Witch of Blackbird Pond,*
was set in Wethersfield, Connecticut, a town in which
she had lived for twenty years. "I was fascinated by
the 'meadows' in Wethersfield," she told me, "and
began to imagine there an old woman who lived
alone and was suspected of being a witch; then a
young girl who was lonely and unhappy. I happened
upon an account of the children who used to be sent
from Barbados, an island in the West Indies, to be
educated in Boston and wondered what would happen
if a girl from that sunny and luxurious island had come,
not to Boston, but to the small Puritan town of
Wethersfield in 1685, with its narrow, hard life domi-
nated by the meeting house. That imaginary girl became Kit Taylor in the novel. I suddenly saw a reason
why this girl might be unhappy in this bleak Puritan
atmosphere. Finally the other characters gathered
around these two and began to play out the story.
Mercy was my imaginary picture of an invalid aunt I
never knew but learned about from my mother."

For *The Bronze Bow,* her third novel, she went far
afield from her New England setting. *"The Bronze Bow*
was a deliberate attempt to bring Bible times alive for
a group of seventh grade Sunday school pupils whom
I was teaching. For all of us the life and people of
ancient Palestine which we were studying seemed very
dim and far away. Actually the first century A.D. was
an exciting, colorful, and violent age. To make the

period come alive, I began to imagine a group of young people who grew up learning to hate their Roman conquerors, who longed for freedom for their country, and who heard and came to know the great teacher of Galilee. I began the book with a heroine but soon realized that life for a girl in those days was far too sheltered and that if I wanted an adventurous tale, I must deal with a hero. One of my imaginary young people suddenly took the story into his own hands and became Daniel, the book's hero.

"Research for this book took nearly two years. I could not visit the Holy Land, but I read histories and travel books till I could almost see it for myself. Years later when I did go to Israel, I was overjoyed to find that the hills I had envisioned were really there and that the Sea of Galilee looked much as I had imagined it."

I asked Ms. Speare if she had a personal favorite among the three books. "This is impossible to answer," she responded, "for all books that one has written come to seem more and more unreal as the years go by, and it is always a surprise to open one and read a page. Perhaps I had more real fun writing *The Witch of Blackbird Pond* than I did with the others."

She then commented on her work habits: "My stories always begin with a person or a group of people who suddenly take on life and become very real to me. Then the long research begins for background, history, and the like. Gathering the material for a book takes me a year or more. While I am taking pages of notes in libraries and museums, the story slowly grows in my mind. When I finally begin to write, I know in general what my characters are to do and how their story will end, though many surprising changes always occur on the way. I work very slowly, doing only a few pages a day and trying to make each sentence say exactly what I mean. Sometimes I reach a blind spot, a sort of gulf, and for weeks I cannot see how I can possibly get my characters across to the other side where I want them to be. But sooner or later, almost by magic, a bridge appears. Some bit of history, some ancient custom, or perhaps just the sort of person one character has turned out to be suggests a way, and presently we are all safely across.

"Every book has been completely written at least three times, which does not count, of course, the daily reworking of pages. Except for the first book, I have never tried out the ideas on anyone."

Mr. and Ms. Speare live in the Connecticut countryside. Their house is surrounded by woodlands with a small pond where wild ducks come to feed. Both are ardent birdwatchers. Their children are both grown. Alden, Jr. is a professor of sociology at Brown University; Mary is married to a doctor and lives in California. The Speares have three grandchildren.

"Our favorite possession is our golden retriever, Daniel, named for the hero of *The Bronze Bow*. Like us, he is growing old," said Ms. Speare.

* Dorothy Sterling

Books by Dorothy Sterling fall mainly into two categories — those dealing with science, particularly the biological sciences, and those that explore little known aspects of Black history.

Her first books for children were sparked by her own children's interests. *"Sophie and Her Puppies* (Doubleday, 1951) came about because Sophie was our dog and the puppies were born on my daughter Anne's bed," she told me. "The book was really a disguised sex education, how-puppies-grow book. It was illustrated with photographs by Myron Ehrenberg, a close friend.

"Because of my son Peter's interest and fascination with caterpillars, I, too, became intrigued with them. But I couldn't find even an adult book that would identify the creatures he brought home or even tell us about their life-cycle, so I wrote *Caterpillars* (Doubleday, 1961). Similarly, after summers on Cape Cod hunting for books to answer our questions about the sea and shore animals and plants, I wrote *The Outer Lands* (Natural History Press, 1967)."

As Ms. Sterling's children grew older and their interests widened, she continued to write books relating to their experiences. The children's involvement in scout troops provided her with backgrounds for her first two mysteries—*The Cub Scout Mystery* (Doubleday, 1952) and *The Brownie Scout Mystery* (Doubleday, 1956).

Ms. Sterling explained how her own life experiences led her to write books about Black life and history: "I started writing books on Black history and the Black experience quite by accident. I was looking for a dramatic subject for a book for girls. I knew even then, before the women's liberation movement, that I didn't want to do a book about a nurse or somebody's wife like Abigail Adams or Eleanor Roosevelt. I wanted to write about a woman who had made it on her own.

"Someone suggested Harriet Tubman. I found Earl Conrad's biography of her (*Harriet Tubman: Soldier and Abolitionist,* International Publishing Company, 1942) and was hooked. Not only was she a marvelous subject for a book for young people, but the research I did on her life gave me a whole new perspective on American history. First of all, I felt cheated. I had gone to two of the best women's colleges in the country and had never *heard* of Harriet Tubman—of Frederick Douglass, Sojourner Truth, Robert Smalls, or their contemporaries. The more I read, the more concerned I became. Here was a whole segment of our past that had been kept from me. It was also being kept from my children and everyone else's children as well."

Freedom Train: The Story of Harriet Tubman (Doubleday) was published in 1954. The following year the author went to South Carolina to work on a biography of Robert Smalls, a slave who became a Civil War hero and later a congressman from South Carolina.

"When my editor read the final manuscript of *Captain of the Planter: The Story of Robert Smalls* (Doubleday 1958), she was rather reluctant to publish it. It was one thing to write about Harriet Tubman, but to tell the often brutal, tragic story of Black disenfranchisement and the birth of Jim Crow was something else. All southern markets would be closed to the book, and my editor wondered about the northern markets too. Fortunately for me she sent the manuscript to Arna Bontemps. He was so enthusiastic about it that it finally was published."

After completing *Captain of the Planter,* Ms. Sterling traveled through the South to talk with Black and White youngsters who were entering integrated schools for the first time. Myron Ehrenberg and his camera equipment accompanied her. The trip resulted in more than she had imagined; together the team produced *Tender Warriors* (Hill and Wang, 1958), an adult book consisting largely of students' own words and interviews with their parents. Despite prior Supreme Court decisions concerning integration of southern schools, the civil rights movements of the 1960s had not yet become forceful and effective, and the book soon went out of print.

Ms. Sterling was so emotionally involved with the children that she went on to write her popular *Mary Jane* (Doubleday, 1959), a fictionalized account of a

Black girl's first year in an integrated junior high school in Arkansas. *Mary Jane* remains one of Ms. Sterling's personal favorites.

"I can still remember that I was so tense and excited while I was writing *Mary Jane* that my legs, wrapped around the typewriter table, ached at the end of a day's work," she recalled. "Looking back on this book there is now, and has always been, one thing that bothers me. That is the 'happy ending.' I knew then that it shouldn't end happily, but no one was putting unhappy ending in kids' books in 1957, and there was enough opposition to publishing it anyway. It's far, far too optimistic in terms of what's happening today and far too simplistic. I had more hope at the time of an integrated solution to racial problems, and so did the kids I talked with in the South."

Mary Jane, however, has become a staple in libraries here and abroad; it has been translated into at least seven foreign languages including German, Russian and Czechoslovakian.

Ms. Sterling is equally well known for her titles dealing with Black history. *Forever Free* (Doubleday, 1963) tells of the Emancipation Proclamation; in *Lift Every Voice* (Doubleday, 1965, co-authored with Dr. Benjamin Quarles) four biographies are presented — Booker T. Washington, W. E. B. Du Bois, Mary Church Terrell, and James Weldon Johnson; *Tear Down the Walls: The History of the American Civil Rights Movement* (Doubleday, 1968) is a stirring account.

"I was prematurely pro-Black," she declared. "I

rode with the tide for a few years and now find my-self almost alone again telling editors and salesmen that research into Black history can't stop now because there's still too much to find out and write about. As you know, publishers tend to look at Black history as a fad that has run its course, and this makes me gnash my teeth."

Ms. Sterling remains an active voice in the area of civil rights. She was a founding member of the Rye, New York, Council for Human Rights and is currently a consultant to three major publishers on multi-ethnic books, including serving as consulting editor with Milton Meltzer on Scholastic's "Firebird Books," a series designed for young readers to help them understand some of the less familiar events in American history dealing especially with the experiences of minority Americans.

Dorothy Sterling was born on November 23, 1913, in New York City. Her childhood interests were al-ways geared to nature. "I was marked as a nut very early in life because I preferred bugs to baseball. I have always hated sports. I swim and walk—but that's it," she exclaimed. "We moved to West 79th Street in Manhattan when I was ten. I remember spending long, happy hours in the Museum of Natural History only two blocks away. I had a recurring dream—that I was going to be locked in the Museum one night; I wasn't sure if that was good or bad. I also wandered alone in Central Park—then it was safe to do so. I was a fairly lonely kid who read a book a day."

After high school she attended Wellesley College and Barnard College. She graduated from Barnard at the height of the Depression. "After more than a year of job hunting, the Federal Writers' Project rescued me from my private depression. When Congress threatened to abolish the arts projects, I marched on a picket line and shouted for jobs. This was *the* movement of my day, and I'm glad I had the chance to be part of it."

On the Writers' Project she met and married Phillip Sterling, who is currently writing books for children also. While raising her family, she continued to work in the field of publishing, doing all sorts of jobs on the staffs of several magazines.

During the winter months the Sterlings live in a triplex garden apartment in Greenwich, Connecticut, which also serves as their studio and library. "This is the first time we have had all our books in one place, cataloged according to the Dewey decimal system," she remarked. "But Greenwich doesn't feel like home. It's between the New England Thruway and the Boston Post Road and next to an incinerator. Our real home is on Cape Cod where we spend five months a year and will probably live year-round in the near future. There we have a magnificent view of Wellfleet Bay, can watch the sun rise and set, and can see sea gulls swoop down. I'm an ardent gardener, indoors in winter and outside in summer. Growing tomatoes in Cape Cod's sand is a real achievement."

The Sterlings' home is shared with a middle-sized

poodle named Jack who is "both a pest and a lot of fun." Their children, now married, are both professors; they have two grandchildren.

I asked Ms. Sterling about her life now that her children are grown. "I like being an adult," she replied. "I loved having kids and love my husband. I even like to cook now that there are just two of us to cook for and am into Chinese cooking this year. But mostly I like to write books. I put in a full five-day week and sometimes more at my typewriter. In my free time I'm usually reading for something I'm working on. My husband works on the far side of our big bookcase. We edit each other's stuff and have a good solid companionable relationship.

"I prefer wearing pants to dresses and have been pro-women's liberation since I was eight years old. I am consumed with envy of today's young women who are so free to say, do, and wear whatever they like. My daughter and her contemporaries have liberated me, so that I now wear a natural graying-blonde hairdo, omit the make-up, which I never really liked to use, and generally feel comfortable about dressing simply and casually.

"Perhaps they don't want to know it, but there's one thing I'd like to tell kids. That is that writing is hard work, not just inspiration. I'm troubled by the letters I receive from kids full of romantic notions about the glory and glamour of being a writer. I try to explain that it's a full-time job, enormously time-consuming, and enormously satisfying *when* the book is *done.* Also, it's a very lonely job with too little contact with people."

Also by Ms. Sterling

Trees and Their Story (Doubleday, 1953).

Insects and the Homes They Build (Doubleday, 1954).

Creatures of the Night (Doubleday, 1960).

Fall Is Here! (Natural History Press, 1966).

✳ Mary Stolz

No child has ever asked me if authors get toothaches, but if one does, I can factually say, "Yes, authors do get toothaches. And I know one who's got one!" The day I interviewed Mary Stolz (Stoles), she was suffering from a bad toothache but wasn't going to go to the dentist until she had to.

I first met her in Chicago, Illinois, at the 1972 American Library Association convention. There Harper & Row, gave a party to honor several of their authors — William Armstrong, Arnold Adoff, and Mary Stolz. At the party I made a date to visit her in her Connecticut home.

It was quiet when I arrived at her large white home on Bird Song Lane in Stamford. There were few sounds other than those usually provided by mother nature in a suburban setting. Ms. Stolz greeted me at the door—toothache and all. Our visit lasted for hours. She even forgot about the aching tooth.

Mary Stolz was born in Boston, Massachusetts, and grew up in New York City where she attended the Birch Wathen School, a private institution on New York's East Side. Early in life she became an avid reader. "I read everything," she told me. "I was particularly interested in history because it teaches that no passion is peculiar to one part of mankind. The bomb is peculiar to us, but we may perhaps have a better chance of controlling it than men had of controlling the plague. I also loved poetry, novels, and drama. Children ask me sometimes what book I'd take to a desert island, but I think I couldn't go to a desert island unless it had a public library on it."

Ms. Stolz attended Columbia University for awhile and later went to the Katherine Gibbs School where she learned to type. "And thank goodness," she stated. "I might never have been a writer if I hadn't learned to type. Can you imagine writing everything in *longhand?*"

First jobs included selling books at Macy's department store in New York City and working as a secretary at Columbia's Teachers College.

"In 1948, when I was living in New Rochelle, New York, I got sick with arthritis," she recalled. "I was in the hospital for three months and was very depressed." To keep her occupied, her doctor suggested that she "write something long." The doctor was Dr. Thomas C. Jaleski. "He was a good psychologist. Since he'd suggested I write something, I did." Thus, she produced her first novel for teenagers, *To Tell Your Love;* it was published by Harper & Row in 1950.* The doctor's patient also became his wife.

Since 1950 Ms. Stolz has written books for all ages. Growing children can find one of her books to meet their age and interest level from the time they are just learning to read through to adulthood. For young readers she has written *Emmett's Pig* (1959) and *Belling the Tiger* (1961), a variation of the story of two mice selected for the job of belling the house cat. *Belling the Tiger* was selected as a 1962 Newbery Honor Book.

Middle-grade girls and boys devour her "Barkham Street" books—*A Dog on Barkham Street* (1960) and *The Bully on Barkham Street* (1963)—as well as her novels, such as *Juan* (1970), *The Noonday Friends* (1965), a 1966 Newbery Honor Book, and *A Wonderful, Terrible Time* (1967).

Teens read and reread her novels, which include *Who Wants Music on Monday?* (1963), *Ready or Not* (1953), its sequel *The Day and the Way We Met*

---

*All titles have been published by Harper & Row.

(1956), and her recent *Leap Before You Look* (1972).

Adult readers have seen the author's name on stories that have appeared in such popular magazines as *Ladies' Home Journal, McCall's,* and *Redbook.* One of her stories that appeared in *McCall's,* "The Baby Blue Expression," was bought by Alfred Hitchcock for his television series.

Over one million readers have come to know this author's work in just two decades.

One thing that Ms. Stolz provides her audiences is realism. Much of her fiction is based on fact—things that happened to her seven nephews and one niece and, when he was younger, her son Bill, who figures in many of her books. For example, when her sister Eileen's son, Emmett, was a little boy living in an apartment, he wanted more than anything else to own a pet pig. He had a collection of piggy banks but had never even seen a live pig. His parents solved the problem by arranging to "board" a piglet on a farm, and they often took Emmett to visit his pig. This experience formed the basis of *Emmett's Pig,* a popular title in Harper's "I Can Read Book" series.

Her themes deal with real life—family relationships, love, struggles, divorce, social problems, sex, and the many pains and delights of growing up.

Her "Barkham Street" books are quite unusual. The first, *A Dog on Barkham Street,* tells about boys and and their attitudes toward life. Edward is terrified by Martin, the bully who lives next door. The story is told from Edward's point of view. In *The Bully of*

Barkham Street, not a sequel but a companion volume, the same story is related from the bully's viewpoint. Using the two books with children can spark tremendous thought and serve as a springboard to excellent discussions.

In 1970 *Juan* appeared. This story of an eight-year-old Mexican orphan came about after a visit to San Miguel de Allende in Mexico. Ms. Stolz and her husband were staying in this small quaint village in a hotel near an orphanage. They wanted to do something for the children, but there were over eighty of them. She and Tom decided to take the whole crew, along with adult chaperones, on a picnic.

"We got the necessary permission. There were only three adults and a few teen-age girls with the whole bunch of children. But they were wonderful. One of the children was Juan, a handsome and marvelous boy. At the end of the day's outing he threw his arms around me. I'll never forget this child. Never."

The book captures Ms. Stolz's experiences and will capture the hearts of readers.

Her more than thirty-five titles have all been published by Harper & Row. She has great respect and affection for her editor, Ursula Nordstrom, whom she affectionately calls "Urse."

"Over these many years, Urse and I have become close friends. She is a great editor, with an uncommon talent for friendship, which is wonderful for her writers and artists. My own respect for her judgement has led me to discard any manuscript that she really thinks unworthy. The way she puts it is, 'Mary, this will lend no lustre to your name nor to Harper's.' Naturally, I should like my work to be as lustrous as possible, so I listen to her and consider any unaccepted manuscript simply a finger exercise.

"I love to write. It's an exciting, satisfying, frustrating, and altogether wonderful craft or art. I still get a thrill when I sit down and type page one, Chapter One. After finishing a book, I can still smell the foods I wrote about and I can see the family's furnishings in their various rooms. I know the characters as if they were friends. They're all still there—real."

She quizzes her family to find out everything she is going to write about, every detail. In *Leap Before You Look,* for example, she tells of a daily bus ride to school. She asked her niece about each detail, from how the driver acted to what the riders might think about on their daily trip. She gets it all—this is why her writing is keen and sharp, down to the essential taste of morning coffee.

Ms. Stolz prepared lunch for me. She loves to cook and what a cook she is. Her chutney was the best I ever tasted—it was so good that I suggested she bottle it and sell it commercially.

After lunch she showed me through the house. The walls are adorned with fascinating curios from travels, particularly Mexico, and paintings galore, most of them done by her husband, an accomplished amateur painter. The grounds surrounding the house show the love and care that Dr. Jaleski puts into them. Flowers, plants, shrubbery and rock gardens abound. Land-scaping is his pastime along with painting; both relieve the tensions of his work as a heart specialist.

Ms. Stolz loves cats and always has had one. At present there is Eleanor, a fifteen-year-old named for her two favorite Eleanors—Eleanor of Aquitane and Eleanor Roosevelt. She really enjoys her family; her conversation constantly refers to her husband, mother and aunt, who are twins, her sister, brother-in-law, niece, nephews, and, of course, her son.

"Bill served with the Peace Corps and the Food for Peace program in Brazil. There he met a *glorious* Brazilian, Maria Franca. They were married, and now we have a beautiful blossom, a two-year old grand-daughter, Johanna. They live in New York City; we see one another often."

To describe Ms. Stolz I can use one word—chic. She talks fast, moves quickly, and somewhat reminds me of a young Bette Davis. If she were to appear in a Holly-wood film she might well portray Ms. Gavin, the mother, in her *Leap Before You Look*. She's like Ms. Gavin in some ways, but unlike her in others. She's warm and outgoing, yet protective of her personal self. She's witty and charming, yet angry and full of rage and pain over the state of the world. Vietnam haunts her; the upset stomach of the country bears down hard on her thoughts.

Before I left, Ms. Stolz excitedly showed me the plans of a new home she and Tom are building in Sarasota, Florida. But her exhilaration seemed a bit forced, as though she were selling herself solidly on the desirability of the move.

The day spent with Ms. Stolz was a memorable one. As I bade her goodbye, she told me to wait a minute, dashed back into the house, and came out with a present—a jar of chutney! "Keep it in the fridge for a few months," she told me. "It will settle well then."

I listened. It's really too good to eat anyhow.

Several weeks after my visit I received a letter that read in part:

Should mention that we panicked at the penultimate moment and cancelled building that house in Sarasota. When it came time to sign with the builder, we realized that it was not all a delicious dream but something we were actually going to do, and that would mean leaving all our people up here and this house. WE CAN'T DO IT. So, now we own a piece of land on the bay in Sarasota and some beautiful plans for a house that will never be built. Still, it was fun, most of the way. See you again, I hope.

I hope so, too!

Also by Ms. Stolz

(All published by Harper)

For younger readers

Say Something (1968).

The Story of a Singular Hen and Her Peculiar Children (1969).

For middle-grade readers

Pigeon Flight (1962).

Fredou (1962).

The Dragons of the Queen (1969).

✳ ✳ **Sydney Taylor** ✳ ✳

Sydney Taylor is one of those rare human beings who was born, bred, and still lives in New York City. Her home as a child was on New York's Lower East Side. It is no wonder that she recreated this area's atmosphere in her popular series for middle-grade readers, "All-of-a-Kind Family."*

Ms. Taylor recalled her childhood life in this area: "The East Side was in many ways an extension of the ghettos in middle Europe. Most families lived in small, crowded, cold-water flats in five-story tenements. We were luckier. Though there was still no heat nor hot

---

*All titles have been published by Follett.

water, our four rooms were in what was called a private house—a two-story building. We could even boast of a bathroom all to ourselves instead of just a communal toilet on a floor, though it still was outside in the hall. In winter time it was so cold that mama had to bathe us in her kitchen washtubs.

"There was poverty, sickness, and unsanitary conditions, with the breadwinners working ten, twelve, and fourteen hours a day for meager wages. But over and above all, was the intoxicating joy in the freedom long denied the immigrants in their 'old countries.' The realization of unlimited opportunity, if not for themselves but at least for their children, released a dynamic force and energy so long dormant in these newcomers. After all, here in this new land schools were free and libraries open to all. With their great respect for learning, these Jewish immigrants regarded teachers and librarians almost reverently. And all of these feelings were imparted to the children.

"We were six children in our family at that time — five girls and one boy, with me the middle sister. Mama and papa worked hard, and their day began early. So did ours. Household chores and even short practice periods on the piano before going to school were the order of the day for us.

"But there was much fun, too. Of course there were no radios, no televisions, and movies, then in their infancy, cost a nickel for two people. Even so small a sum was not easy to come by. Toys, too, were a luxury, so our supply was limited. Thus our whole world of the imagination lay inside the covers of books or in our own heads. We created our own fun and games.

"All the ancient Jewish festivals were celebrated in traditional fashion, filling us children with wonder and awe on the solemn occasions and with boundless joy on the happy ones. Families and friends were close-knit. Lives were intertwined with those of our neighbors. Everyone was ready to help in times of trouble."

The first book in the series, *All-of-a-Kind Family* (1941), relates the story of Jewish life during the early 1900s. The family is called "all-of-a-kind" because there are five girls and no boys. The boy comes along in *More All-of-a-Kind Family* (1954). The series came about because of Ms. Taylor's only child, Jo. "When Jo was little," she told me, "I would sit beside her bed at night and try to make up for the lack of a big family by telling her about my own. Jo loved the stories about how papa and mama worked and how the five little girls helped out. She was delighted with the tales of our good times together and the enjoyment of simple pleasures. She loved the stories so much that I decided to write them all down especially for her. The manuscript went into a big box and lay there. But my husband was not satisfied to let the story stay there."

During the summer of 1950, while she was away working at a children's summer camp, her husband heard about the Charles W. Follett Award. He took his wife's manuscript from the box and sent it off to the publisher. Some time later Ms. Taylor received a letter from an editor stating that Follett wanted to publish the work. "I didn't know what the editor was even talking about. I told my husband, and the whole story came out."

The book went on to win the second annual Charles W. Follett Award and the Isaac Siegel Memorial Award given by the Jewish Book Council of America. The third book in the series, *All-of-a-Kind Family Uptown* (1958), continues the family chronicle and depicts the children growing up.

Ms. Taylor described her work habits: "I don't have a steady working time. I start writing when the mood seizes me. Once launched, however, I work continuously until it's finished. Sometimes the ideas come through the air like acrobats—with the greatest of ease —but sometimes I just have to scrounge. I rarely try out my ideas on children since I feel they are impressed too much by one's manner of presentation."

Ms. Taylor is slim, barely five feet tall. Among her favorite possessions is a family photograph of mama, papa, and the five little girls, which hangs on the wall in her workroom alongside the original book illustration by Helen John of the five little pinafored figures.

For thirty years she has worked as director of dance and dramatics in a children's camp for girls from seven to eleven years of age. Her hobbies are dance, yoga, travel, reading, and taking care of her apartment on West 24th Street.

The newest book in her series, *All-of-a-Kind Family Downtown,* was published in 1972. She gave a word of advice about it: "Chronologically it belongs between the first and second books, even though it is the latest to be written.''

Children now beginning the series will not be affected by this, but all of us adult readers will want to go back and reread the series in chronological order!

Also by Ms. Taylor

(All published by Follett)

A Papa Like Everyone Else (1966).

For beginning readers

Mr. Barney's Beard (1961).

The Dog Who Came to Dinner (1966).

* * **P. L. Travers** * *

Helen Piers

March 1, 1972, came into New York City like the gentlest of lambs. The thermometer hit a record-breaking high. I walked up Fifth Avenue in the mid-afternoon stopping in at several of my favorite bookstores to hunt for one of P. L. Travers' "Mary Poppins" books. How could I visit this author—one whose stories I grew up on—without obtaining her autograph? To my dismay, not one copy of *Mary Poppins* was in stock. Disappointed, I returned to my office at Scholastic. But lo and behold, like the East Wind that blows through the first chapter of *Mary Poppins* (1934)* a copy of *Mary Poppins in the Park* turned up via Phyllis Braun, Scholastic's Arrow Book Club editor.

Late that afternoon I went to visit P. L. Travers, Mary Poppins' creator. She was in New York City for a short time before returning to her home in Europe. Her temporary lodging on New York's Upper East Side was in a large, new apartment building. I must admit that I was a bit uncomfortable approaching this author. I had read a great deal about her—how she prefers anonymity and how careful she is to protect her innerself. But once I had met her, I didn't encounter any problems. She is kind, warm, gay, and puts one at ease within a split second's time.

P. L. Travers was born in 1904 in Australia. Her father was Irish, her mother of Scottish descent. Though brought up in Queensland and Sydney, home for her was Ireland and England—two countries where she still spends much time.

At the age of three she was reading and while a youngster devoured works by Shakespeare, Dickens, Thackeray, and Scott, right along with Buffalo Bill

---

*Unless otherwise noted all books mentioned have been published by Harcourt Brace Jovanovich.

comic books and paperbound fairy tales that she could buy for a penny.

"Ours was a reading, articulate family, full of communication; lonely, perhaps, since there were very few families like ours in my early childhood. The family was inventive, imaginative, even perhaps poetic. Life was very hard financially after my father died," she related, "but I was able to go to England and later Ireland at an early age and had the good fortune to be befriended both as a person and a writer by AE (pseudonym for George Russell), particularly, and also James Stephens and W. B. Yeats, both of whom liked my poetry.

"Throughout my young life writing was no more important than my other childish avocations. I can't remember a time when I didn't write, but then, I never called it writing. It never seemed important in that sense. I thought of it more as listening, then putting down what I had heard. Nobody in my family called it writing; in fact, nobody was either pleased or proud. I feel that was rather a good thing for me because I was never made to feel that I was anything special."

While she was still very young AE, the Irish poet and economist, published some of her poems in the *Irish Statesman*. This was the beginning of a lasting friendship. "It was AE and W. B. Yeats who largely licked me into shape as a writer, much as mother cats lick their kittens into the shapes of cats," she declared.

Discussing her classic, *Mary Poppins,* she told me that she is not quite sure of the character's genesis, "if, indeed, there was any genesis. Perhaps Poppins just 'growed' like Topsy." While living in England in a small, thatched manor house in Sussex and convalescing from an illness, she began to "listen for" the character and the story. Her friend, Hendrik William Van Loon, the late author who won the very first Newbery Medal in 1922 for *The Story of Mankind* (Liveright, 1921), was of the opinion that far from P. L. Travers thinking up Mary Poppins, it was Mary Poppins who had thought up Mary Poppins! And the author clearly leans toward Van Loon's theory.

Upon publication *Mary Poppins* became an immediate success. In following years P. L. Travers wrote four more volumes about the extraordinary nanny— *Mary Poppins Comes Back* (1935), *Mary Poppins Opens the Door* (1943), *Mary Poppins in the Park* (1952), and *Mary Poppins from A to Z* (1962). All of the books have been illustrated by Mary Shepard and, like Alfred Hitchcock in his films, P. L. Travers appears once in each of her books, tucked somewhere into the illustrations as an anonymous bystander.

The books were so well established that they hardly needed Walt Disney Studios to promote their principal character; they have been translated into every major language in the world. For a long time the author refused Mr. Disney's various offers, but in 1960 she at last gave in and agreed, since the film was to be done in live action, to let him have a go at it. Thus Mary Poppins rose up from the printed page to become a

movie star. The author is quite happy with the result-
ing film "but not entirely," she confessed. "The film
is good entertainment, glamorous and colorful, but
it has very little relation to the books. All the inward-
ness and the truth have been removed; only the skin
remains."

A child once wrote to her stating that Mary Poppins
in the film, played by Academy Award-winning actress
Julie Andrews, had behaved "in a very indecorous
manner." The author felt she knew exactly what the
girl meant. "I am sure it was the scene where the
director allowed Ms. Andrews to do the can-can on
the roof and display all her Edwardian underwear.
Mary Poppins, as the child and I very well knew, could
cheerfully have danced a can-can had she felt like it,
but her skirts, in such a case, would have known the
proper way to behave and clung demurely 'round her
ankles."

P. L. Travers' hope, however, is that the film will
bring more people to the books. And although the film
did not completely please her, something that sprang
from it clearly does. Two roses have been named
after the unprecedented nanny and one after the
author. "There is a beautiful, huge, golden-hearted
yellow Mary Poppins rose in England and in the
United States, and also a pink one in the States;
there's a blushing, deep rosy Pamela Travers, too. If
Dr. Dennison Morey of California, the man who
named the roses had asked, 'May I call a cabbage

after you?' I'd have been pleased. After all a cabbage, too, is quite beautiful. But a rose—my favorite flower —how wonderful!" she exclaimed.

Being a Mary Poppins fan I just had to ask P. L. Travers if her character would ever again grace the pages of a new book. She answered me with another question, "Is there any reason why she should? We know quite a lot about her already." She pondered for a moment and added, "I don't know. Someday perhaps."

I also wanted to know why the author decided to write for children. She scowled at such a suggestion. "But I don't write for children at all. Does anybody? Who would dare? Like Beatrix Potter I write to please myself and luckily for me, some children seem to be pleased, too. *Mary Poppins* was never meant to be a children's book. It was just *a book* like any other. To me literature seems to be all one stream, and I would like to think *Mary Poppins* is floating in the stream."

There have also been three non-Poppins books: *I Go By Land, I Go By Sea* (Dell, 1967) dealing with the evacuation of children from England to America before the United States' entry into World War II; *The Fox in the Manger* (Norton, out-of-print), based on an old carol about Christmas Eve, and the recently published *Friend Monkey* (1971).

"*Friend Monkey* came about as a result of long brooding on the idea of Hanuman, the monkey lord of the Hindu myths, who could never do anything by halves," she told me. "When I was well-started on the book, the manuscript, by an unfortunate accident, disappeared; it couldn't be found anywhere. But after a long period of disappointment I eventually began again, and in fourteen months there he was!"

I asked the author if she had a favorite among her books. "One's favorite book is like the new baby in a family. It needs one more; it is nearest to newness. So I suppose at this moment, in 1972, *Friend Monkey* comes first, since he was only born on November 3, 1971. There are bits in all my books that have favorite moments for me. But ask me again in five years time," she laughed. "I'll know more about it then."

P. L. Travers is not a stranger to the United States. During World War II she spent two summers here living on an Indian reservation. In 1966 she served as writer-in-residence at Radcliffe College and later at Smith and Claremont Colleges. She gave informal lectures and talked with students at a series of "at home" sessions.

In England she lives in a tiny book-filled Georgian house in the Chelsea section of London where she has a cherry tree in a large pot at the door to commemorate Cherry Tree Lane where the Mary Poppins books take place. She grows roses and herbs in her back garden. She also has a house in Dublin, Ireland.

"I try not to have favorite possessions but to be like a bird on the wing," she told me. "People always come first with me. After that it's the joy of working on something that I like and believe in. I like life to be full of friends, with moments of aloneness for working. You know, I don't think authors matter very much. It's their books that count. Maybe all authors should be anonymous. Being born, living, and dying, and to do them all as well as possible. That's what I would like."

As a child she believed that the writers of her favorite books were, if not dead, lurking about playing harps in the clouds. "I'm always very complimented when people say to me, 'I thought you were dead.' And perhaps as an author I've never been alive. I remember when Beatrix Potter died. It gave me a really frightful shock. For me she hadn't been a living person, and now, here she was—dead. How dreadful!"

She uses her initials, P. L., rather than her full name, Pamela Lyndon, because she has always objected to the sentimental connection so often made between women and children's books. She hopes that people won't bother to wonder if the books were written by a man, woman, or kangaroo! "One of my favorite authors," she stated, "is the person who through the ages has been known by the name of Anon (anonymous). You will find this name everywhere in anthologies, and it is far and away the one I like best. Few people wonder what the A. A. in A. A. Milne, stands for or the W. B. in W. B. Yeats. Yet everybody wants to plunge into my secret world. The initials simply mean, 'Knock for a moment at the door. Let me be sure if I'm in or out!'"

But I was glad P. L. Travers let me into her world. Before I left her apartment, she told me about a boy who was asked by his teacher to write an essay on his favorite book. "The essay was short but very concise," she said with a twinkle in her eyes, and his teacher thought so well of it that she kindly sent it to me. It read:

The Lord is the Father of all things and Mary Poppins is the Mother of all things and they are married or have been married and they are both a miracle.

✳ Mary Hays Weik

Hartwig Berger

I first met Mary Hays Weik (Week) at a cocktail party at the apartment of her daughter, Ann Grifalconi. Ms. Grifalconi is an author-illustrator of children's books; we have collaborated on two books and are friends-beautiful.

The first thing I noticed about Ms. Weik was how much she and her daughter look alike. Seen together one would just know they are related.

In June, 1972, Ms. Weik came to my office to talk with me. She didn't want me to visit her apartment for she uses it "for home and not for an office." She isn't an easy woman to pin down nor to get talking about herself. When she does talk, she speaks in a stream-ofconsciousness way, jumping from one thing to some very different topic in less than a few seconds.

Her book *The Jazz Man* (Atheneum, 1966) was recognized as a 1967 Newbery Honor Book. It is a haunting story about Zeke, a nine-year-old crippled Black boy living in Harlem. Both his parents work all day, and he stays home alone. The reason why he is alone and not attending school or being watched over is never really explained in the book. I asked the author why. "Because he's crippled and he stayed away from school, that's all," she answered.

One day Zeke's father loses his job. He drinks a great deal, and one day his mother leaves both of them. Zeke's father goes away too, leaving him on his own. Zeke's friendship with a jazz man, a neighbor, ends too, when the jazz man goes away. The story ends on an unusual note, one that has to be read to be fully captured.

Although honored by the Newbery Committee, the book has received a number of negative comments from critics; some have called it a book of despair, a book filled with ambiguity, a book symbolizing hopelessness, even death. I asked Ms. Weik about such remarks. "Oh! Those institutionalized comments make me so angry!" she responded. "It's pitiful! Can't anyone believe there's a second chance in life? I get letters from children about this book where I can just see teachers planting these ideas into their heads. They just have no hope. Zeke could have been anybody, anywhere. And he is! He'll become something in life—anything—for, you see, his mother and father really love him."

The book was inspired by a woodcut Ms. Grifalconi made of a Black musician. Although Ms. Weik went to school with Noble Sissle, the Black orchestra leader and composer, and knew Eubie Blake, a jazz musician (the team had produced a successful off-Broadway musical, *Shuffle Along,* in 1921), they had nothing to do with her writing *The Jazz Man.*

"Consciously?" I asked her.

"Consciously or unconsciously, what difference does it make?" she replied.

Strangely, the woodcut her daughter did resembled Eubie Blake—yet Ms. Grifalconi had never seen him.

Recalling the development of the book Ms. Weik told me: "I love the book because it seemed the most real. And because it was fun working with Ann, though I never saw what she was doing. I didn't see the artwork until it was finished. But the characters looked exactly as I imagined them."

The illustrations were done in woodcuts. The original woodcut that sparked the idea for the book was not included, however. This was Ms. Grifalconi's first attempt at illustrating a book in this medium. She did the cuts on old orange crates. Ms. Weik wrote the text in "one of a few afternoons. It wasn't for children. It just happened to fit into that category. Like my other writings, the ideas come by accident. I let my stories write themselves. The characters determine how and where it goes."

Her first book for children "was something about building a house. I don't remember it. I don't even have a copy of it, and I never want one. It was published by Knopf. I did it on assignment, and the money came in handy," she confessed.

Ms. Weik was born in Greencastle, Indiana. "Growing up there was like forever. My mother, to whom I was deeply attached, died when I was twelve years old. I lived alone after that with my father, a Lincoln biographer, and my older brother. I lived on a kind of island filled with books and grew up with a man's viewpoint on life.

"I left the place as fast as I could. As a matter of fact, I left the day after I graduated from college."

Interested in becoming a journalist, she wanted the big city—Chicago—but her first job was in Evanston, Illinois, which is as much Chicago as Paramus, New Jersey is New York City. Her story about her first news assignment shows the warm and human inner feelings of the author.

"I was assigned to a big scoop—a murder story. I met with the mother of the murdered son. She told me everything. It was pitiful. She opened up to me so. When I returned to the office, the editor asked me if I got a good scoop. 'I didn't get anything,' I told him. 'She wouldn't talk.' "

The following years of her life were like a ping-pong game, moving from one place to another and usually ending up back in Greencastle.

"I had to go back often because my father was ill. He used to mail me the hometown newspaper each week. I don't know why. We both hated it. One day on the way to the post office, he was hit by a car and suffered a great deal from the accident. I returned to Indiana to care for him."

While there she continued writing. "There was nothing else to do there!," she exclaimed. She sold a short story that gave her enough money to go to New York City. She settled in Greenwich Village, wrote stories, and worked as an editor on various magazines. Back and forth to New York she went. One time she married, stayed there, and began to raise a family — Ann, and a son, John, who is currently a city planner and teacher at Rhode Island University. She was divorced and had to work hard to raise her children during the Depression years.

"But they were happy times," she recalled. "People were different then than they are now. Today everyone is alienated from each other. Alienation has hit us all. I wish all people would learn that the most fun you'll ever get out of life is talking with strangers, getting involved with people."

Ms. Weik now lives in an apartment in New York's East Village. "But for all I see," she told me, "it could be on a farm a million miles from nowhere."

She likes people, enjoys traveling, and adores Vienna, which seems "like a place she had known in another life." But she doesn't believe in reincarnation. She likes "to fool around on the piano." She doesn't own a television set; "the only things good are the advertisements."

At the time of this interview, Ms. Weik had just

finished *A House on Liberty Street* (Atheneum, 1972), a story about her grandfather, a '48er emigrant German baker who died before she was born. Ann Grifalconi did the illustrations. Again Ms. Weik didn't see them until the book was published.

*
* *Sister Noemi Weygant
* *

Sister Noemi Weygant is a multi-talented poet-photographer who was born in Ada, Minnesota, and named Ida Weygant. She spent most of her childhood on a Montana homestead in the Judith River Basin area, living a free, un-inhibited life close to the land. Her love of nature is reflected in her childhood memories and in her poetry.

> SPRING IS . . .*
> Oh come,
>   oh run
>   to the woodlands with me.

---

*From *It's Spring!* Westminster Press, 1969.

Listen,
 see how everything,
 everywhere,
  is blooming,
  nesting,
  sprouting,
  growing,
  leafing,
  blowing,
  feathering,
  mating,
Spring is being new.

Spring is—I love you.

Spring is—love.

"I can never remember when I was not raising children for I was the baby of a family of nine and had many nephews my own age or younger. When I was very young my father, who was a pharmacist, became ill, and it was decided he should take a homestead in Montana to regain his health. Several older brothers had already taken homesteads there, and so my mother, my brother Louis, and I boarded a train for Montana within a year after my father had made his claim. My father soon recovered his health and returned to his profession. My mother loved the ranch and stayed on with my brother and me. Believe it or not, we did a good job of it and were totally happy children. The cowboys gave us ponies to ride. The log cabin was built in the basin of Wolf Creek with rim rocks towering up about us on all sides. Then on the ranch land we could ride to the top of a high butte and view seven mountains. I could milk cows as well as herd them by the time I was nine, teach calves to drink, and do many other farm chores. I enjoyed all of this.

"Though I was a tough little girl, surviving many a bucking that threw me to the ground, I would never wear trousers because boys wore them. I loved being a little girl. And I loved my dolls. I had a few toys, and each night I would cover them up with a tarpaulin in the event of rain. My mother frowned on this and feared some night a rattlesnake might crawl under the tarpaulin for warmth, so she built me a playhouse in the trees. I cherished that playhouse more than words can express.

"I was very much in love with a little boy who came down to play house with me; and maybe—maybe—had my mother not brought me to Duluth and his parents later departed to some unknown city or state, we might really have married when we grew up as we planned to. I had only one ambition then—to marry a rancher and raise twelve children. I ended up as a nun, and by choice. God works in strange ways.

"I became grafted to the land, but mother, deploring the fact that my brother and I were growing up so ignorant, brought us to Duluth where my father was located so that we might become educated. I was twelve at the time, and since no one had any idea where to put me, I was placed in the seventh grade.

I adjusted to city life easily and am still fond of Duluth.''

After graduating from the University of Minnesota and working for a short time in advertising, in 1947 she entered the Saint Scholastica Priory of the order of Saint Benedict in Duluth. Because of her lifelong interest in photography, she became the convent's photographer.

"Even as a child I was interested in photography," she said. "My big sister, a schoolteacher, would come home for summer vacations with a box camera, and I could never leave it alone. I was not allowed really to take pictures, but I would pretend and pretend and decided then that someday I was going to become a photographer. When we came to Duluth, I could not rest until I had a box camera. But it was not until I was out of college that I could begin to pursue photography in earnest. When I came to the convent, I brought my darkroom along with me. But it was really in the convent where I matured as a photographer.''

She found time to explore the one hundred sixty acres of fields and woods around the College of Saint Scholastica with her camera in hand. Often she laid beside a pond for hours to catch the correct sunlight on a sleeping frog or waded through deep mud for a shot of a caterpillar poised on a green stem. She captures in her full-color photographs nuances of form and color that allow the viewer to see the world of nature—her world—in a fresh way. Her talent has been recognized widely; she has won more than forty awards from many associations, including the Minnesota Professional Photographers' Association and the Professional Photographers of America.

"I do want to say about my photography that most people think I photograph only nature. Before I entered the convent, I specialized in children. I will photograph anything really if the opportunity is there. *In a Promise* (Augsburg Publishers, 1968) contains only pictures taken on deserted farms."

In her children's books, beginning with *It's Autumn!* (Westminster Press, 1968), the reader is taken on exciting trips through nature via poetry and her full-color photography.

"Poetry," she told me, "has been a source of creative joy since childhood. I've always written poetry but never tried seriously to sell it. My journals are filled with poems. I have no idea whether they are good or not.

"In my journals I combined photography and poetry for a long time. Then I had an exhibit at the University of Minnesota. Reverend Herbert Brokering saw my pictures, called me, and inquired if I would consider collaborating on a project. Thus our first book, *In the Rustling Grass* (Augsburg Publishers, 1964), was born.

It's Autumn! (1968), *It's Spring!* (1969), *It's Winter!* (1969), and *It's Fall!* (1970; all published by Westminster Press) developed spontaneously.

"I was walking through the woods alone when I came to a big brown stump on which dozens of little fungi, like huts, were growing. Suddenly I was speaking to everything in the forest, or were they speaking to me? I never really decided to write for children. I always wanted to write. Even out on the prairies of Montana or viewing Lake Superior for the first time when we came to Duluth, I prayed I might someday write. I am childlike in my disposition, so relating to children has always been easy for me. I relate equally well with young people of college age, too."

Besides the four children's books, she found time to collaborate on five other books with Reverend Brokering. The most recent, *Green Ghetto* and *More Than a Dream* (St. John's Liturgical Press, 1972), contain photographs Sister Noemi took during the summers of 1968 and 1969 while teaching in a poor area of Chicago.

"I am told I am the most controversial personality in the College. That is because, despite the fact that I really try to live a true Benedictine life, and I think I do, something of the West is still in me. My theme song remains, 'Don't Fence Me In,' and my nature has always been free and joyful. I am what a German professor called, 'an apple-cheeked woman.' I have few fears or frustrations. I am far too fond of eating; I love good food. I have kind of a lust for living in every possible way. It has always been so with me. I am independent and while I love to teach, I find faculty meetings, committee meetings, and the like very boring. I don't read half the notices put into our faculty mailboxes."

Currently she is totally absorbed with a farm. "It is not really my farm, but a friend gave it to me to live on.

Or maybe I talked him into giving it to me. But it is un-heard of that a sister would have a farm, and yet it is accepted that Sister Noemi have one for she always does everything that is different. It really was good-for-nothing, just a shack, but with the help of students we are making the most charming, rustic, old-fash-ioned retreat out here you could ever imagine. The house clings to the earth like a mushroom in summer; in winter it's so buried in snow, it is like an igloo.''

Just recently she found a deserted barn. "And, oh, my dear friend, the barn is fantastic!'' she exclaimed. "Long, dim, once handsome and filled with life, stalls for a bull, calves, heifers, steers, and milk cows. One day the original owner died, and all the animals, in-cluding horses, were sold and the barn was left empty. Everything was left just as the owner left it—a hatchet on a bale of hay, a knife stabbed into an upright beam, a can of salve for sore teats, a blade to clean out hoofs, milk stools in the corner, chains and rope and twine and rubber, and all of it now draped with spider webs. I warned a student companion to be careful and not destroy the festooning of the spiders. Exploration has only started. One day I hope to do a book on the farm for I discovered that it is one of the oldest in the vicinity —the first in Hermantown.''

Of her present life she commented: "My adult life is a triple one. There is the Benedictine life as a nun —prayers, retreats. There is the professional life—pho-tographer and teacher. And there is *my* life—the wood-lands, two little kittens named Butterfly and Snowflake, and many friends. I am a member of the Zonta International Club, a club for professional women. I belong there just as much as I do chopping wood out in the barn on the farm. I love to drive, and one of my highest hopes is to have a car someday."

I received a standing invitation from Sister to have a picnic at her Duluth farmhouse. Not being as nature loving as she is, I'll wait for a spell until the shack is restored some more. Until then she will have to settle for a picnic in a Duluth hotel. Knowing her, it won't make a bit of difference. She might even bring some ants along to give our inside picnic authenticity!

✳ E. B. White

Donald E. Johnson

It is difficult to believe that Elwyn Brooks White has only produced three books for children: *Stuart Little* (1945), *Charlotte's Web* (1952), and *The Trumpet of the Swan* (1970; all published by Harper). Like Dr. Seuss, E. B. White has become a household name for providing millions of young readers with these enchanting tales.

E. B. White was born on July 11, 1899, in Mount Vernon, a town near New York City. He attended public schools in Mount Vernon, graduated from Cornell University in 1921, worked in New York City for a year, and then traveled about. After five or six years of trying many kinds of jobs, he joined the staff of *New Yorker* magazine. This was in 1927 when this now prestigious magazine was still in its diaper stage. Mr. White regularly contributed satire, poems, essays, and editorials. His connection with *New Yorker* proved to be a particularly happy one; he has continued to write for the magazine ever since and is still on the staff, working from his home in Maine.

His first book, *The Lady is Cold* (Harper), a book of adult poetry, appeared in 1929. From that time on his writings have appeared regularly. Titles include *Is Sex Necessary?* (Harper, 1929), a book of essays co-authored with the late James Thurber, and *Farewell to Model T* (Putnam, 1936) with R. L. Stout.

In 1938, Mr. White moved to his farm in Brooklin, Maine. It is here where all of his juvenile books were written. *Stuart Little,* his very first, tells of a heroic little mouse with human qualities who was born to the Little family, *real* people-people. The parents and their first son, George, accept the situation rather calmly and make the necessary adjustments to raise a mouse son. Mr. White created the book in the hope of amusing a six-year-old niece but before he finished it, she had grown up! "It took about twelve years to do Stuart," he recalled, "but most of the time I did not think I was writing a book. I was busy with other matters."

The text was submitted to Ursula Nordstrom, Harper's juvenile editor. Ms. Nordstrom remembered the difficulty of finding an artist to do justice to the text. "The drawings for *Stuart Little* posed a tremendous challenge. I tried several well-known artists but was horrified by most of the results. Some drew Stuart as a rather Disney-like creation; others drew him in extremely contemporary clothes. From time-to-time I sent Mr. White samples. He agreed they were all impossible.

"Garth Williams was the eighth artist we tried. Garth had not yet illustrated a book. He loved the manuscript and asked for a couple of weeks to work out his characterization of Stuart. As he worked, and as we talked about the book on the phone, I began to feel a little relaxed for the first time about the problem of the illustrations. It was a thrilling day when his sketches came in. Mr. White loved them as much as I did."

Seven years later Mr. White and Mr. Williams teamed up again to produce the modern classic, *Charlotte's Web*, the tale of Charlotte, a large, grey spider who sets out to save the life of Wilbur, a pig and her dearest friend. In a promotion piece Mr. White tells how *Charlotte's Web* came about:*

*Available free from Harper and Row, Inc., 10 East 53rd Street, New York, N.Y. 10022.

I like animals and my barn is a very pleasant place to be, at all hours. One day when I was on my way to feed the pig, I began feeling sorry for the pig because, like most pigs, he was doomed to die. This made me sad. So I started thinking of ways to save a pig's life. I had been watching a big, grey spider at her work and was impressed by how clever she was at weaving. Gradually I worked the spider into the story . . . a story of friendship and salvation on a farm. Three years after I started writing it, it was published. (I am not a fast worker, as you can see.)

Young readers had to wait almost another two decades before *The Trumpet of the Swan* appeared. "I don't know how or when the idea for *The Trumpet of the Swan* occurred to me," he remarked. "I guess I must have wondered what it would be like to be a trumpeter swan and not be able to make a noise."

About his writing he has commented:**

Sometimes I'm asked how old I was when I started to write, and what made me want to write. I started early —as soon as I could spell. In fact, I can't remember any time in my life when I wasn't busy writing. I don't know what caused me to do it, or why I enjoyed it, but I think children often find pleasure and satisfaction in trying to set their thoughts down on paper, either in words or in pictures. I was no good at drawing, so I used words instead. As I grew older, I found that writing can be a way of earning a living . . . .

Are my stories true, you ask? No, they are imaginary

**Ibid.

tales, containing fantastic characters and events. In *real* life, a family doesn't have a child who looks like a mouse; in *real* life, a spider doesn't spin words in her web. In *real* life, a swan doesn't blow a trumpet. But real life is only one kind of life—there is also the life of the imagination. And although my stories are imaginary, I like to think that there is some truth in them, too—truth about the way people and animals feel and think and act.

Awards and honors bestowed upon Mr. White could well fill several pages. To name a few, *Charlotte's Web* was designated a 1953 Newbery Honor Book and in 1958 received a Lewis Carroll Shelf Award as a book "worthy enough to sit on the shelf with *Alice in Wonderland.*" In 1963 President John F. Kennedy named Mr. White as one of thirty-one Americans to receive the Presidential Medal of Freedom—the highest honor a civilian can receive from the government in time of peace. In 1970 Mr. White was given the Laura Ingalls Wilder Award for both *Charlotte's Web* and *Stuart Little.* This award is given to "an author or illustrator whose books, published in the United States, have over a period of years made a substantial and lasting contribution to literature for children." (This award is named for Ms. Wilder for her own lasting contributions of "The Little House" series published by Harper & Row.) In 1971 Mr. White received the National Medal for Literature given by the National Book Committee. He also holds honorary degrees from many colleges and universities.

Besides all this *Stuart Little* has been televised by NBC, and *Charlotte's Web* has been made into a motion picture.

I asked Mr. White if there was one award in particular that was the most meaningful. He replied, "The best award is a letter from a child or an adult."

In his acceptance speech for the Laura Ingalls Wilder Award (published in *Horn Book,* September 1970, p. 350), he declared:

> I have two or three strong beliefs about the business of writing for children. I feel I must never kid them about anything. I feel I must be on solid ground myself. I also feel that a writer has an obligation to transmit, as best he can, his love of life, his appreciation for the world. I am not averse to departing from reality, but I am against departing from the truth.

The author and his wife, Katherine, a now retired *New Yorker* editor whom he married in 1929, live in a clapboard house in a Maine village, "an area that is rural, wooded, seagirt and friendly." His favorite possessions are "two terriers, four geese, and a twenty-foot sloop." He enjoys sailing and being around many kinds of animals.

He has no personal favorite book, never decided to write specifically for children, doesn't really know how he gets ideas, never had any formal writing training, reworks his material, and *never* tries out an idea on youngsters. He has a son, three grandchildren, a stepson, stepdaughter, six step-grandchildren, and three step-great-grandchildren. "At last count, that is," he exclaimed.

As a final question, I asked Mr. White if there was anything else he felt a child would like to know about him. "Sure," he said, "but I'm not telling."

He really wouldn't discuss his writing much. Of *Charlotte's Web* he has said, "I haven't told why I wrote the book, but I haven't told why I sneeze either. A book is a sneeze."

If his books are sneezes, we should all give him a great big "God bless you" and secretly hope a coldbug bites him a bit more often.

✳ ✳ ✳ Maia Wojciechowska

Maia Wojciechowska (My-ya Voi-che-hov-skah) is a one-of-a-kind entity in the field of children's literature. She is candid and outspoken. Her comments about life and the world of books are widely quoted, laughed at, and scorned—but listened to. She is thin, zesty, and as earthy as a Melina Mercouri or an Anna Magnani. She may also be the only female author to have fought in the bullring! And she *is* a woman!

"I just got married again," she exclaimed. "Marriage is the normal state for a woman, and I love being one."

Life for Ms. Wojciechowska began on August 7, 1927, in Warsaw, Poland. Her father, Zygmunt, was a wartime chief of staff for the Polish Air Force. She grew up all over Poland, France, Portugal, and England. In 1942 Ms. Wojciechowska came to the United States with her parents and two brothers when her father was assigned to this country as an air attaché to the Polish Embassy. "The book I just finished, *Till the Break of Day* (Harcourt, 1972), goes into all this," she explained. "Of course the war scared all of us who were young, but also it provided a fantastic time in which adults were the fools."

After spending one year at the Immaculate Heart College in Hollywood, California, she worked at a potpourri of jobs including masseuse, restaurant hostess and waitress, translator and broadcaster for Radio Free Europe, and for a short while as an undercover detective. "I was about to develop a new theory of shadowing by letting the subject follow me, but unfortunately the same day I lost him," she laughed.

Prior to becoming a controversial writer and spokesman for today's youth via such books as *A Single Light* (Atheneum, 1964), *Tuned Out* (Harper, 1968), and her Newbery Award-winning book, *Shadow of a Bull* (Atheneum, 1964), she wrote several books under her first married name, Maia Rodman. These included *Market Day for Ti Andre* (Viking, 1952), a book for young readers, and *The Loved Look: International Hairstyling Guide,* published by the American Hairdressers in 1960.

It was *Shadow of a Bull* that brought this author's name to the fore in publishing circles. The book's central character is Manolo Olivar, a boy who is expected to fight his first bull at the age of twelve and like his father, Juan, he is also expected to become a great bullfighter in Spain. It was first a short story that developed after the author saw "a boy who looked like Manolete" (a famous bullfighter).

Ms. Wojciechowska commented on receiving the prestigious Newbery Medal for this work: "People who give prizes and review books don't know what they're doing. It's all a matter of personal taste. *Shadow of a Bull* is really a short story and should have stayed a short story. A major women's magazine rejected it for some ridiculous reason, so I decided to make it into a book. The magazine editors said they liked it but they published only one children's story a year. 'Nuts to them,' I said. 'Who reads their old magazine? The hell with the mothers sitting around waiting for one story a year. I'll do it as a children's book, for children.' "

She did! "Now everyone expects me to write *The Son of Shadow of a Bull*, but I won't do it. I'd die of boredom." Since its publication it has been translated into many languages including Africaans, Japanese, and Serbo-Croatian.

Ernest Hemingway, the late noted author, once commented that Ms. Wojciechowska is more knowledgeable about bullfighting than any other woman alive.

In 1972, a second book dealing with Spain's most

popular sport appeared, *The Life and Death of a Brave Bull* (Harcourt). She wrote this easy-to-read account to explain to Americans the depths of courage and strength involved in this time-honored Spanish custom. It is her hope that her portrayal of the fierce pride and courage in the face of death shown by a brave bull and a great matador will make readers appreciate this oft-misunderstood ritual. For years she has been angry with Munro Leaf who wrote the picture book classic, *The Story of Ferdinand,* (Viking, 1936) because she feels, "Ferdinand is an imposter —not a real bull. Picture books should tell the truth!"

The basic purpose in her writings is to leave the reader with a thought, idea, or a question; each of her works contain the subtle message that human beings have a choice in life. Her books express a concern for the problems and central truths of living in today's real, sometimes wildly confusing world.

Tuned Out candidly explores the use of drugs. "I wrote it to scare small kids and to make the older ones think," she declared. *A Single Light,* which is also set in Spain, relates the story of a deaf mute, abandoned by her father, who is searching for some meaning in her own life. *Don't Play Dead Until You Have To* (Harper, 1970) describes Byron, a teen-ager and his four-year friendship with Charlie, an unhappy younger boy whose parents are separated. This book is her own personal favorite "because it kept me on my toes trying to bring off a full-length book in monologue as a sort of a feat or tour de force or whatever."

Shelton L. Root, Jr., wrote of the novel in *Ele-*

mentary English magazine: "One thing is certain, whether or not the book is appropriate for children, it is one that every adult who is concerned about children and their literature ought to read."

Regarding her work habits, she told me: "I'm disorganized. My best work is done in a bathtub while reading somebody else's book. I shape my characters, develop my plot, and so on inside my head. My typing is lousy. When I know where I'm going, I can work at the typewriter for hours. I rewrite at least twice."

She is fluent in four languages, her native Polish, English, French, and Spanish, and understands Russian, Italian, Portuguese, and missal-Latin. She plays and teaches tennis, loves skiing where there are no liftlines as at Alta, Utah, or Santa Fe, New Mexico. "I also love walking in the woods and being with someone I like or being with a child I don't even like, for he listens. My most precious possession is time, and it's being continually stolen."

Ms. Wojciechowska lives in New Jersey in a small, two-room house next to a tennis court, two ponds, and a river "thirty minutes from New York City but still wild enough for a herd of deer I see each day out of my window." Her husband, Richard Larken, is "a great chess player." She has one daughter, Oriana, from her previous marriage to Selden Rodman, a writer-anthologist.

Remarks from Ms. Wojciechowska's works might one day fill a *Wojciechowska Book of Familiar Quotations*. Consider the following from *Don't Play Dead Until You Have To:*

School: "All they do in school is wreck your mind."

Death: "Well, the thing is, I wish he had made it plain that dying can be about as noble a thing as a human being can do. But Ross said, 'that's bullshit, living is noble. Dying isn't.' "

Truth: "How many times does a little kid hear just the simple truth without a lot of bullshit?"

God: "I'll go looking for God in people. Because you were right about that too. People aren't perfect; it's not their job to be. But if I don't find traces of God in people, I won't find God anywhere."

Or these directly from Ms. Wojciechowska:

Family life: "I always had problems with my mother whom I loved but never quite managed to like, but adored my father, fought with my brothers, loved being a trouble-maker. I had a very strong fantasy life, which I think is missing in these drug-oriented times."

Writing for children: "I write for children because I find children more exciting as an audience than adults. I think I'm more a teacher than a writer, trying in my books to point out what is important enough to pay for and stay away from everyday 'non-character shaping stuff.'

I try to write for one particular kind of child. I once saw an ugly girl on the subway completely escaping into the world of books. I thought to myself, 'Here is someone who is going to grow up to be a magnificent human being but is having a difficult time.' I'm writing for her and all the others like her."

Education: "I always had problems in school. I hated the way things were taught and how kids were all grouped together to the detriment of their individuality. Our educational system has bogged down completely, and it is a very strong and determined child who can survive the assaults on his intelligence, the assaults that start at the kindergarten level and continue through college. There has never been a love affair between me and education, especially since the time when at eleven I was asked by a teacher what I was doing. 'Thinking,' I replied. 'Stop it!' said my teacher."

Books: "Every book for young kids is a propaganda piece, and as they absorb, so should they be given. On high school reading lists these days, everything there was published as adult fiction. There's so little written directly to and for children.

J. D. Salinger's *Catcher in the Rye* should have been published as a kid's book."

Critics will continue to debate and question her work for years to come. But hopefully readers will have more books by her to debate.

Also by Ms. Wojciechowska

Odyssey of Courage: The Adventures of Alva Nunez Cabeza de Vaca (Atheneum, 1965).

The Hollywood Kid (Harper, 1967).

Hey, What's Wrong with This One (Harper, 1969).

The Rotten Years (Harper, 1971).

Through the Broken Mirror with Alice (Harcourt, 1972).

✳ **Elizabeth Yates**

Bradford Bachrach

One summer evening Elizabeth Yates was on her way to attend the Amos Fortune Lecture Series in the little town of Jaffrey Center, about seven miles from her home in Peterborough, New Hampshire. Before attending the lecture, she went to the churchyard on the hilltop to see Amos Fortune's grave. Toward the far stone wall she saw his slate gravestone. Beside it stood one for his wife, Violet. Ms. Yates read the inscriptions of both markings:

Sacred
to the memory of
AMOS FORTUNE
who was born free
in Africa a slave in America
he purchased liberty
professed Christianity
lived reputably and
died hopefully
Nov. 17, 1801
Aet. 91*

---

*Aet means "at the age of."

Sacred
to the memory of
VIOLET
by sale the slave
of Amos Fortune by
marriage his wife by
her fidelity his friend
and solace she died
his widow
Sept. 13, 1802
Aet. 73

Ms. Yates recalled the experience for me: "I stood by the stones in the cemetery in Jaffrey and I wanted to know more." For one year she did research on the life of Amos Fortune, a man who lived from 1710 to 1801, a man once an African prince who became a slave in Boston, a man who at the age of sixty bought his freedom and helped others to do the same.

Ms. Yates studied his papers, his will, and African slave trading and saw his home and the personal items that had been left. After her notes grew an inch thick, she began writing the story. In 1950 *Amos Fortune, Free Man*** was published, and it went on to win a host of honors including the 1951 Newbery Award and in 1953 the first William Allen White Children's Book Award whose recipient is selected by the annual vote of Kansas school children in grades four through seven.

**Unless noted, all titles have been published by Dutton.

I asked the author how she felt on winning the Newbery Medal. "I was not aware that there was such an award," she replied, "and receiving it was a total surprise, quite belying what people like to say about 'this coveted award.' My feeling always has been that it went to Amos more than to me, and for this I am glad."

Recently the book has received some negative criticism because of the way the central character is portrayed. I asked Ms. Yates if she would write the text differently if she were to write it today! "No," she answered. "How could I? I did the best that I could do with the material that was available, with the research, with the memory that still lived in Jaffrey where he had spent his last twenty years. I am aware that he has been referred to recently as an Uncle Tom, but I described the kind of life he lived in a small New Hampshire town. If it was gentle, graceful, and to some, subservient, that's what he was, and how could I change his essential personality? No new material has come to light about him since my book was published. Dutton has just sent me a copy of the twenty-third printing, March 1972."

The same criticism of the book was given to the dramatized version of the story produced by Miller-Brody Productions, Inc. I wanted to know the author's reaction to this.

"The Miller-Brody company sent me a record, and when I first played it, I thought I was really hearing Amos Fortune's voice. To me it is utterly beautiful, especially the tiny details. The music is deeply moving.

It has been played over and over to my friends, to children visiting me, to many different people. It is the only record I've ever worn out and had to replace."

Amos Fortune, Free Man was by no means Ms. Yates' first book for children. Mountain climbing in Switzerland and Iceland, a favorite activity of the couple, sparked her first story, *High Holiday* (A. & C. Black, 1938). The book was published in England but has not been issued in the United States.

Elizabeth Yates was born the second youngest of seven children on December 6, 1905 in Buffalo, New York. The most memorable days of her youth were the long summers spent on her father's farm in the rich, rolling country south of Buffalo. "There were always others to play with, and we lived in a house filled with books. There were always animals around—horses of our own, dogs, and farm animals. There were fields, woods, hard work, fun, long hours of quiet, long hours of adventuring.

"I would go off on my horse for a day at a time, rambling through the countryside, a sandwich in my pocket and the knowledge that any fresh running stream would give us both a drink. I was never lonely, for there was the horse to talk with and in my head I was writing stories. On the next rainy day I'd climb the ladder to an unused pigeon loft, my own secret place, and there I wrote down in a series of copybooks all that I had been thinking."

From kindergarten through twelfth grade she attended the Franklin School in Buffalo. This was followed by a year at boarding school and a summer abroad. Then there were three years in New York, from 1926–1929, where she did every kind of writing from newspaper accounts and book reviews to articles and stories. While in New York she met and then married William McGreal, an American whose business was in England. About this time a poem of hers was published in Franklin P. Adams' *The Conning Tower*. The next ten years were spent mainly in London with frequent travel throughout Europe.

In 1939 the McGreals returned to the United States because of a recurrent and serious eye problem Mr. McGreal suffered from. They found an old farmhouse in Peterborough, New Hampshire, surrounded by sixty-seven acres of land. They modernized this more than one hundred fifty-year-old house and named it Shieling from memories of the Isle of Skye and the shepherds' shielings—a type of shelter.

That winter Mr. McGreal had an operation, but it was a failure and left him blind. His encounter with blindness is told in Ms. Yates' inspiring book, *The Lighted Heart* (1960).

In 1943 *Patterns on the Wall* appeared, a story set in New Hampshire in 1816 about Jared Austin, an apprentice and then journeyman painter. Seven years later *Amos Fortune* appeared. Since 1950 Ms. Yates has written a number of books for both children and adults including such children's stories as *Carolina's Courage* (1964), a tale of a young girl's hazardous journey in a covered wagon when the West was inhabited by Indians, *Children of the Bible* (1950), a retelling of the childhoods of favorite Bible characters, and *Someday You'll Write* (1962), a nonfiction book to interest youngsters in the craft of writing.

"My work is about equally divided between fiction and biography for adults and books for children. I never really decided to write for children. It simply is that some stories seem to be the sort of ones that are tellable for girls and boys.

"I am at my desk mornings from about 8:30 until about 1:00 p.m. Research for a book often requires long hours in libraries, sometimes travel and interviews. My first draft is done in longhand with sharp pencils on yellow legal pads. The revision is my favorite stage of work when words are in hand and the whole can be brought to my idea of perfection; then the finished copy is typed and goes off to the publisher. I have often done additional work at an editor's request and told children a story that has become a book."

Ms. Yates never had any type of formal writing training. "Practical experience was my teacher."

Physically the author is five-feet seven-inches tall, weighs one hundred forty pounds, and has brown eyes and hair. "Philosophically," she commented, "my best thoughts and the ones that sustain me are expressed in my books."

Although Mr. McGreal died in 1963, his wife still maintains the Peterborough farm. "The farm is a good walking mile from the center of a small town with a population of about 3,500. The hills, woods, fields, running brooks, deep lakes, and friendly country people have made up my world. My dog, Sir Gibbie,

a sheltie, is a beloved companion. Every summer a
flock of seven hens completes the family. Also during
the summer there is canoeing, swimming, climbing,
friends and good talk, reading, and trips—wilderness
trips with the Sierra Club down the Colorado River;
a pack trip in the Smoky Mountains, with the Wilderness Society, or a canoe trip in the Border Waters
area of Minnesota and Canada with a stalwart friend.
In wintertime I go snowshoeing in the woods. The
natural world, with those who love it too, is the one I
like most for adventuring in now.

"During the good growing months I am a delighted
gardener. I'm also actively involved in civic affairs. I'm
a trustee of our local Peterborough Town Library, the
first in the world to be supported by taxation, and a
member of the State Library Commission, along with
other such activities."

"Which is your favorite book?" I asked Ms. Yates.

"I love them all and have no favorites," she answered. "Each one had the best I could do and could
give it while working on it, and each one represented
something I very much wanted to express. The most
recent, like the youngest child, is the nearest to me and
the one I feel most tender about. In this case it's *Sarah
Whitchers's Story* (1971)."

Also by Ms. Yates

Prudence Crandall: Woman of Courage
(Dutton, 1955).

Sir Gibbie (Dutton, 1963).

With Pipe, Paddle and Song (Dutton, 1968).

Skeezer: Dog with a Mission (Harvey House, 1973).

Appendix

Newbery Award-Winning Books

The Newbery Medal is named in honor of John Newbery, an 18th century bookseller and publisher. The Medal is presented annually by a committee of the Children's Service Division of the American Library Association to "the author of the most distinguished contribution to American literature for children." The list below cites the year the book received the award, the title, the author and publisher.

Note: * denotes the author is included in this volume; ** denotes that the author is mentioned; † denotes interview in *Books Are by People* (Citation Press, 1969).

1922 *The Story of Mankind.* Hendrik Van Loon. Boni & Liveright.**

1923 *The Voyages of Doctor Dolittle.* Hugh Lofting. Lippincott.

1924 *The Dark Frigate.* Charles Boardman Hawes. Little, Brown.

1925 *Tales from the Silver Lands.* Charles J. Finger. Doubleday.

1926 *Shen of the Sea.* Arthur Bowie Chrisman. Dutton.

1927 *Smoky, the Cowhorse.* Will James.
      Scribner.**

1928 *Gay Neck.* Dhan Gopal Mukerji. Dutton.

1929 *Trumpeter of Krakow.* Eric P. Kelly.
      Macmillan.

1930 *Hitty, Her First Hundred Years.* Rachel
      Field. Macmillan.

1931 *The Cat Who Went to Heaven.* Elizabeth
      Coatsworth. Macmillan.*

1932 *Waterless Mountain.* Laura Adams Armer.
      McKay.

1933 *Yung Fu of the Upper Yangtze.* Elizabeth
      Foreman. Holt.

1934 *Invincible Louisa.* Corneila Meigs. Little,
      Brown.

1935 *Dobry.* Monica Shannon. Viking.

1936 *Caddie Woodlawn.* Carol Ryrie Brink.
      Macmillan.*

1937 *Roller Skates.* Ruth Sawyer. Viking.

1938 *The White Stag.* Kate Seredy. Viking.

1939 *Thimble Summer.* Elizabeth Enright. Holt.

1940 *Daniel Boone.* James H. Daugherty.
      Viking.†

1941 *Call It Courage.* Armstrong Sperry.
      Macmillan.

1942 *The Matchlock Gun.* Walter D. Edmonds.
      Dodd, Mead.*

1943 *Adam of the Road.* Elizabeth Janet Gray. Viking.

1944 *Johnny Tremain.* Esther Forbes. Houghton.

1945 *Rabbit Hill.* Robert Lawson. Viking.

1946 *Strawberry Girl.* Lois Lenski. Lippincott.†

1947 *Miss Hickory.* Carolyn Sherwin Bailey. Viking.

1948 *The Twenty-One Balloons.* William Pene du Bois. Viking.

1949 *King of the Wind.* Marguerite Henry. Rand McNally.

1950 *The Door in the Wall.* Marguerite de Angeli. Doubleday*

1951 *Amos Fortune, Free Man.* Elizabeth Yates. Dutton.*

1952 *Ginger Pye.* Eleanor Estes. Viking.*

1953 *Secret of the Andes.* Ann Nolan Clark. Viking.*

1954 *. . . And Now Miguel.* Joseph Krumgold. Crowell.

1955 *The Wheel on the School.* Meindert De Jong. Harper.*

1956 *Carry On, Mr. Bowditch.* Jean Lee Latham. Houghton.*

1957 *Miracles on Maple Hill.* Virginia Sorensen. Harcourt*

1958   *Rifles for Waitie*. Harold Keith. Crowell.*

1959   *The Witch of Blackbird Pond*. Elizabeth George Speare. Houghton.*

1960   *Onion John*. Joseph Krumgold. Crowell.

1961   *Island of the Blue Dolphins*. Scott O'Dell. Houghton.

1962   *The Bronze Bow*. Elizabeth George Speare. Houghton*

1963   *A Wrinkle in Time*. Madeleine L'Engle. Farrar.*

1964   *It's Like This, Cat*. Emily Neville. Harper.*

1965   *Shadow of a Bull*. Maia Wojciechowska. Atheneum.*

1966   *I, Juan de Pareja*. Elizabeth Borten de Treviño. Farrar.*

1967   *Up a Road Slowly*. Irene Hunt. Follett.*

1968   *From the Mixed-Up Files of Mrs. Basil E. Frankweiler*. E. L. Konigsburg, Atheneum.*

1969   *The High King*. Lloyd Alexander. Holt.*

1970   *Sounder*. William H. Armstrong. Harper.*

1971   *Summer of the Swans*. Betsy Byars. Viking.*

1972   *Mrs. Frisby and the Rats of NIMH*. Robert C. O'Brien. Atheneum.

1973   *Julie of the Wolves*. Jean Craighead George. Harper.*

Index

Editor's Note: The book and series titles given are ones about which some fact is noted; titles merely listed within or at the end of interviews are not indexed. An asterisk (*) indicates a full interview in Mr. Hopkins' earlier volume, *Books Are by People.*